Haun
Heritage

MW00795765

Heritage, Tourism, and Community

Series Editor: Helaine Silverman

University of Illinois at Urbana-Champaign

Heritage, Tourism and Community is an innovative new book series that seeks to address these three interconnected areas from multidisciplinary and interdisciplinary perspectives. Manuscripts are sought that address heritage and tourism and their relationships to local community, economic development, regional ecology, heritage conservation and preservation, and related Indigenous, regional, and national political and cultural issues. Manuscripts, proposals, and letters of inquiry should be submitted to *helaine@uiuc.eduhelain*

The Tourists Gaze, The Cretans Glance: Archaeology and Tourism on a Greek Island,
Philip Duke

Coach Fellas: Heritage and Tourism in Ireland,
Kelli Ann Costa

Inconvenient Heritage: Erasure and Global Tourism in Luang Prabang,
Lynne Dearborn and John C. Stallmeyer

Heritage that Hurts: Tourists in the Memoryscapes of September 11,
Joy Sather-Wagstaff

Speaking for the Enslaved: Heritage Interpretation at Antebellum Planation Sites,
Antoinette T. Jackson

Faith in Heritage: Displacement, Development, and Religious Tourism in Contemporary China,
Robert J. Shepherd

Haunted Heritage: Cultural Politics of Ghost Tourism, Populism, and the Past,
Michele Hanks

Haunted Heritage

The Cultural Politics of Ghost Tourism, Populism, and the Past

Michele Hanks

WALNUT CREEK, CALIFORNIA

LEFT COAST PRESS, INC.
1630 North Main Street, #400
Walnut Creek, CA 94596
www.LCoastPress.com

Copyright © 2015 by Left Coast Press, Inc.

All rights reserved. No part of this publication may be reproduced,
stored in a retrieval system, or transmitted in any form or by any
means, electronic, mechanical, photocopying, recording, or otherwise,
without the prior permission of the publisher.

ISBN 978-1-61132-225-5 hardback
ISBN 978-1-61132-226-2 paperback
ISBN 978-1-61132-227-9 institutional eBook
ISBN 978-1-61132-657-4 consumer eBook

Library of Congress Cataloging-in-Publication Data:

Hanks, Michele.
  Haunted heritage : the cultural politics of ghost tourism, populism,
and the past / Michele Hanks.
      pages cm — (Heritage, tourism & community ; 7)
  Includes bibliographical references and index.
ISBN 978-1-61132-225-5 (hardback) —
ISBN 978-1-61132-226-2 (paperback) —
ISBN 978-1-61132-227-9 (institutional ebook) —
ISBN 978-1-61132-657-4 (consumer eBook)
  1. Haunted places—England—York. 2. Ghosts—England—York.
  3. Parapsychology—Investigation. 4. Tourism—Social aspects.
  5. Heritage tourism. I. Title.
  BF1472.E53H36 2014
  133.109428--dc23

Printed in the United States of America

∞ ™ The paper used in this publication meets the minimum require-
ments of American National Standard for Information Sciences—
Permanence of Paper for Printed Library
Materials, ANSI/NISO Z39.48–1992.

Image of Whitby Abbey on title page by Archangel12 (Whitby Abbey)
[CC-BY-2.0 (http://creativecommons.org/licenses/by/2.0)],
via Wikimedia Commons

CONTENTS

ILLUSTRATIONS

ACKNOWLEDGEMENTS

This project would not be possible without the support and contributions of a number of people. I am deeply indebted to the ghost tourists, ghost hunters, and paranormal investigators who participated in my research. Their kindness and generosity of spirit made this research possible, and their friendship and insights strengthened my understanding of the practices of ghost tourism. Many thanks to the tour producers and museum professionals who generously shared their time with me and allowed me to access their tours and events.

My mentors supported, encouraged, and guided me through the process of this research. Virginia Dominguez has offered intellectual guidance, mentorship, and inspiration since the very start of my academic career. Her support encouraged me to pursue this project. Jane Desmond and Matti Bunzl have generously shared their insights and wisdom with me. Helaine Silverman has championed this project and book from its beginning. I am extremely grateful for her intellectual support and practical encouragement throughout the research and writing process.

My friends and colleagues in the Department of Anthropology at the University of Illinois at Urbana-Champaign and the SAGES Program at Case Western Reserve University have kindly read and commented on drafts of this work and encouraged me to push forward with it. Many thanks to Tim Landry, Lauren Anaya, Lisa Nielson, Brad Ricca, Kelly St. Pierre, Amy Absher, Annie Pecastaings, and Barbara Burgess Van-Aken.

Many thanks to my family and friends. From collecting books of ghost stories for me to attending ghost walks, they have offered enthusiastic support and useful help throughout this project. Special thanks to Noreen Mahon, Thomas Hanks, Lucy Hanks, Mary Tressider, Karen Grant, Michael Parsonage, and Paul Carr.

Many thanks to Mitch Allen at Left Coast Press for his help throughout this process. I am also grateful to Jerryll Moreno for her wonderful copyediting.

Funding from the North American Conference on British Studies, Phi Kappa Phi, and the Departments of Anthropology at the University of Illinois at Urbana-Champaign and the University of Iowa supported the field research for this project.

GHOST TOURISM AND THE PRODUCTION OF HAUNTED HERITAGE

Located between the Pennines, the North York Moors, and the Yorkshire Wolds is the city of York, reported by Ghost Research Foundation International in 2004 to be the most haunted city in the world. Some claim that 504 ghosts haunt the city (BBC 2004; Readicker-Henderson 2008); some ghost tourists suggest that this only scrapes the surface of its ghost population. York's most famous ghosts are the Romans who haunt the basement of the Treasurer's House, the former home of Treasurer of the York Minster, the imposing Gothic cathedral in heart of the city. Like many, I first learned of the Roman ghosts on one of York's many ghost walks in the summer of 2006. After winding our way through the darkening streets of the city, I and other tourists traipsed after the tour guide to a stately home. There our guide stood in front of the home's gates and told us the story of Harry Martindale, an apprentice plumber, who saw something remarkable while working in the basement of the house in 1953.

Martindale was alone in the basement installing a heating system when he suddenly heard the sound of distant music. He found this unusual because the walls of the basement were quite thick, and he had never heard music before. Assuming it was just a loud radio nearby, Martindale continued his work. The music seemed to grow closer though. Suddenly, tired-looking horses and a group of men dressed in unusual clothing emerged out of the wall. The men and horses were only visible from the knees up; Martindale noticed that they seemed to walking on their knees. They did not look at Martindale or seem to notice his presence. They walked across the room and then vanished into the opposing wall. Afraid that people would think he was crazy, Martindale did not immediately share his story with anyone; he abandoned plumbing and became a York police officer.

When he eventually shared his story in the 1970s, the significance of his encounter was clearer. The men and horses that he saw might have been Romans. Many believed this because archaeologists had discovered the remains of the Roman Road Via Decumana Roman underneath the Treasurer's House. That they walked on their knees seemed logical. The Roman

Haunted Heritage: The Cultural Politics of Ghost Tourism, Populism, and the Past by Michele Hanks, 11–31. © 2015 Left Coast Press, Inc. All rights reserved.

Road was buried under layers of waste and development, which obscured their lower legs.

The story of Harry Martindale and the Roman soldiers is an exemplary ghost story. Martindale was an ideal witness: skeptical and reliable. The identity of the ghosts was established and corroborated by eventual archaeological and historical research.

As I began to research ghost tourism in England, I heard this story many times, and I was initially shocked by the multiple variations and interpretations of the story. One guide told the story as proof that ghosts were real. The National Trust, who now owns the Treasurer's House, presented Martindale's encounters as a way of making the Roman past engaging and fun to the public. A ghost walk guide pointed to the story as a means of critiquing the authority of archaeological researchers and heritage officials. For him, it signified that anyone could unearth new information about the past through encounters with the ghostly. Some local ghost hunters pointed to the National Trust's control of the Treasurer's House and the haunted basement as a demonstration of their disenfranchisement from the past. For these people, the Roman ghosts signified a particular orientation toward the past while providing a language for considering the current management and presentation of the past.

In Britain at the turn of the twenty-first century, ghosts seemed to be everywhere. They emerged on television as the subject of reality programs, the protagonists in dramas, and the enticing inhabitants of historic sites on travel shows. Ghosts appeared in haunted homes, castles, pubs, hotels, museums, train stations, and shops, and perhaps surprisingly, people sought out these ghosts. People wanted to learn about these ghosts and, in some cases, encounter the ghosts for themselves. This book examines the touristic practices that this quest for the ghostly engendered.

When I began my first period of fieldwork, I was surprised by how pervasive and public ghosts were. Upon my arrival in England in 2006, the Heathrow Express train into London played a stream of interesting facts about London, including the fact that Anne Boleyn's ghost haunted the Tower of London. When I arrived in York, which would become the base for my fieldwork, the walk from the rail station to my first apartment was overrun with signs advertising ghost walks. As I walked through the city center of York on my first night, I was overwhelmed by the presence of ghost walk guides loudly telling ghost stories as they navigated their teeming masses of tourists to competing sites. Ghost tourism seemed shockingly present. With time, I came to realize that these hyper-present forms of ghost tourism were only part of the broader practices of ghost tourism. While ghost walks are highly visible, companies' offered and self-formed groups pursued more intimate encounters with ghosts during overnight visits to haunted buildings.

Ghosts sustain a wide range of touristic engagements. Ghost tourists had a dizzying range of options available to them in their quest for the ghostly. They could visit a heritage site or museum that incorporated ghosts into their retelling of the past, spend the night in a hotel that advertised its ghostly occupants, partake in a ghost walk to learn a town's ghost stories, participate in an overnight ghost hunt that promised to bring them into contact with ghosts, or join a local ghost hunting club who sought out their own knowledge of and experience with ghosts. This range of touristic engagements, I argue, constitutes ghost tourism.

Ghost tourism includes any form of leisure or travel that involves encounters with or the pursuit of knowledge of the ghostly or haunted. The practice of seeking out ghosts as part of tourism is not entirely new. Historian Owen Davies (2007) suggested that it was a largely twentieth-century practice. This book does not address this history; it focuses primarily on the contemporary practice of ghost tourism and their attendant cultural politics.

Throughout this book, I focus on three forms of ghost tourism: (1) ghost walks, (2) commercial ghost hunts, and (3) non-profit ghost hunts and paranormal investigations. Ghost walks are the most ubiquitous and publicly noticeable form of ghost tourism; they are usually hour-long walking tours through historic city centers led by guides who tell ghost stories. Commercial ghost hunts are overnight excursions to haunted buildings that aim to enable participants to encounter ghosts. Commercial companies organize and sell these events. Non-profit ghost hunts and paranormal investigations closely resemble commercial ghost hunts. Like commercial ghost hunts, they occur overnight in haunted places; however, they differ in that they are organized by local ghost hunting or paranormal investigation groups. Groups refer to these events as ghost hunts or paranormal investigations depending on the nature of the planned activity. Many enthusiasts dismiss ghost hunts as events geared toward believers who seek thrilling paranormal experiences and praise paranormal investigations as research-oriented ventures. Ghost tourism focuses almost exclusively on what I would call "public ghosts." While Fenella Cannell (2013) has highlighted the role of family ghosts in creating ancestors and understanding family history, the ghosts found in ghost tourism are almost never associated with tourists' families. These ghosts, instead, are profoundly public in the sense that tours present the ghosts' lives and stories as a matter of local, regional, or national history rather than family history.

These varying forms of tourism are united in foregrounding ghosts or less commonly the paranormal. As I will show throughout this book, tourists problematize the idea of a ghost far more than one would expect. However, for the sake of a working definition, I will use the term ghost to refer to a being who lived and died in the past but emerges in the present with the physical capacity to speak, touch, influence, or appear to spectators. While many would use terms such as soul (Davies 2007) or spirit to define a ghost, the tourists whom I came to know tended to avoid such words because of their association with spirituality and religion. While most forms of ghost tourism foreground ghosts, some emphasize the paranormal instead. Scholars have written significantly on the nature of paranormal beliefs ranging from ufology to Bigfoot (Bader, Mencken, and Baker 2010; Rice 2003). The ghost tourists I met used the term paranormal in a far more restrictive fashion. For them, the paranormal referred to the range of actions associated with ghosts: mysterious sights, sounds, or perceptions. However, it was not *necessarily* grounded on the idea that a dead person was causing the events.

The touristic practice of seeking out knowledge about or encounters with either the ghostly or the paranormal necessarily raises questions about people's ideas about the past, their understandings of the mechanisms underlying the appearance of ghosts, and their motivations for pursuing such encounters. As I explored the world of ghost tourism, I realized that three concepts organize its terrain: experience, knowledge, and heritage. These interrelated concepts structure the practices of ghost tourism. The first two concepts, experience and knowledge, are highly noticed concepts by ghost tourists. The last concept, heritage, is less explicit but equally important.

Ghost tourists explicitly seek knowledge of ghosts, which can take the form of ghost stories either of distant historical figures or people from the recent past who experienced a haunting. Ghost walk guides, museums, commercial ghost hunt leaders, local ghost experts, and mediums can provide tourists with such knowledge. The nature of this knowledge, however, is complex. By hearing a ghost story on a ghost walk, is a ghost tourist learning about an episode from the past or the nature of life after death? At the heart of this knowledge is a dialectical tension between knowledge of the past and knowledge of occult. As I will show throughout this book, different tourists and different tour experiences manage this tension in varied ways.

At the core of ghost knowledge, though, is experience. Tourists invoke the term *experience* as a gloss to refer to contact with a ghost. The nature of this contact is variable; however, it constitutes the foundation of ghost knowledge. Every ghost that I learned about in ghost tourism became an object of knowledge and discourse through someone's experiential encounter with it at some point in either the near or distant past. To know a ghost required either experiencing one or hearing about someone's experience with one, and many tourists were not content to simply hear of other people's encounters with ghosts. They sought out their own encounters with ghosts as a means of exploring the nature of ghosts, reflecting on the nature of life after death, and exploring the past. This desire engendered forms of tourism, designed to bring participants into contact with ghosts, such as commercial and non-profit ghost hunts. Ultimately, experience is recursively tied to knowledge of ghosts and the projects of ghost tourism. A tension emerges between knowledge and experience in ghost tourism, and this tension complicates understandings of the past, as well as understandings of who has the epistemological authority to narrate the past.

The experiential nature of ghosts and ghost knowledge is different than many of the ways of knowing the past that commonly constitute heritage. Ghost tourists explicitly challenge the expertise of orthodox sources of information regarding the past, such as archaeologists or historians. Experiencing a ghost, tourists and tour providers alike contend, requires no special expertise or prior knowledge; but such encounters provide privileged glimpses into the past. This book examines how this reconfiguration of historical expertise challenges or reaffirms dominant notions of the English national past.

Ghost tourism's dialectical tension between experience and knowledge ultimately produces a type of haunted heritage. Ghosts, like heritage itself, represent the past, but they are never automatically or simply born of the past. This book argues that ghosts constitute a type of disembodied heritage. The touristic quest for ghosts is marked more frequently by absences than presences, by incomplete and sometimes incoherent narratives, and by a sense of disquiet and unsettledness on the part of the tourists. This disquiet reflects tourists' engagement with their national past while also providing them with a rhetorical and embodied means of critiquing popular representations of the past. Ghost tourists pursue the past in a myriad of ways but invariably find partial, fragmented glimmers of it. I will trace the ways in which the ensuing haunted heritage disrupts known narratives of the past while also destabilizing the authority of historical experts.

The practices of ghost tourism may seem like an unusual topic for academic research. In *Specters of Marx*, Jacques Derrida famously remarked that:

> There has never been a scholar who really, and as a scholar, deals with ghosts. A traditional scholar does not believe in ghosts—nor in all that could be called the critical space of spectrality. There has never been a scholar who, as such, does not believe in the sharp distinction between the real and the unreal, the actual and the inactual, the living and the non-living, being and non-being. (1994, 11)

Since 1994, this situation has changed somewhat. Scholars in history (Hazelgrove 2000; Owen 1989, 2004) and literary studies (Gordon 1997; Richardson 2003) answered Derrida's call, exploring the generative work of spectrality; however, that much of this work addressed ghosts in history or literature is not accidental. Doing so enables us to set aside the troubling question of the persistence of belief and interest in ghosts in the contemporary world. This book attempts to address just these questions. What does this turn to haunted heritage reveal? How does what Derrida called the "critical space of spectrality" in ghost tourism support and reconfigure understandings of history, national belonging, and knowledge itself? Engaging haunted heritage, I will argue, is a creative means of refashioning the past, but more importantly reconfiguring regimes of historical expertise.

Ghosts and Ghost Tourism in England

The touristic engagement with ghosts is not unique to England. Ghost walks are the most globally ubiquitous form of ghost tourism available in cities throughout the world like Prague, Singapore, Venice, Amsterdam, Melbourne, and Montreal to name only a few. Ghosts and haunted sites figure more prominently in some city's destination image than others though. For example, in the US, cities like Gettysburg, Savannah, and New Orleans have higher-than-normal concentrations of ghost tours. While I have not systemically studied such ghost walks, I have taken ghost tours in a number of cities in the course of my own tourism in both North America and Europe. There are many parallels to English ghost tourism, particularly a shared fixation on the past, especially the dark past; however, each ghost tour seems particularly bound to its city and country of origin. As historians and anthropologists have demonstrated, occult manifestations are invariably tied to the particular time and place that produces them (Comaroff and Comaroff 1999; Johnson 2013; Mantz 2007; Sanders 2003; Smith 2001). Ghosts, like many forms of heritage, reveal more about the social world that produces them than the historical era from which they originate.

While ghost tourism is undeniably a growing sector of the global tourist market, two aspects of English ghost tourism are unique: its emphasis on experiential encounters with ghosts and the volume and scale of ghost tourism. In the UK, more so than anywhere else in the world, tourists seek out first-hand experiences with ghosts, and both commercial and non-profit groups have emerged to respond to this demand. In 1999, the first commercial ghost hunting company was founded. Today, there are many companies that sell opportunities to spend the night in a haunted venue and seek out ghosts. Similarly, during the 2000s, a number of non-profit, local groups were formed to facilitate encounters with ghosts. According to one estimate, there were 1,200 such local groups in 2006, while there had only been 100 such groups in 1995 (Winsper, Parson, and O'Keeffe 2008). Other countries, such as the US, also include experiential dimensions. For example, there are commercially run opportunities to ghost hunt in cities like Gettysburg and Savannah. Some former penitentiaries and reformatories have also begun to sell their own ghost hunting experiences. For example, the Mansfield Reformatory in Ohio regularly holds ghost hunts on its property. While there are undoubtedly similarities, it seems that the structures and practices are somewhat different. Properties in the US more often present themselves as haunted and hold ghost hunts. In the UK, intermediary parties, which are either commercial or non-profit ghost hunting groups, mediate this process. A comparison of these forms of tourism would undoubtedly contribute greater insight into the management of haunted heritage; however, it is beyond the scope of this book. While ghosts factor into the tourist economies of many countries, the volume and scale of English ghost tourism are unusually high. There is a vast range of widely available touristic experiences—including ghost walks, commercial ghost hunts, non-profit ghost hunts, and museums that incorporate ghosts.

The presence of ghosts in English heritage and tourism owes much to the long cultural history of ghosts, as well as their contemporary cultural standing. Ghosts are an established feature of English popular culture. Some have estimated that English authors have written 70 percent of all published ghost stories (Mitchell 2010). While the accuracy of this figure is questionable, the English have certainly produced some of the most famous and enduring fictional ghosts throughout history, such as Hamlet's father, The Canterville Ghost, and Jacob Marley. Of course, ghosts do not only appear in the classic literature of Shakespeare, Wilde, or Dickens. Contemporary popular culture is saturated with depictions of ghosts in fiction, as well as non-fiction. Fictional television programs, such as *Being Human* and *Doctor Who*, and books, such as the *Harry Potter* series, are very popular English productions that all feature prominent ghost characters. Several of these forms of popular entertainment, especially the *Harry Potter* series, have given rise to their own forms of tourism. Although most ghost tours make no or few references to such forms of popular culture, these fictional depictions certainly help to create an audience for ghost tourism by associating ghosts with entertainment and narrative.

Ghosts are not limited to popular culture though; they are also a matter of popular belief. During the course of my fieldwork, I regularly encountered individuals outside the community of paranormal knowledge producers who actively expressed an interest or belief in ghosts. In fact, when I described the purpose of my fieldwork in England to most people, they responded either with a story about a haunting or ghost in their own home or one in their immediate circle of family or friends. While they often considered my primary informants' interest excessive, they did not find belief in ghosts especially remarkable. For example, when I described the nature of my research to my landlord, a man in his forties, he volunteered that he was not sure if he believed in ghosts; however, his sister believed that there was a ghost in her house. Similarly, one night while returning very late from a ghost hunting meeting in Halifax, I had a conversation with a train conductor between Leeds and York. He asked why I was in England, and when I explained, he enthusiastically began to tell me about various paranormal encounters he had over the course of his life. During the course of my fieldwork, I experienced many more encounters such as these. While they are by no means a systematic form of research, they do suggest that there is widespread interest in or acceptance for the ghostly or paranormal.

While ghosts have been present in English culture for a long time, people's understanding and experience of them have changed radically across time. Historians have done significant work tracing the presences of ghosts in premodern England (Finucane 1996), as well as in the modern era (Bennett 1999; Davies 2007; Gorer [1923] 2011; Timms 2012), and they have demonstrated that notions of the ghostly varied significantly across historical era. While many analysts of modernity anticipated a decline in belief in ghosts due to secularization and the popularization of science, this has not happened. Davies suggests that belief in ghosts may actually be tied to secularization. As religious belonging becomes increasingly flexible and fluid in the UK (Bruce 1995; Davie 1994; Engelke 2012), ghosts are "examples . . . [of the] individualistic, flexible, and pluralistic [nature of secularism, which is] no longer tied to institutions or denominations" (Davies 2007, 244). Of course, not all ghosts or spirits are unassociated with religious institutions. The Spiritualist religion, which traces its history back to 1840s, embraces the reality of spirits as proof of survival of life after death.

An Ipsos poll conducted in 2003 found that 38 percent of Britons believed in ghosts. Similarly, a 2005 Gallup poll found that 40 percent of Britons believed that houses could be haunted (Lyons 2005). Considering these findings, it seems likely that most English people either believe (to some degree) in the paranormal (or some element of) or know someone who does. Davies observed that "since the 1950s, opinion polls have shown a consistent rise in ghost-belief among the British" (2007, 241). He suggested that these polls primarily reflect people's lack of embarrassment about their belief in ghosts. Davies suspects that "ghost belief has become more socially acceptable" (2007, 241).

Scholarly assessments of ghost belief (Davies 2007), as well as polls, tend to treat belief as an obvious or static category that is an easily measured entity. Anthropologists have long recognized that belief is a "thorny concept" (Engelke 2002, 3), and they have approached it carefully (Needham 1973). Particularly within the confines of secularism, belief becomes a challenging, dynamic state to trace. As Bruno Latour (1999, 2010) and others (Jones 2003; Taylor 1989, 2007) have argued, modern rationality is grounded in a distancing from positions of belief. Charles Taylor has noted that a certain ethics of belief persists in secularism; one should only believe what one has adequate evidence for (Taylor 1989, 403–4). These elements of secularism profoundly shape the projects of ghost tourists. Throughout this book, I demonstrate the ways in which ghost tourism provides an embodied means of evidencing ghosts. The unfixed, dynamic nature of belief in ghosts drives the practices of ghost tourism.

Scholarly Engagement with the Ghostly: The "Spectral Turn"

This proliferation of ghosts in the public sphere has corresponded to what some have called a "spectral turn" (Blanco and Peeren 2013; Luckhurst 2002) in the social sciences and humanities. This is due in no small part to Jacques Derrida's influential text, *Specters of Marx* (1994). Derrida, who was inspired by Marx and Engels's famous claim that "a spectre is haunting Europe—the spectre of communism" ([1888] 2012, 33), argued for the importance of spectrality and hauntology as interrelated ways of addressing amorphous presences in the world. The notion of spectrality, a difficult concept to specifically define, grapples with the ways in which the past lingers in the present and makes itself known. Derrida's notion of hauntology, with which he aims to replace ontology, dealt with similar concepts. Colin Davis explains hauntology "replac[es] the priority of being and presence with the figure of the ghost as that which is neither present nor absent, neither dead nor alive" (2005, 373). Many have criticized Derrida's mode of engaging Marx and his attempt to bring together deconstruction and Marxism. Terry Eagleton (1999) and Aijaz Ahmad (1999) viewed Derrida's spectral turn as offering little in the way of redirecting Marxism, and they questioned the idea that deconstruction was truly a "radicalization of Marxism" (Ahmad 1999, 101). Fredric Jameson went further, calling Derrida's notion of hauntology "a ghost echo if ever there was one . . . which promises nothing tangible in return" (1999, 39). While Derrida's ideas gained little traction with Marxists, they did attune scholars to questions of the ghostly.

Derrida's efforts generated significant scholarly interest, in literary and critical theory circles at least, in ghosts as metaphorical and literal presences in texts. Colin Davis praised Derrida's "rehabilitation of ghosts as a respectable subject of enquiry" and observed that it "has proved to be extraordinarily fertile" for literary scholars (2005, 273). Turning to spectrality has led scholars to evaluate and consider the textual practices of authors (Castricano 2003), as well as the presence and significance of ghosts in fiction. Such a range of deployments led Martin Jay to observe that the "uncanny [has] become a master trope available for appropriation in a wide variety of contexts" (1998, 157).

This trope has become so powerful that scholars who focus on issues of historical memory and social transformation deploy the rhetoric of hauntings, ghosts, and specters to signify the present absences they seek to illuminate, particularly in the arenas of postcolonialism (Bergland 2000; Stoler 2006), displaced cultural identity (Brogan 1998) and racial memory (Gordon 1997). Gordon, in her influential *Ghostly Matters*, explicates the relationship among ghosts, memory, and the past. "Haunting," Gordon claimed, "describes how that which appears to be not there is often a seething presence, acting on and often meddling with taken for granted realities" (1997, 8). Gordon suggested that the ghost has a special role to play in making history. She argued that "the ghost is not simply a dead or a missing person, but a social figure, and investigating it can lead to that dense site where history and subjectivity make social life" (1997, 8). I agree with Gordon's conceptualization of ghosts and draw on it throughout this manuscript; however, I also aim to show that the search for ghosts does more than simply mediate people's relationships with their pasts. In "making social life," a turn to ghosts also allows for reconfigurations and rearticulations of power, knowledge, and authority.

Other scholars have effectively expanded on Gordon's connection between ghosts and memory. Judith Richardson, in her excellent analysis of the history of haunting in New York's Hudson Valley, expands on this idea of ghosts as elements of forgotten or traumatic memory by highlighting the productive qualities of ghosts. She argued that the region's "restless history . . . created a sense of social and historical tenuousness that was crucial to producing ghosts" (Richardson 2003, 23). The rootlessness of immigrants to the area, combined with the physical features of the landscape, produced a bevy of silent, seemingly incomprehensible ghosts. These ghosts provided the new residents with a way of grappling with their disconnect from the past. For

Richardson, hauntings are about "historical consciousness" and ghosts constitute "an alternate form of history-making" (2003, 3–4). Throughout this book, I expand on Richardson's claim of ghosts as a kind of "history-making," and show how this "history-making" allows for shifts in power in the present.

Much of the emergent literary and historical engagement with spectrality treats ghosts as metaphorical rather than actual presences. The idea that anyone might believe in ghosts as real rather than metaphorical entities is almost entirely absent. This is not accidental. Maria del Pilar Blanco and Ester Peeren suggest that this spectral turn was predicated on a transformation in popular belief in ghosts. The scientific interest in "proving or disproving the reality of spiritualist feats and related phenomena such as telepathy . . . prevented the ghost's figurative potential from fully emancipating itself" (Blanco and Peeren 2013, 3). Much of the spectral turn, including Derrida's invocation of spectrality and hauntology, treats ghosts and spirits as nothing more than metaphors. This position is not surprising. A commitment to rationality and a distancing from belief as a way of knowing are constitutive of Western modernity (Jones 2003; Kapferer 2001; Latour 2004, 2010; Styers 2004). As Bruno Latour has insightfully remarked that "a modern is someone who believes that others believe" (2010, 2). Many interpret belief in general, and belief in ghosts in particular, as indicators of less than fully formed rationality. Few literary and historical scholars who have contributed to the spectral turn have grappled with the lived realities of believing in or encountering a ghost. Some have gone so far as to limit such encounters to the "fringes" of the modern world (Blanco and Peeren 2013, 3).

Of course, social scientists, especially anthropologists, geographers, and sociologists, have participated in the "spectral turn" (Luckhurst 2002), and they have tended to address ghosts as real, as well as metaphorical presences. Anthropologists have turned a critical eye to ghosts. Drawing on ethnographic research, they have reiterated the role of ghosts in the work of historical mourning and memory. Many anthropologists have examined how contemporary experiences of the ghostly, from encounters to storytelling, offer a language for critiquing the conditions of everyday life while also grappling with broader forces of history (Gustafsson 2009; Johnson 2013; Trnka 2011; Wardlow 2002). For example, in 2009, Mai Lan Gustafsson powerfully showed how contemporary Vietnamese people contend with ghosts from the Vietnam/American war as a means of understanding their own social suffering while aiming to release ghosts from their suffering. Much of this work is indebted to Jean Comaroff and John Comaroff's 1999 influential analysis of occult economies in which they contend with the puzzling question of the presence and persistence of enchanted world views in modernity. Comaroff and Comaroff suggested that such enchantments and occult manifestations are a construction of people's attempts to come to terms with the practices and consequences of neoliberalism and millennial capitalism. This notion that a turn to the occult or ghostly indexes an attempt to understand broader sociopolitical currents is a recurrent thread in anthropology and beyond. As I show in this book, the English engagement with ghosts can be understood in these terms as well, although only partially. As I show in chapter five, the pursuit of haunted sites can be read as a response to neoliberal social transformations in England in particular and Europe in general; however, its logic differs from occult economies. The logic at work bears far more in common with broader English and European efforts at "heritagization."

Much of the anthropological scholarship on ghosts and hauntings focuses on places outside the North Atlantic world. Scholars have focused on ghosts, the occult, and the uncanny in South Asia (Gustafsson 2009; Johnson 2013), Africa (Comaroff and Comaroff 1999), and the South Pacific (Trnka 2011; Wardlow 2002). While this scholarship acutely attends to the meaning of local encounters with ghosts and spirits, the absence of more scholarship on ghosts and the paranormal in the North Atlantic world is revealing. Perhaps it remains easier to engage ghosts as metaphors in the North Atlantic and as actual presences elsewhere. It is only quite recently that sociologists (Bader, Mencken, and baker 2010) and anthropologists (Cannell 2013) have addressed ghosts closer to home in the US and UK. In this book, I seek to contribute to such scholarship by examining how English touristic engagement with ghosts constitutes a type of heritage.

Ghosts, Tourism, and Heritage

Ghost tourism has attracted academic interest only in the very recent past. Scholars have examined the performative qualities of ghost walks (a type of walking tour) in the US (Gentry 2007; Thompson 2010) and Britain (Hanks 2011a), the role of ghosts in constructing Scotland's destination image (Inglis and Holmes 2003), and the possibility of ghosts as deterrents to tourism (Rittichainuwat 2011). Many of these previous studies (Gentry 2007; Hanks 2011a; Inglis and Holmes 2003; Thompson 2010) have foregrounded the role of ghost walks in their analyses. This book expands on this approach by addressing a broader range of ghost touristic practices, including ghost hunts and the incorporation of ghosts into museum and heritage sites. Based on my observations and conceptualization of ghost tourism as the pursuit of knowledge of or experience with ghosts, it engages several significant areas of tourism and tourism research: heritage studies, pilgrimage, dark tourism, and thrill-seeking. While it does not neatly fit in any one of these domains, its practices touch on or intersect with them.

Ghosts are intimately tied to the idea of heritage; both concepts are grounded in contemporary attempts to understand and represent the past. Attempts to know the past are necessarily partial (Clifford 1986; Haraway 1988) and often complicit in current politics (Lowenthal 1985). This is very much the case for haunted heritage. While contestations and erasures occur in many articulations of cultural heritage (Silverman 2011), haunted heritage and ghost tourism sustain multiple interpretations of the past while enabling the formation of new modes of historical expertise. Experiencing ghosts leads to new insights into the past, which are sometimes unsupportable in the known historical record. Encountering a ghost also produces new experts who, having seen ghosts, may present themselves as historical and, in some cases, scientific experts. Some of these spectral encounters affirm known elements of the past; this was the case in Harry Martindale's encounter with Roman ghosts in York. His experience confirmed the known historical record, and positioned it as interesting and mysterious. As I show, there are many ghosts who do similar work to confirm known historical narratives; however, for every instance in which ghost encounters confirm the known historical record, there are many that contest it, sometimes in unsustainable ways. For example, Clara, a ghost hunter I came to be friends with during the course of my research, often made historical claims based on her encounters with ghosts. As we walked through the city of York one day, Clara explained to me that thousands had died here from the Bubonic plague; she had seen their ghosts. When I asked her to clarify when this had happened, she told me that it was as recent as the 1940s—a fact most historians would heatedly contest. When I expressed skepticism about this, pointing to the lack of historical support, she emphasized that she had seen the ghosts. "Historians can lie," she explained to me. In Clara's case, ghosts acted a means for envisioning, encountering, and authoring radically new versions of the past.

Some would call Clara's history-making a type of "pseudohistory" (Melleuish, Sheiko, and Brown 2009; Shermer and Grobman 2009). Melleuish, Sheiko, and Brown characterize pseudohistory as:

> subverting established truths. Its authors, who generally come from outside the History . . . seek to attack the conventional wisdom of the professionals and to demonstrate its folly. They move to use their particular expertise to establish a new, allegedly superior explanation, usually founded on highly speculative, and invariably unreliable, interpretations of evidence (2009, 1484).

These historical claims often focus on the extraordinary and tend to include references to conspiracies, UFOs, and the occult. Some direct attention to the political dangers associated with such pseudohistories (Shermer and Grobman 2009) and point to their association with emergent forms of nationalism and populism (Melleuish, Sheiko, and Brown 2009). In my examination of the production of haunted heritage, I too note its potent connections to populism and nationalism. Rather than debating the legitimacy of the ensuing understandings of the past, I focus on the agency and motivations of ghost tourists and specifically on what types of nationalism and modes of populism they engage.

In addition to the questions of historical accuracy, touristic engagements with ghosts also raise questions about popular perceptions of authenticity. The tourists I met sought out authentic spirits of the past, authentically English places, and authentic experiences in the present. Anthropologists and tourism studies scholars have debated how to engage the concept of authenticity. Dean MacCannell (1973, 1999) influentially argued that tourists, driven by a lack of authenticity in their lives, seek out authenticity in tourist encounters. Scholars, such as MacCannell (1999) in his early work, adopted at times an essentialist approach to authenticity, assuming an authentic/inauthentic divide. Scholars (Bruner 2005) have criticized this approach. As Kjell Olsen observed, "the idea of the authentic implies a vocabulary that presupposes that the original is better than its counter concept, the copy" (2002, 162). Today, most scholars, in anthropology, at least, agree that the concept of authenticity is, as Edward Bruner eloquently put it, "a red herring, to be examined only when the tourists, the locals, or the producers themselves use the term" (2005, 5). Even MacCannell himself has come to embrace such a notion. Writing in 2008, he emphasized that even in his earlier works his primary concern was with the *staging* of authenticity rather than authenticity itself (MacCannell 2008, 336).

Scholars have debated the consequences of this quest for objectivity. Bruner, writing about authenticity at the New Salem heritage site in Illinois, observed that there were two ways to interpret the question of authenticity: pessimistically or optimistically (2005, 167–68). The pessimistic view casts museums and heritage sites as exploitive institutions creating false historical consciousness and fostering social alienation, while the optimistic interpretation highlights the "utopian potential for transformation" (Bruner 2005, 168). Eric Gable and Richard Handler explicitly take the more pessimistic view. They see "authenticity as a model for, rather than a model of, a reality" (1996, 576) and suggest that it often reaffirms problematic and politicized imaginings of the past. The practices of ghost tourism traverse this interpretive divide. On ghost walks, tourists and guides playfully handle the authenticity of ghost stories. The reality of the stories is, perhaps, secondary to the pleasure in hearing them and the questions they raise about belief. On both commercial and non-profit ghost hunts, though, the treatment of authenticity differs significantly. Tourists desire authentic encounters with ghosts and, as a result, authentic encounters with the past. Here, the grounds for authenticity shift radically from those discussed by Gable and Handler (1996) or Bruner (2005). Some tourists ground their understanding of historical authenticity on encounters with ghosts then, in turn, assess the authenticity of the sites. Following Handler, I treat discourses of authenticity as objects of scholarly inquiry. I aim to trace ghost tourists' concerns regarding objectivity and reveal their sociopolitical significance.

The engagement with spirits that forms the core of ghost tourism shifts the grounds for discussions of authenticity. Tourists simultaneously engage what they see as authentic encounters with and knowledge of ghosts, which in turn structures their understandings of the real past. Anna Karlstöm noted that "spirits seriously [act] as constitutive elements of heritage" (2013, 398). The idea that spirit contact or spirit possession leads to new forms of historical consciousness is not a new insight. Spirit possession, which Janice Boddy usefully generalized to mean "the hold exerted over a human being by external forces or entities more powerful than she" (1994, 407), has powerful ties to history-making. Anthropologists of spirit possession have demonstrated that contact with or possession by spirits can produce understandings of the past that contend with colonial legacies (Stoller 1995), engage family history (Lambek 1998), and more. As Jeanette Mageo noted in 1996, "the characters that emerge in possession often embody era-specific voices" (1996, 76). She noted that possession could be understood as a form of historical discourse. She argued that Samoan possession acts as a form of moral history-making where the possessed encounter lessons from the past that enable them to grapple with problems in their lives. Michael Lambek, in 1998, demonstrated that spirit possession in Madagascar produced a form of historical consciousness at odds with "Western" conceptions of history. "Historical consciousness," he wrote, "is not reducible to a single attitude, but arises through the interplay of multiple voices. It is neither single nor static, but open" (1998, 109). I note that he contrasted this with a sense of history found in the "West," writing that "unlike the dominant mode in the West, where history recedes and the historian goes back, the Sakalava past is carried forward" (1998, 121). While the practices of encountering a ghost differ in important ways from those of spirit possession, there are nonetheless parallels. English ghosts, like the spirits who possess people in Madagascar and

Samoa, convey historical information and instill particular forms of historical consciousness. This book shows how tourists engage this form of historical consciousness and the types of implicit critiques of the current political economic climate grounded in it.

Given the centrality of encounters with spirits to ghost tourism, it might appear to be a form of pilgrimage, which is a profoundly spiritual activity (Badone and Roseman 2004; Eade and Sallnow 1991; Morinis 1992; Turner and Turner [1978] 1995). However, ghost tourism, although tied to supernatural belief, is an avowedly non-religious one. Of course, there has always been slippage between the categories of pilgrim and tourist. As Turner and Turner put it "a tourist is half a pilgrim, if a pilgrim is half a tourist" ([1978] 1995, 20).

Recognizing the ambiguity and exchange between these categories, scholars have increasingly emphasized the significance of secular pilgrimage. Noga Collins-Kreiner (2010) compellingly suggests that pilgrimages should be dichotomized into the religious and the secular. Drawing on this expanded scope of pilgrimage, Kenneth Hyde and Serhat Harman define it as "travel to, and communion with, a specific, non-substitutable physical site that embodies and makes manifest the religious, cultural or personal values of the individual, the deeply meaningful, or a source of core identity for the traveler" (2011, 1347). Secular pilgrimage can include travel to a wide range of destinations from Star Trek conventions (Porter 2004) to surfing destinations (Krause 2012). There has been significant emphasis on places of memorialization, such as battlefields like Gallipoli (Hyde and Harman 2011; Osbaldiston and Petray 2011), and sites associated with dead celebrities, like the Strawberry Fields memorial to John Lennon in New York City (Kruse 2003) or Elvis Presley's Graceland (Aldermann 2002).

That sites associated with death and dying figure prominently should not be surprising. Following John J. Lennon and Malcolm Foley (2000), these places have become known as the sites of "dark tourism." For them, dark tourism focuses on "the presentation and consumption (by visitors) of real and commodified death and disaster sites" (Foley and Lennon 1996,198). While others have used terms such as *negative sightseeing* (MacCannell 1989), *tragic tourism* (Lippard 2000), and *thanatourism* (Seaton 1996), *dark tourism* has become the central term in popular and academic discussions of tourism. In the years since the publication of Lennon and Foley's *Dark Tourism* (2000), little consensus has emerged about the motives and nature of the practice, leading some to question its utility as a category (Bowman and Pezzullo 2010). Some scholars conceive of the practices of dark tourism as "an intimation of post-modernity" (Lennon and Foley 2000, 11) emerging after World War II, while others trace its origin to much earlier in the Middle Ages (Seaton 1996). A variety of sites constitute dark tourism, including sites of terrorism, such as Ground Zero or Oklahoma City (Sather-Wagstaff 2011; Sturken 2007) and battlefields (Dunkley et al. 2011), as well as sites of manufactured death, like the Dungeon attractions in the UK (Stone 2009). Understandings about the underlying motivations of dark tourists remain equally diverse. Some see it as a meaningful way of grappling with death (Stone and Sharpley 2008; Venbrux 2010), a productive way of contending with national tragedies (Sather-Wagstaff 2011), or as a superficial way of minimizing tragedy (Sturken 2007).

The place of ghost tourism within this dark tourism spectrum is confounding. On the one hand, the practices of ghost tourism are explicitly grounded on death. After all, ghosts emerge only after death. On the other hand, the focus of ghost tourism remains on ghosts, who explicitly transcend death. While tragedy and death figure prominently in its practices, tourists seek the ghosts engendered by these tragedies; in a very literal sense, they are looking beyond death. This is not to say that there are not grotesque, violent stories present in ghost tourism; however, based on my observations I suggest that knowledge or experience of ghosts motivates most tourists. I show that ghost tourism provides a means for tourists to consider questions of life after death and contemplate their relationship to the past; addressing death is part of this project, but paradoxically not a significant part. Ultimately, ghost tourism engages questions of spirituality and pilgrimage, heritage and historicity, and science and death. In doing so, it produces a type of haunted heritage that critiques and refashions known elements of the past and historical expertise.

Approach and Methods

This book is based on extended fieldwork with paranormal investigators, ghost hunters, ghost tourisms, ghost enthusiasts, and ghost tour operators, as well as critical evaluations of ghost literature and museum and heritage sites. I conducted research for this project during the summers of 2006, 2007, and 2012 and eighteen months of fieldwork between 2008 and 2009. Initially my research focused only on ghost tourism, but it evolved into a more specific concern with paranormal investigators' understandings of science and technology. My research involved participant observation on a range of paranormal activities including commercial ghost hunts, non-profit ghost hunts, and ghost walks. I also devoted significant time to attending the meetings and activities of ghost hunting and paranormal investigating groups. I conducted multiple semistructured interviews with ghost hunters, paranormal investigators, and the tourists who purchased commercial ghost hunts and ghost walks. While my primary ethnographic focus was on tourists and participants on these ghost events, I also interviewed guides, as well as the people who ran the haunted venues that tourists sought out.

My research on commercial and non-profit ghost hunts took a different course. My approach to ghost tourism differs in some key ways from many other ethnographies of tourism. For obvious structural reasons, most anthropologists of tourism must contend with rapidly changing tourist populations. Many anthropologists have the experience of staying in one tourist destination and encountering a stream of new tourists on a daily or weekly basis. My research differed in that I became attached to particular ghost hunting or paranormal investigation groups that staged non-profit ghost hunts, and this directed me in terms of what sites I analyzed and which ghost hunts I observed.

The four main groups that I mention in this book are Eastern Ghost Researchers (EGR), Central Paranormal Investigators (CPI), Dark Night Researchers (DNR), and Ghost Doctors. Each group had between two and twenty-five members and regularly held private and public ghost hunts. EGR was based in Middlesborough, a large town in the Teesside area. During the course of my research it had roughly 15 regular members; EGR held group-only investigations two to three times a month and typically offered one public investigation a month. CPI was the largest paranormal investigation group that I worked with; they had twenty-five regular members in 2008. Based just outside Manchester, they held monthly group and public investigations. DNR was the smallest paranormal investigation team, with just two regular members but many collaborators. Based outside Hull, they staged private investigations in collaboration with other investigation groups, particularly EGR, throughout the North East. Ghost Doctors, based outside Leeds, was a small ghost hunting group of seven members who held regular private and less frequent public investigations. In each of these groups, members varied in age between 22 and 67. The majority of team members were in their 30s and 40s. There was a fairly even distribution of men and women members. I spent significant time with these four groups and attended their meetings and private and public investigations. I came to know many of the members very well during the course of the research. These groups staged investigations and ghost hunts both near home and further afield. I joined them on these events throughout the North East. The majority of the investigations occurred in York, Newcastle, and the Teesside area.

Similarly, my research with commercial ghost hunting companies focused on only two of the many existing companies. I purchased tickets to their events, observed their ghost hunts, and interviewed producers and tourists alike. Sometimes these were fairly short, structured interviews. In other instances, I came to know some of the regular attendees quite well and developed a broader sense of their involvement in ghost tourism.

Ghost tourism generally attracts largely domestic tourists. Out of the forms of ghost tourism I examined, ghost walks attracted the most internationally diverse crowds; I met and interviewed several Australians, Americans, and Canadians on ghost walks. But the bulk of ghost walk participants were British. Ghost walks in major cities, like London or Edinburgh, tended to attract more international visitors. All of the members of paranormal investigation or ghost hunting groups were English, and with one exception, were white Britons. When they staged public events, the attendees were entirely English, with the exception of three American college students who happened upon an event. They joined for part of it but left early. I was typically the only non-British person present. Similarly, British companies organized the commercial ghost hunts for overwhelmingly British audiences.

In the years that I have studied the practices of ghost tourism and paranormal knowledge production, friends, colleagues, and strangers have all asked me if I believe that ghosts are real. My answer invariably disappoints them. The goal of my project has never been to evaluate or criticize the reality of ghostly phenomena at the heart of ghost tourism. There is already significant skeptical and scientific literature that critically evaluates the reality of such claims (Hines 2003; Shermer 2001). Instead, I am interested in the cultural practices that emerge out of people's desire to know or experience the ghostly. Like other anthropologists who study the occult or spiritual, my aim is to analyze the meanings that people construct and contest through their engagements with the ghostly. As a result, in writing about my research here, I have avoided applying terms such as "allegedly" or "reportedly" to people's claims of their own supernatural experiences or the status of haunted buildings.

Outline of the Book

This book aims to map the practices of ghost tourism and show how they contribute to an understanding of haunted heritage that destabilizes established forms of epistemic authority and reorders the past. To do this, I analyze how different ghost tourists mobilize understandings of the spectral.

The first chapter, "Constructing Haunted Destinations: An Analysis of Ghosts on TV, in Travel Literature, and in the Museum," examines contradictory definitions of the ghostly and their epistemological and political consequences. I contrast two popular understandings of ghosts as either fully formed historical figures or inchoate experiential entities. Tour producers, travel writers, and museum officials strategically embrace notions of ghosts as fully formed historical beings, which in turn allows them to position ghosts as an uncontested element of the past. In contrast, I trace the emergence of understandings of ghosts as experiential, partial beings in paranormal reality television, which in turn supports the diversification of historical expertise.

Chapter two, "Discourses and Enactments of Belief and Transformation on Ghost Walks and Commercial Ghost Hunts," maps varying ways of engaging and enacting belief in ghost tourism. It demonstrates that belief is a dynamic concept with the capacity to support a range of touristic positions. Comparing the performative nature of belief in two forms of ghost tourism reveals the ways in which the moral economies of secularism position belief as an internal, evidence-based process.

While ghost walks and commercial ghost hunts sell the opportunity to learn about or encounter ghosts, some paranormal enthusiasts view such ventures as crass forms of commercialized thrill-seeking. In chapter three, "Staging Ghost Hunts: The Roles of Knowledge, Expertise, and Science in Ghost Tourism," I shift my focus from the commercial modes of ghost tourism to the non-profit dimensions. Members of ghost hunting and paranormal investigation teams stage events intended to facilitate contact with and research about ghosts. Their ability to know the paranormal and their recognition as experts on the paranormal hinged on these events. Because of the increasingly commercialized nature of ghost hunting in England, staging these events becomes increasingly complex. Ghost hunters and paranormal investigators must stage public events to support their own research and financially afford access to desirable haunted locations. I show that paradoxically staging these public ghost hunts, which investigators and ghost hunters view as less pandering or inauthentic than commercial events, provides them with the performative means necessary to publicly enact their own brand of paranormal expertise.

Chapter four, "Encountering the Ghostly: Mediumship, Populism, and the Articulation of Amateur Expertise," continues to trace the shifting nature of expertise—in this case historical expertise—in ghost tourism. I examine the practices of mediumship in commercial, as well as non-profit, ghost hunts. Mediumship, an embodied means of coming to know spirits of the past, provides persuasive grounds for imagining and articulating new forms of historical knowledge. Mediums' visits to museums and heritage sites become opportunities to explore their encounters with spirits while offering new interpretations of the known past. I trace the audiences and impacts of these competing narratives of the past and reveal that rather than offering a compelling counterpart to established historical narratives, they fragment the known historical record and position it as partial and imperfect. Mediums, then, emerge as experts on par with historians, archaeologists, and heritage officials.

The final chapter, "'This is the Real England': Discourses of Authenticity, National Belonging, and Difference," tackles the question of what constitutes a haunted site. While a site's association with dark history or paranormal activity certainly contributes to its reputation as haunted, I reveal that the term "haunted" functions as a politicized aesthetic that locates sites as authentic or inauthentic. Ultimately, this rhetoric of authenticity mediates discourses of national belonging.

CHAPTER ONE

CONSTRUCTING HAUNTED DESTINATIONS: AN ANALYSIS OF GHOSTS ON TV, IN TRAVEL LITERATURE, AND IN THE MUSEUM

The ghost of Edward II's favourite, Piers Gaveston, haunts Scarborough Castle (open to the public). Gaveston was captured here and taken to Warwick for execution. His headless ghost is malicious. It haunts the broken battlements and rushes at trespassers foolhardy enough to visit the castle at night.

—John Brooks, *The Good Ghost Guide*

Occasionally, *if they are lucky*, people walking . . . by the walls of Scarborough Castle see the headless spirit of Piers Gaveston rushing towards them, ghostly blood still gushing from the severed arteries in its neck. . . . Those who fail to notice this ghost approaching them are pushed violently over the cliff's edge. . . . It has always been something of a mystery as to why Gaveston's ghost should choose to haunt Scarborough Castle shoving innocent holiday makers to their deaths. One possible explanation is . . . the fine sea views, the healthy airs, or the multitude of tourist attractions for which the Old Town of Scarborough is now rightly famous.

—Michael Wray, *The Haunted Coast*

Scarborough Castle has seen many reports of the ghost of a man beheaded in the 14th century walking the paths. One version of the story says he tries to lure visitors to the edge of the cliff and then pushes them off.

—Spirit Seekers Tour Site

Haunted Heritage: The Cultural Politics of Ghost Tourism, Populism, and the Past by Michele Hanks, 33–58. © 2015 Left Coast Press, Inc. All rights reserved.

Different ghost guidebooks present a single ghost, Piers Gaveston, in significantly varying ways. One ghost guide presents Gaveston in a matter-of-fact fashion that positions him like any other tourist attraction. A collection of regional ghost stories, sold in a tourist shop near the Castle, tells a flowery, historically detailed account of Gaveston's story that includes details of his life, death, and spectral motivation. Finally, another tour company offers a brief and vague version of Gaveston's story that fails to mention him by name and emphasizes reports of experiential elements of his haunting. Gaveston's ghost is not unique. Most English ghosts are recorded, presented, and circulated in a variety of media formats, including collections of ghost stories, ghost guidebooks, and television shows about the paranormal—to say nothing of literature produced by tour companies to attract tourists. Both Gaveston's ghost and the nature of the haunting at Scarborough Castle appear more coherent and consistent across the media selected here than many other ghosts; guidebooks often present competing suites of ghostly traits, stories, and experiences.[1]

The above stories with their variations in rhetorical emphasis and content reveal a central tension in popular depictions of ghosts in contemporary England. At one end of the spectrum, ghosts appear as fully formed entities complete with a known history that intersects with the given historical record. On the other end, they appear as anonymous, lurking beings characterized primarily through contemporary tourists' embodied experiences of them. In short, there is no unified understanding of ghosts. Ernesto Laclau suggested that spectrality can be "found in this undecidability between flesh and spirit; it is not pure body—for in that case there would be no spectrality at all; but it is not pure spirit either—for the passage to the flesh is crucial" (1995, 87). As such, there must always be an interminability and uncertainty surrounding the ghostly. In this chapter, I argue that the interplay of understandings of ghosts as either historically grounded figures or inchoate beings that are experientially known fuels the practices of ghost tourism, particularly in the context of established heritage sites. This dynamic tension, I argue, also obscures the existential, ontological, and spiritual questions raised by the presence of ghosts: does life after death exist, and if so, what is the evidence of it? By avoiding such thorny questions and instead positioning ghosts as either historical reality or experiential thrill, this rhetorical tension renders ghosts as safe, available components of English heritage. Organizations like the National Trust and English Heritage embrace these understandings of ghosts and incorporate them into their depiction of heritage, while some ghost tourists rely on the same media to problematize the idea of ghosts.

This diverging image of ghosts circulates through public culture shaping the goals and ideals of paranormal tourists and the character and desirability of paranormal destinations. This chapter examines the role of three key elements of public culture that influence and shape paranormal tourism: guidebooks to haunted locations, paranormal reality television, and the brochures and literature of the ghost tourist industry. I argue that these three interrelated forms of public culture, while offering varied accounts of ghosts and the past, collectively contribute to several important elements of paranormal tourism: (1) the construction of a particular epistemology of the past grounded in experience; (2) an understanding of experience as a popularly available resource; and (3) an understanding of paranormality grounded in travel and difference.

That public culture shapes and informs ghost tourism is no surprise to scholars of tourism. As John Urry noted "places are chosen to be gazed upon because there is an anticipation. . . . Such anticipation is constructed and sustained through a variety of non-tourist practices, such as film, TV, literature, magazines, videos, which construct and reinforce the gaze" (1990, 3). In recent years, studies of the impact of film, literature, and television on tourism in general (Beeton 2005; Deery 2004; Hudson and Ritchie 2006; Mordue 2009) and perceptions of English heritage in particular (Higson 2001, 2003) have highlighted the importance of popular media in shaping tourism. Communication studies scholars (Maller and Lundeen 1933; Sparks and Miller 2001; Sparks and Pellechia 1997), as well as popular critics (Dawkins 2000; Randi 1992; Shermer 2001), have also long been interested in the role of the media in fostering and sustaining "paranormal belief." There has been less attention to the ways in which these mediated images mobilize varying levels of paranormal belief or interest into culturally elaborated and orchestrated action, as is the case in ghost tourism.

Genres of Ghost Media

From literature to film, ghosts appear in a wide range of media. As I noted in the introduction, scholars have begun to analyze the significance and meaning of such literary representations (Gordon 1997; Richardson 2003). While a broad range of popular imaginings certainly contribute to tourists' understandings of the ghostly and their travel practices, the role of "reality-based" understandings is less well understood. In particular, guidebooks and travel shows play an especially important role in crafting the practices and paradoxes of ghost tourism.

Guidebooks are a staple of all forms of tourism. Specialized guidebooks abound, offering specialty guides for tourists interested in food, art, architecture, walking, literature, and more. Ghosts constitute a component of that market. Of course, the inclusion of ghosts in travel guides is far from a new development. For example, in 1855, Harriet Martineau's *A Complete Guide to the English Lakes* mentioned several haunted homes and businesses. More recently, travel guides, such as *Lonely Planet England* (2005), include information about ghost tours and haunted sites. However, books that specifically chronicle the ghosts in a particular area have become an ubiquitous form of publication.

Such books that tell ghost stories were common during my research in England. I found them in gift shops at touristic, historic, and archaeological sites, as well as in official tourist offices and individual bookshops.[2] Stylistically, these books ranged from beautifully produced, mass published texts to smaller volumes published by local or regional presses. These books also vary in content. Some books offer brief accounts of locations with an emphasis on the type of paranormal activity visitors might encounter there. Others tell complete ghost stories that emphasize the narrative and folkloric value of the tales and minimize visitors' potential for paranormal experience. In each case, these texts play an important part in defining the scope and scale of ghost tourism in Britain.

There are two dominant genres of ghost books produced for the touristic market: books of ghost stories and encyclopedias of hauntings.[3] The former focuses on providing detailed accounts of well-known ghost stories. The latter focuses on providing an encyclopedic catalogue of ghosts in a country, region, or nation. While the conventions of each genre vary, they share an emphasis on recounting the history and nature of paranormal experience, although each type of book tends to focus on a slightly different component.

Anthologies of Ghost Stories

Collections of ghost stories are commonly found in gift shops and bookshops. These books tend to privilege complete stories of ghosts and provide information about the history of the ghost, the emergence of the haunting, and experiential details. These books can emphasize varying degrees of realism. For example, in the introduction to *Classic Devon Ghost Stories*, the compiler, Paul White, explains that "the stories in this book have come from many sources, most notably Sir Ernest Bennet, Mrs. Bray . . . [and others]. They have been selected for readability rather than psychical authenticity, and you certainly do not need to believe in ghosts and apparitions in order to enjoy them." (1996, 1). White's introduction articulated the divide that this genre of text navigates. Such texts are not produced with avid ghost hunters in mind; rather, they are produced for casual tourists or enthusiasts who enjoy the historical and atmospheric dimensions of ghosts. Despite this, they do not discount the possibility of actual encounters with the ghostly.

The stories chronicled in White's volume typically include information about their source, as well as a detailed account of the ghost story in question, often in period writing. Of course, not all anthologies offer such detailed information regarding the origin of a story. In one example, *Ghosts and Ghouls of the East Riding*, Michael Wray (2004) simply launches into ghost stories without recounting their historical origins. The characters and contexts of the story emerge without much contextualization. In another instance, he begins a ghost story by noting "it was evening in the little village of Harpham. . . . An old widow was looking sadly out of her cottage window" (Wray 2004, 5). He goes on to explain that the widow's son, a drummer, was murdered and thrown into a well and that the sounds of drumming can still be heard from the well. While this story is a fairly typical ghost story, the rhetorical construction of the tale is worth noting. By beginning the story with the widow looking out the window, Wray establishes himself as an omniscient narrator. This has the effect of rendering the ghost story as folklore rather than psychical reality.

Such rhetorical style serves to highlight the romantic, atmospheric components of ghost stories. Some may interpret these stories as reliable accounts of past hauntings. For example, Wray includes some of the necessary information for tourists to visit and experience the hauntings on their own; however, it is not the main focus of his text. Ultimately, these texts tend to present ghosts as fully formed and reasonably well-known entities, and they give the impression that there is a known canon of fully formed ghosts occupying the landscape. Museums and heritage sites find this vein of understanding very useful in articulating their model of the haunted past.

Encyclopedias of Hauntings

Encyclopedias of hauntings tend to include a greater number of brief accounts of ghosts with special focus on the experiential elements. Entries detailing the specificities of particular haunted sites constitute anywhere between a paragraph and several pages in length. These entries rarely attempt to include all of the history of the site. They also tend to avoid the flowery or romantic language found in some collections of ghost stories. They emphasize sites that have regular paranormal activity, and their descriptions treat the activity as real and reliable.

In many ways, Derek Acorah's *Haunted Britain and Ireland* (2006) is representative of the genre and particularly noteworthy given his fame among paranormal enthusiasts.[4] In the introduction to his guide, he introduces readers to several types of manifestations of ghosts and hauntings, as well as some of the ways in which people can pursue them. (These articulations are very much in line with what shows, such as *Most Haunted*, emphasize as ideal research techniques.) Acorah makes it clear in his introduction that it is a guidebook intended to help paranormal enthusiasts or ghost hunters pursue their interest in the paranormal. John Brooks's *The Good Ghost Guide* is also typical of this approach. Publishers fashioned the guidebook, which is taller than most books, to look like emblematic guidebooks like *Fodor's*, which are a convenient size for travel. *The Good Ghost Guide* goes so far as to remind readers that "although this book mentions times and places where ghosts are reported to appear, no guarantees are offered" (Brooks 1994, 7 [figure 1.1]). The inclusion of this disclaimer speaks to several key assumptions about the purpose of the volume. Most notably, its goal is to direct tourists to ghosts and, even more importantly, facilitate their encounters with a ghost.[5]

In recent years, with the increasing popularity of ghost hunting as a hobby, local researchers increasingly produce such guides and include firsthand accounts of their own embodied experiences and research. One excellent example of this approach is *Otherworld North East: Ghosts and Hauntings Explored* (Liddell 2004). In it, Tony Liddell, an archaeologist and paranormal investigator, presents 40 haunted locations, 16 of which include paranormal investigation case studies. While Liddell includes elements of ghost stories and history, the emphasis here is on the experiential elements of the hauntings. A related trend is evident in online databases of ghosts and hauntings maintained by ghost hunting and paranormal investigation groups, such as websites like *Ghost Village* and *Real Ghosts and Haunted Places in Britain*. These websites follow the encyclopedic approach and emphasize the experiential dimensions of haunting. For instance, the website *Real Ghosts and Haunted Places in Britain* describes its approach this way.

> You may wonder what I mean by the term 'real ghosts?' I mean, not only the traditional phantoms that you may think of when you hear the word 'ghosts,' but also screaming skulls, headless specters and phantom black dogs. Phenomena that seems to be peculiar to Britain. These British ghosts don't all have to be visible in order to be 'real.' Ghosts can be heard, smelt, seen or felt or they may make their presence known in some other way and here you will find ghosts of this sort as well as poltergeists and, 'things that go bump in the night.' (Real British Ghosts.com)

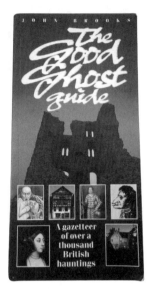

FIGURE 1.1 The Good Ghost Guide, like standard guidebooks such as Fodor's, seems designed to fit easily into a travellers' bags. It provides information about the location of haunted sites as well as their availability to the public and the type of hauntings housed there.

This website's emphasis on experience and the breadth of the sensorium is representative of much online coverage. In addition to such overview sites, local ghost hunting and paranormal investigation groups also produce smaller encyclopedias of hauntings on their websites with special focus on their personal encounters.

Additionally, presenters from reality television programs increasingly publish their own guides to haunted locations, as well as paranormal investigation.[6] As individuals emerge as celebrities in the ghost hunting field, increasingly they have begun to publish first person accounts of their experiences that act as de facto guidebooks. For example, in 2007 Jason Hawes and Grant Wilson, from the American television show *Ghost Hunters*, published *Ghost Hunting: True Stories of Unexplained Phenomena from The Atlantic Paranormal Society*, which provides first person accounts of their research at various haunted sites. The increasing presence and popularity of these books demonstrates the pervasive role of paranormal reality television in constructing understandings of hauntings.

TV Programs

Since the late 1990s, there has been an abundance of television programs focused on the paranormal or ghostly in both the UK and the US. These shows played an important role in reviving and reinventing popular interest in the paranormal. They have also played an important role in promoting, constructing, and guiding ghost tourism. Programs such as *Most Haunted*, *Ghost Adventurers*, *America's Haunted Hotels*, *Most Terrifying Places in America*, and *Ghost Hunters* foreground a documentary approach to the paranormal, and they are wildly popular in Britain and the US. There is a long history of television programs that focus on the paranormal or spooky. In the past, these programs tended to be explicitly fictional, in the case of shows such as *The Twilight Zone*, *The Outer Limits*, *The Munsters*, *The Addams Family*, *Dark*

Shadows, Casper, and *Scooby Doo.* They also ranged from frightening to funny. In recent years, fictional stories that include paranormal elements have proliferated even further. For example, *The X-Files, Passions, Supernatural, Fringe, True Blood, Dead Like Me, Pushing Daisies, Medium, The Ghost Whisperer,* and *Being Human* have found devoted cult and popular audiences. While such programs, many of which focus explicitly on the lives of ghosts, certainly contribute to popular interest in the ghostly, I believe that the phenomenon of paranormal tourism is more thoroughly grounded in a different popular cultural trajectory.

Since the 1960s and 1970s, there have been programs that focus on the paranormal in a nonfictional context. These programs tend to share stories of bizarre or unexplained encounters with possibly paranormal forces. Among the most popular and influential are *In Search Of . . ., Arthur C. Clarke's Mysterious World,* and *Strange but True.* These shows tended to focus heavily on eyewitness narratives of the paranormal, including first-person testimony of supposed events, but rarely include any footage of the events themselves. Media studies scholar Vincent Campbell has suggested that a hallmark of most paranormal documentary is the absence of visual evidence. He noted that "perhaps the most striking feature of many documentaries on paranormal topics is the treatments of visual evidence. The most pressing problem for several of the programmes assessed was the lack of visual 'evidence' of the subject matter" (Campbell 2000, 149). Importantly, Campbell's analysis of paranormal documentaries focused exclusively on cryptozoology and ufology, forms of inquiry that often fail to yield visual evidence. Programs such as *In Search Of . . .* and *Arthur C. Clarke's Mysterious World* focused heavily on general unexplained phenomena, UFOs, and monsters like the Loch Ness Monster.

Most Haunted

There was a seismic shift in the representation of the paranormal on television in the early 2000s with the introduction of the British program *Most Haunted.* Its first episode premiered on May 25, 2002, on Living, a British television channel.[7] Fourteen seasons of the program aired between 2002 and 2010. The program featured a regular cast of "investigators" who visited a new haunted site each episode to investigate the paranormal. It also generated a second, less regular show, *Most Haunted Live!* The regular participants in *Most Haunted* included a presenter, a historian, parapsychologists, and a medium or psychic. Turnover, of course, took place over the years.[8] Historian Owen Davies noted in 2007 that the program "presents sensational, telegenic live investigations" (2007, 97). Each episode of the show typically featured the cast visiting a haunted site where they spent the night investigating. Mediums played a prominent role on the program, and their interpretations of a site's haunting featured very heavily. The show also included a skeptical or scientific voice in the form of a parapsychologist.[9]

The representation of paranormal activity and research found on *Most Haunted* resonated heavily with paranormal investigators and ghost enthusiasts across Britain and, later, the US. It contributed to the emergence of self-fashioned paranormal investigators, a widespread form of amateur research in Britain. It also popularized the practice of engaging in a particular type of tourism at potentially haunted sites. Prior to *Most Haunted*, there were abundant ghost walks throughout England that provided tourists with scary or playful ghost stories. After *Most Haunted*, however, tourists became interested in a more experiential form of ghost tourism that foregrounded their own encounters with the paranormal. To understand this, it is necessary to examine the format of *Most Haunted* and its role in constructing a particular understanding of paranormal experience, history, and destination image.

Most Haunted mirrors and explicates many of the strategies that link place and history throughout the genre of ghost guidebooks. Some of the sites visited in this show were already very popular ghost tourism destinations, such as Edinburgh's Mary King's Close and the Edinburgh Vaults. Other sites, such as Sunderland's North East Air Museum, had a reputation for paranormal activity in local circles; however, *Most Haunted* brought them much wider national and international attention.

The episodes typically include an historical exposition of the site focusing heavily on its darker elements. For example, during the opening scenes of an episode about Tutbury Castle in Staffordshire, the following is offered as a broad historical and paranormal introduction:

> Tutbury Castle has stood here since 1070 and has been involved in some of the most dramatic events in almost a thousand years. Mary Queen of Scots was held here as a prisoner three times, and Charles I and his nephew Prince Rupert were offered shelter here during the Civil War. And Oliver Cromwell ordered that the castle be dismantled for harboring the king. Some of the ruins were repaired after the restoration in 1662 leaving the castle as you see it today. Witch burnings, the ghost of a huge man in full Tudor armor, a hooded figure, and one terrifying room that had to be closed to the public as people were fainting for no apparent reason. Too much paranormal activity has been reported here for it to be ignored. (Fielding 2003, *Most Haunted* Season 2, Episode 2)

This introduction to the Castle knits threads of paranormal activity and historical significance together seamlessly and, in doing so, renders the past as paranormal. In the first part of the introduction, Yvette Fielding, the presenter, briefly describes some of the famous occupants of the Castle. Then, she lists some of the paranormal events. The producers of the program, including Fielding, clearly see a relationship between the historical list and the paranormal occurrences; however, it is not rendered explicit. She assumes that there is a casual relationship between the two, an assumption that undercuts much of the ghost literature.

This episode of *Most Haunted* moves from Fielding's initial introduction to an interview with Leslie Smith, the Castle's curator. Smith echoes Fielding's implied logic in her description of the Castle's past and its paranormal activity:

> This castle is nearly a thousand years old. Some of the greatest names in English history have been here. At one point we think as many as 600 soldiers were here and 400 were looking after them. It was a fortified town and because of that obviously a lot of lives, a lot of passions, blood and thunder, siege, death, and torture, so what do you expect? If there's going to be residue from the other side, it's bound to here. And we do have ghosts here. (Smith, Season 2, Episode 2)

Smith argues that because the Castle's history can be traced far back into the past and because it has been the site for many dramatic historical episodes, there is likely to be "residue from the other side." Both Smith and Fielding suggest that sites, which have housed a variety of historical eras and periods, are likely to boast hauntings. This emphasis on the past emerges again and again in paranormal tourism. The history that both Smith and Fielding recount, while intertwined with the ghostly, corresponds closely with the known historical record. This suggests that encounters with the ghosts present at Tutbury confirm the known historical record rather than contest it. While this may seem like an obvious observation, it is both significant and, as I will show later, highly contested.

Other guides also assume that hauntings are closely tied to the known historical record. This is the case even when writers describe anonymous ghosts whose identities are not explicitly grounded in the historical record. For example, consider Derek Acorah's description of a ghost who haunts the Royal Victoria County Park in Southampton. His description of the site could fit in any guidebook. He praises it as a "haven for many different kinds of wildlife . . . and bird species" and observes that events, such as "football and cricket matches, bus and caravan rallies, craft fairs, and dog shows," attract roughly 360,000 visitors a year (Acorah 2006, 192). Acorah then notes some interesting elements of the site's history. It was "once the grounds of the Royal Victoria Hospital, which became the country's main military hospital after it opened in 1863" (2006, 192). The Hospital has since been destroyed; however, it engendered the key haunting associated with the site. Before addressing the haunting, Acorah included some interesting historical details unrelated to the haunting, such as Florence Nightingale's dislike of the grandness of the architecture. Then, he delved into the history that contextualizes the haunting: "thousands of patients were treated there" (Acorah 192, 192).

Finally, Acorah turned to the ghost in question. He wrote that "the site of the former hospital is haunted by a lady in a grey crinoline dress. She is said to be the ghost of a young Victorian nurse who gave her soldier boyfriend a fatal overdose by mistake. When he died, she climbed the chapel tower and jumped to her death. Afterwards, her appearance in the hospital was considered to be a sign that someone would die that next morning" (2006, 192–93). While the details of the historical woman are questionable, her ghost story serves to reveal the history of the former hospital. In Acorah's account, the history of the hospital and a description of its modern day park occupy more textual space than the description of the ghost. Such textual choices illustrate how ghosts can be used to make history interesting and accessible.

Theme of Travel

These guides, regardless of genre, implicitly or explicitly assume that encountering a ghost requires travel. This is not a straightforward assumption. Despite most ghost hunters' explicit claims that a haunting may occur anywhere (including your own home), all forms of ghost tourism are grounded on the assumption that travel is necessary to access a haunting. While the reasons for this are complex, part of the reason may stem from these textual representations of hauntings.

Consider what Acorah says about the purpose of his guide: "no matter where you live or how little you are prepared to travel, there will always be somewhere worthy of a visit if you are on the hunt for a ghost or two" (2006, 2). Here, it should be clear that Acorah imagines ghosts and paranormal experience as requiring and motivating travel. The tourists conjured in this description are interested primarily in ghosts.

Additionally, Acorah's invocation of travel is worth considering. His observation that "there will always be somewhere worthy of a visit if you are on the hunt for a ghost or two" reveals an important and pervasive assumption in ghost hunting and paranormal tourism. An interest in ghosts or a desire to encounter them appears to necessitate some form of travel. While Acorah emphasized that tourists and enthusiasts need not travel far to find a ghost, he implies that some travel is necessary. Desirable and intriguing hauntings, then, occur outside the home. This representation of ghost tourism also demonstrates the assumption that tourists want to encounter *public* rather than *private* ghosts. While tourists' own ghosts of dead family members may haunt homes, the spirits who haunt public sites are more widely known figures often tied to major historical events. These guidebooks, then, reiterate that ghost tourism's focus is public history rather than private, genealogical knowledge. This emphasis on travel suggests that some ghosts are more worthy of notice than others and that some histories are more significant that others, claims that I show in chapters four and five that ghost tourists themselves contest.

The rest of Acorah's text is structured with the idea of travel in mind. He divides the book into sections focusing on England, Wales, Scotland, Northern Ireland, and the Republic of Ireland. England, Wales, and Scotland are each divided up into particular regions. For example, England is divided into Eastern England, London, Northern England, the Midlands, and Southern England. At the start of each section, Acorah briefly describes the landscape and history of hauntings as well as any literary depictions of hauntings associated with the region. Many other guidebooks mirror this organizational scheme.

Such encyclopedias are, in many ways, invitations to travel. Many explicitly list visitor information for particular sites. John Brooks's approach, in his 1994 *The Good Ghost Guide: A Gazetteer of Over a Thousand British Hauntings*, is especially noteworthy. In his introduction to the guide, Brooks included very specific visiting instructions.

> Inclusion of an entry in this book does not mean the haunted area is open to the public. The words 'open to the public' in the text indicate places that charge an entry fee and may be open only at specified times. It is advisable to check fees and times with local tourist authorities. Pubs and hotels present no problems. (Brooks 1994, 7)

From his introduction, it is clear that Brooks anticipates readers relying on his text to help them plan trips to particular haunted sites. He also includes a handy key providing easy-to-use indicators of the nature of a haunting. The markers in the key broach the divide between ghosts-as-stories and ghosts-as-experiences. They signal experiential elements of hauntings, such as ghosts that "make scheduled appearances" and that "bring harm to the onlooker" (Brooks 1994, 7). At the same time, the markers ground ghosts in known, narrative capacities, such as a "World War ghost" or a "spectral army"

(Brooks 1994, 7). Presenting these traits in the form of a key emphasizes the fixedness of these characteristics. It harkens to the keys found on maps, which geographers have long noted are politicized attempts to articulate and instill particular visions of geographic, social, and political order (Harley 2009). Invoking the language and visuality of maps reiterates the fixedness of the hauntings in question. This apparent stability allows for the emergence of sustained, regular ghost tourism; however, from the perspective of ghost hunters, it also overstates commonly understood levels of determinism.

Brooks's assessment on the availability of particular sites is especially revealing. While describing how to access particular sites, Brooks empha- sizes that not all sites may be open to the public. While he eventually urges tourists to "respect privacy" (1994, 7), this initial presentation represents an important tension in ghost tourism. He suggests that there are some sites that are open to ghost tourists and some that are not. While this is the case in many forms of tourism, for ghost tourists, especially ghost hunters and paranormal investigators, restrictions on access emerge as a point of con- testation and frustration (see chapter five). While encyclopedic guides like Brooks's are clear invitations to travel, other ghost guides function in a less explicit fashion.

Guidebooks and Legend-Trips

It is possible to view the networked understandings of ghosts present in these books and television episodes as legends and incitements to legend- tripping. Folklorists have argued that forms of mass media including tele- vision shows (Dégh 2001; Koven 2007), films (Koven 1999), and books can all act as either legend-tellers or forms of legend ostension. In the former, a storyteller recounts a narrative about a legend to an audience while in the latter they are "shown as direct action" (Koven 2007, 184). So, in the example of Wray's 2004 book of local ghost stories described earlier, Wray acts as a storyteller. At the same time, as Koven (2007) persuasively argues, the show *Most Haunted* acts as an ostension of folklore by focusing on cast members investigating. These written guides, folklorists argue, as well their televised counterparts, spark individuals to engage in legend-trips.

Folklorists use the term legend-trip to refer to the practice of visiting the site of a local legend to engender a supernatural or extraordinary experience. Scholars have often pointed to the centrality of the practice among teenagers (Bird 2002; Ellis 1989; Goldstein, Grider, and Thomas 2007). The structure of a legend-trip, as S. Elizabeth Bird argued, is two-fold: "the telling of the story, followed or accompanied by the visit to the site, and the tests of bravery this usually involves" (2002, 539). The role of the guidebooks, in this model, is clear; they provide the story or its ostension, effectively guiding tourists to visit the site in question. Within folkloristic studies of legends and legend-tripping, the activities that occur in the course of a legend-trip are always closely associated with the legend in question. Consider Carl Lindahl's recent description of legend-trips in which he states "such legend quests constitute a sort of ostensive play, an improvised drama in which the players, visiting the site of a haunting or the scene of a crime . . . both recreate the storied events and simultaneously expand the tale by adding their experiences to the core narrative" (Lindahl 2005, 165). Lindahl's explanation is very much in line with how guidebooks and *Most Haunted* present the activities of ghost tourism. They seem to anticipate tourists learning about documented ghost stories and visiting haunted sites with the goal of encountering that particular ghost story. The guidebooks seem to expect that tourists will be interested in the types of experiences canonically associated with the site. In short, guidebooks and television shows actively present ghost tourism as a form of legend-tripping and envision a concrete range of engagements with historically grounded ghosts or canonical experiences. They position tourists as seeking verification of a legend rather than acquisition of personally meaningful knowledge. Ultimately, this understanding of ghost tourism emerges in the text of the guidebooks, as well as its visual instantiation.

Visual Rhetoric of Hauntings

Visuality plays a central role in shaping tourists' expectations of a haunted site. The photographs and images in many of these ghost guidebooks and on paranormal reality television help to construct and affirm images and understandings of hauntedness. The tension between understanding ghosts as either fully formed or inchoate drives the visual depictions of the hauntings and results in visual images that highlight the atmospheric landscape and the historical renderings that are divorced from their contemporary contexts. Ultimately, in these representations, ghosts manifest as glaring social and topographical absences.

Some—although certainly not all—of the guidebooks include beautifully produced photographs of destinations. Richard Jones's 2005 *Haunted Castles of Britain and Ireland* (figure 1.2) and Siân Evans's 2006 book *Ghosts* are excellent examples of this. Both are gorgeous coffee-table books with glossy photographs of haunted destinations; Jones's text includes color and half-tone photographs. Evans's feature only black and white. Several elements of the composition of these photographs deserve comments.

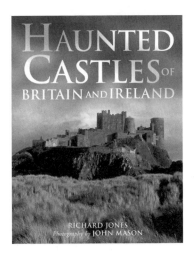

FIGURE 1.2 The cover of Jones's book features a beautiful, evocative photograph of a castle against a cloudy sky. As is the case on many ghost guidebook covers, the photograph does not include any living humans. It focuses instead on the haunted buildings and landscapes.

These photographs cast the English landscape, as well as castles and National Trust sites, as eerie, spooky presences. The perspective of the photographs is also critical. The photographers took many of the pictures from the ground, which results in the built structures looming above the perspective of viewer. In Evans's text, the black-and-white photographs cast the sites in a moody and at times sinister light. Jones's and Evans's text feature multiple photographs that include mist or fog surrounding a particular building. It is unclear what time of day these photographs were taken and if the mists were of a natural or supernatural origin. This ambiguity seems intentional, and it fosters a sense of foreboding and immanent supernatural presence. Interestingly, all of the photographs feature scenes from haunted castles that are owned by England's National Trust or that are publicly accessible. While stories may focus on staff members who encountered ghosts in backstage areas, the visual focus remains squarely on areas that tourists may directly access.

The photographs present in *Ghosts* and *Haunted Castles of Britain and Ireland* visually represent many assumptions regarding the social nature of hauntings. In both texts, there are no people and only the faintest traces of animals in the featured photographs. The houses, buildings, and landscapes are depicted as perfectly preserved but uninhabited domains. While texts, such as Evans's and Jones's, illuminate the role of photograph, this theme of social isolation from the present emerges in many other guidebooks. For example, Brooks's *The Good Ghost Guide* lacks the extensive photographs of Evans's or Jones's texts; however, there are multiple illustrations throughout the text and on the cover. Consider the cover, shown in Figure 1.1, which features looming ruins, two photographs of haunted sites, and four historical paintings or drawings. The text includes additional, similar, images throughout the pages. Nearly all texts mirror this approach; they feature no images of contemporary, living people. These absences are obviously intentional representational strategies. They reveal an implicit assumption that ghosts are from the past, and there is a significant rupture between the past and the present. The only time humans appear in these books is in paintings from other historical eras or in drawn illustration.

The Ambiguities of Evidence

The approach of these guidebooks, as well as the websites and brochures of various ghost tours, is remarkable in its exclusion of photographic depictions *of* ghosts. There is a long history of spirit or paranormal photography in Europe and North America (Brandon 1984; Davies 2007; Kaplan 2003). During the height of the Spiritualist Movement in 1861, William Mumler, a Boston photographer, took a photograph of himself in his studio and, upon developing it, realized that he had also captured the image of his dead cousin. Mumler's photograph sparked a craze, and believers sought photographs of themselves with their dead loved ones in spirit form. The practices of spirit photography seemed to substantiate many of Spiritualists' claims that spirits survived death. Iconic photographs abounded, such as Mary Todd Lincoln sitting with a spectral Abraham Lincoln looming behind her. Of course, such practices attracted many vocal skeptics. Harry Houdini suggested that such photographs could be "faked" in a number of ways, including "double exposures or prepared plates," as historian Ruth Brandon explained (1984, 233). While such critiques eventually led to a decline in the popularity of attempts to photograph full-bodied spirits, other forms of spirit photography emerged to fill the void. For example, photographs of orbs, ectoplasm, and other paranormal substances emerged as popular in the late nineteenth and early twentieth centuries (Marsching 2003; Schoonover 2003). Some forms, such as photographs of orbs, which appear as little balls of light, remain very popular today. Many ghost hunters and paranormal investigators avidly seek to photograph orbs or specs of light that may signify ghostly presences.

Photographs occupy an intensely contested domain in the history of Spiritualism and paranormal knowledge production, as well as its contemporary manifestations. The authenticity and evidentiary stake of photographs of spirits, orbs, or other paranormal phenomena are wildly debated. As historian Louis Kaplan poignantly explained, "photography conjures a state of paranoia and paranoiac knowledge for both skeptics and believers in these photo-apparitions" (2003, 19). He is right. This genre of photography lends itself to such "cantankerous debate" (Kaplan 2003, 20), in part, because of the strong tie between photographs and perceived regimes of truth. Scholars have noted that photographs can act in a dizzying range of ways: artistic expression, personal reminders, methods of objectification, mechanisms of colonizing, as well as scientifically grounded objectification (Dominguez 2007; Sontag 1977; Wilder 2009). In the case of spirit or paranormal photography, the debates are so "cantankerous" because the photographs claim to provide evidence of the ontological reality of the ghostly or the spirit world.

That guidebooks and tourist brochures avoid such photographs reiterates a key component in how they position ghost tourism. The evidentiary nature of spirit or orb photographs is at odds with how guidebooks and touristic brochures present ghosts. I have argued that their representational strategies elevate the experiential and historical dimensions of ghost tourism rather than its documentary possibilities or the ontological status of ghosts. While some ghost tourists are more interested in documenting and pursuing knowledge of the *reality* of ghosts, visual imagery that focuses on the lurking, inchoate presences that *may* titillate visitors sidesteps questions of fraud or pseudoscience and positions these potential encounters with the ghostly in the domain of the touristic or fun. This representational mode allows heritage organizations, museums, and other orthodox arenas to actively position themselves within the touristic market. It also plants the seeds of discontent between ghost tourists interested in the *reality* of ghosts and heritage organizations that present ghosts as matters of folklore or fun.

Most Haunted occupies an interesting position in this tension between representing ghosts as ontological realities or as metaphorical, historical presences. As I have noted, on the show, the team visits haunted sites with the express purpose of investigating the reality of ghosts. Despite this emphasis, the status of evidence in the show is highly ambiguous, and it often presents evidence of someone's experience rather than direct evidence of paranormal reality. In this, they differ from various forms of spirit photography (Kaplan 2003). Viewers observe the show's mediums encountering a variety of spirits, some of whom are known historical figures associated with the sites. For example, in one episode set at Chillingham Castle, Derek Acorah felt the presence of a "Mary." Jason Karl, who was the show's parapsychologist at the time, confirmed that this was a "hit," commenting that "there is a spirit who is associated with Chillingham Castle whose first name is Mary." While such exchanges can certainly be seen as a type of evidence, their evidentiary status is complex and far from straightforward. Many *Most Haunted* viewers maintain a degree of skepticism regarding the veracity of its mediums, especially Acorah. Other types of evidence appear throughout the show. Spirits push, breath on, and touch members of the cast regularly. *Most Haunted* prioritizes the experiences of cast and crew members. Koven argues that "by watching *Most Haunted* we are invited to question the veracity of any of the evidence presented, including that of the show's psychics" (2007, 189). The show ultimately presents the *pursuit* of evidence rather than its collection or evaluation. The vast majority of airtime is dedicated to exploring the site and showing cast members' experiences in the dark. Usually, a small chunk of time is dedicated to presenting the "evidence," in the form of a summary, at the end of the show. While its explicit emphasis on the evidentiary status of ghosts would seem to distinguish *Most Haunted* from other genres of ghost tourist literature, this is not the case. Ultimately, *Most Haunted* constructs *experience and historical narratives* rather than *evidence of the status of ghosts* as the principal goals of investigating and ghost tourism, despite their explicit statements to the contrary.

The Heritage Industry and its Ghosts

This understanding of ghosts as the conduits to history is powerful. Museums and heritage sites have successfully adopted it as a means of broadening their audience and rendering the past accessible. The incorporation of ghosts in heritage and museum sites can take many forms. Sites may offer special ghost tours, include textual descriptions of ghosts associated with the museum, or open up special, haunted areas of the museum to tourists. Even the most elite English heritage organizations, such as English Heritage, National Trust, and Historic Royal Palaces, offer some manner of ghost tourism.

English Heritage, a non-departmental body of the Department for Culture, Media and Sport dedicated to preserving and protecting the historic places of England, has incorporated ghost tours in a number of its properties. For example, in 2011, they hosted ghost walks specifically for adults at Kenilworth Castle in Warwickshire and Bolsover Castle in Derbyshire and ghost walks for children at Pendennis Castle in Cornwall and Dartmouth Castle in Devon. On their website, they advertised these upcoming walks by claiming that

> Hundreds of ghostly apparitions, cold chills, and former residents of our properties are left to roam the empty corridors in the dead of night with only the bats for company. It's a sad fate, but this year you've got a chance to end this neglect by booking on one of our regular ghost tours throughout the winter. Are you brave enough? (English Heritage 2011)

Positioning the ghosts as "former residents" of their castles allows English Heritage to cast the ghosts as historically complete figures. By sharing the stories about these former residents, English Heritage serves its mission of fostering understanding and enjoyment of historic places and environments. Here, again, the historical completeness and concreteness of the ghosts recommends them as features of the heritage complex.

Similarly, the National Trust and Historic Royal Palaces have also actively incorporated ghost tours into their sites. The National Trust, an independent organization dedicated to historic preservation, hosted ghost walks around Halloween at sites like Ham House in Richmond. Historic Royal Palaces hosts regular ghost walks at Hampton Court Palace.[10] Both organizations have incorporated ghost stories into the standard narration of some of their properties as well. For example, Hampton Court Palace features a display explaining about Catherine Howard's ghost. At the Treasurer's House in York, the National Trust prominently features and advertises the well-known Roman ghosts in its basement and even charges guests an extra fee to visit the place they reportedly haunt. These displays deploy ghosts as established figures in the past; their stories serve the greater unfolding of history at the sites. Consider Hampton Court's presentation of its ghosts. In one exhibit focusing on Henry VIII's family, the story of Catherine Howard's ghost casually emerges. Next to a picture of a portrait of her, a sign informs readers that:

> Henry married his queen, Catherine Howard, in 1540. Catherine and Henry spent their honeymoon at Hampton Court. The honeymoon was soon over. Just one year later, also at Hampton Court, Catherine was accused of infidelity and treason. She was put under house arrest in her lodgings in the palace. Senior courtiers gathered together in the Great Watching Chamber to be told of Catherine's treason. According to tradition, Catherine broke free from her guards and ran along the gallery leading to the Royal Pew above the Chapel Royal in a desperate attempt to reach the King and beg for her life. She was dragged, screaming, back to her rooms, and was removed from the palace the following day. She was executed at the Tower of London shortly afterward. It is said that Catherine Howard's ghost still runs along the haunted gallery. (Hampton Court Palace 2009)

This description is remarkable in its calm handling of a fairly upsetting ghost story. Catherine's ghost emerges as an almost unremarkable component of this brief biographical sketch. Indeed, the description of her ghost parallels that of her execution in its matter-of-factness. The site uses tentative language ("according to tradition" and "it is said") to describe Catherine's behavior as a living prisoner and as a ghost, and it does not rhetorically distinguish between these claims. English Heritage emphasizes that both claims are dependent on the observations of historical witness; however, they do not address that the appearance of a ghost poses a significant number of questions about the order of reality while observing a running prisoner does not.

The National Trust presents the Treasurer's House in York and its famous Roman ghosts in a similar fashion. The language in an advertisement inside the Treasurer's House for the special Ghost Cellar tour is straightforward. A sign announces that "in 1953 Harry Martindale saw a legion of Roman soldiers marching through the Cellar of the Treasurer's House. Visit the Cellar with a guide and find out all about this world famous ghost sighting and the history of the Romans in York" (Treasurer's House 2007). The National Trust presents the ghosts of the Roman soldiers as conduits into the past. Hearing their story will inform visitors about the Roman history of York. This positions ghosts as markedly similar to any other colorful figure in the past. Hearing a ghost story, then, is not all that different than hearing a standard historical narrative.

Ultimately, for both groups, a desire for publicity motivates their choice to advocate and publicize their reported ghosts. The retellings of ghost stories found on National Trust, English Heritage, or Historic Royal Palace properties tend to emphasize ghosts as historical figures who fit within an established narrative of the past. The ghosts presented at these sites reach a similarly broad, if not broader, audience than those on ghost walks. Many of the visitors maintain only a casual interest in ghosts. Some of the people who purchased the "Ghost Cellar Tour," a £5-special tour that augments a regular visit to the Treasurer's House, had only a passing interest in the ghostly (figure 1.3). For example, a couple from Harrogate, who purchased the Ghost Cellar Tour, explained their decision to me. The man said, "well, we were keen to see the entirety of the house. We thought the cellar would be interesting as well. It was." When I asked if they had any special interest in ghosts, the woman replied, "No as such, no. I enjoy a good ghost story, but it's not a passion of mine." This is not to say that individuals with serious, more sustained interest in ghosts do not also take ghost walks or visit heritage sites that prominently feature ghosts. They often do as well.

At sites such as the Treasurer's House or Hampton Court Palace, which include descriptions of ghosts into the main narration of their museums through text panels and descriptions, the audience is even wider and more casual. These sites seem to seamlessly absorb ghosts into their presentation of heritage. That ghosts appear as fully formed historical narratives contrib-

FIGURE 1.3 This sign, which stands in the courtyard of the National Trust Treasurer's House in York, advertises the Ghost Cellar. For an extra fee, visitors can take a guided tour of the basement where Harry Martindale saw the ghosts of the Roman soldiers, which I described in the Introduction. Unlike ghost walks, which advertise widely throughout the city of York, this is one of the few advertisements for the Ghost Cellar.

utes in large part to this. Including a story about Romans or Catherine Howard as ghosts does not appear significantly different than including a story about them as historically real beings.

The casual incorporation of these ghosts into heritage sites might strike some as remarkable. After all, many scholars and popular critics closely associate belief in ghosts with forms of irrationality (Dawkins 2000; Maller and Lundeen 1933; Randi 1992; Roig et al. 1998; Sparks and Miller 2001; Sparks and Pellechia 1997). Considering this, how can such respected and elite institutions incorporate ghosts as part of English cultural heritage? In short, by heavily emphasizing ghosts in their historical and folkloric capacity, heritage officials sidestep issues of belief and ontological status. They do not ask visitors to question their beliefs in ghosts, only to learn about the past through ghost stories. The rhetorical construction of ghost narratives allows for this paradox. However, such representations are not unchallenged, as I now explain.

Instability in the Text: Famous/Mundane Sites and the Emergence of New Experts

I have indicated that these guidebooks collectively construct a canon of fixed ghosts, ghost sites, and legends intended to engender legend-trips with little regard for the ontological status of ghosts or the deeper questions tourists may seek to ask. However, the fame of haunted sites is far from fixed. In fact, it changes over time while remaining susceptible to commercialization, commodification, and broad manipulation.

Guidebooks identify famous haunted locations, as well as less well-known alternatives. Ghost guidebooks are as likely to include mundane sites in their collection of noteworthy haunted sites as better-known destinations. For example, in Derek Acorah's collection of ghost sites, he includes places such as Heathrow Airport and several movie theaters.[11] Similarly, John Brooks also includes airports, such as Teeside Airport (now Durham Tees Valley Airport), in his guide.[12]

While guidebooks take a seemingly democratic approach and tend to include a significant number of sites, particular destinations emerge as favorites for ghost tourists. How does this happen? Many haunted sites that are favorites with ghost tourists, commercial ghost hunting companies, and walking tours appear to be fairly recent in origin. For example, it is worth noting that Brooks's 1994 guide to ghosts lacks references to some of the most well-known, and loved, contemporary haunted sites. The guide does not include a reference to the Golden Fleece in York, Castle Keep in Newcastle, or the Edinburgh Vaults, which are all contemporary ghost tourist mainstays. However, it is worth noting that Acorah's 2006 collection also lacks references to these three popular spots.

Not all media has the same impact, especially in the twenty-first century. During its run on LivingTV and even now after its finale, *Most Haunted* and its spin-offs *Most Haunted Live!* and *Most Haunted Extra* played an enormous role in crafting particular haunted sites into desirable touristic destinations. As I mentioned, Koven has argued that the show functioned as a traditional ostension "creating a complex, matrix-like relationship among the supernatural belief traditions, the television show, and those watching that show" (2007, 183). As such, it produced important understandings of ghost lore and shaped viewers understandings of haunted sites. Koven ultimately argued that it acted as form of legend-tripping and a call for others to legend-trip (2007, 185–86). Because Koven focuses almost exclusively on *Most Haunted* as a text, he cannot attend to how followers themselves make sense of the show. As media scholars have noted though, viewers and fans often elaborate on cultural texts in creative, innovative ways (Jenkins 2006, 2009, 2012). Audiences are not simply passive participants who absorb images; rather, they are active agents capable of producing and elaborating on such depictions in a range of ways.

While *Most Haunted*, taken as a text, can function to affirm the ideals of legend-tripping and reiterate the generative tension between ghosts-as-history and ghosts-as-experience, viewers often elaborate and complicate these themes in nuanced ways. In my research with paranormal knowledge producers, many avidly watched *Most Haunted*. Many investigators and ghost hunters initially viewed the show as a compelling representation of paranormal research, as well an exciting showcase of haunted sites (Hanks 2011). As JoAnn, a member of a paranormal investigation team explained, "at first, I watched because I really liked it. It was canny. They went to dead interesting places. They seemed to know what they were doing. I was quite interested in their methods." Eventually, her viewership of *Most Haunted* led her to seek out others in her area who shared an interest in the paranormal; they eventually formed a paranormal research group that was dedicated to researching the *reality of the paranormal*.

The style of investigating found on *Most Haunted* inspired JoAnn and her teammates; however, within a year of forming, they became wary of various aspects of the methodology featured on the program. Thus, JoAnn eventually became an "antifan" (Gray 2005). She explained her enlightened position on the show and argues that "what they're doing is just poor science, really. There are no controls. No way to know what the mediums know. It's a mess. It's a good guide of what not to do. . . . It is still good for the places, though. I'd love to investigate where they get to." JoAnn's experiences as a viewer are representative of many, if not most, in the paranormal community. In JoAnn's narrative, *Most Haunted* transitions from serving as a model of research and a guide to haunted locations to functioning as a counter-example. The cast members fall from trusted experts to exemplars of failure. Interestingly, as I have argued elsewhere (Hanks 2011), this process of transitioning from fan to anti-fan allows paranormal researchers to solidify and "perform" (Carr 2010) their own amateur expertise. In a real sense, their critiques of the show function as a means of repositioning themselves as the legitimate experts and the crew of *Most Haunted* as amateurs.

Paranormal researchers are not the only people who leverage the representations of ghosts, history, and experience into new forms of cultural practice. Owners of sites that appear on *Most Haunted*, as well as in the traditional guidebooks, also have agency in how they present and capitalize on the sites' reputations for hauntedness. Some sites quite literally advertise their association with the show. Consider the self-presentation of the Golden Fleece, a pub in York (figure 1.4). The exterior and entryway to the pub prominently featured photographs, fliers, and signs signaling its association with the show, as shown in figure 1.5. The Golden Fleece also profited from this association by regularly selling investigation and ghost hunting groups' overnight access to their site for a fee. They also collaborated with celebrities in the world of the paranormal like Richard Felix, a former historian on *Most Haunted*, to run periodic ghost tours around the city of York that end in a meal at the pub. For the Golden Fleece, appearing on the show enabled them to engage a new form of tourism and expand their market.

FIGURE 1.4 The Golden Fleece is one of York's most haunted pubs. It has been featured on the television show Most Haunted and it is a perennial favorite among ghost tourists. Many ghost walks stop outside the Golden Fleece to tell stories associated with the pub.

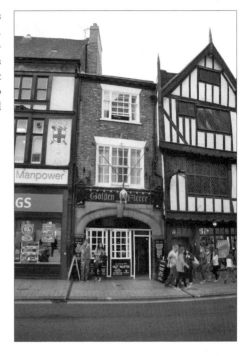

FIGURE 1.5 (left) Inside the pub, the Golden Fleece also advertises its association with the ghostly as well as its connection to shows such as Most Haunted and celebrities within the paranormal tourism community, such as Richard Felix, one of the historians on Most Haunted.

It is important to remember that sites can achieve fame for their hauntedness without appearing on Most Haunted or even in the guidebooks that I mentioned. For example, consider the South Bridge Vaults in Edinburgh. Today, they are a wildly popular haunted destination for a vast array of ghost tourists. Mercat Tours runs regular history and ghost tours in the Vaults. As Mercat's parapsychologists have observed "the vaults have acquired an international reputation for being one of the most haunted parts of Scotland's capital city" (Wiseman et. al. 2003, 196). This reputation is remarkable since the Vault was only rediscovered and opened to the public in 1999. Based on Mercat's aggressive advertising, their tours' overall fit with Scottish tourism

(Inglis and Holmes 2003) and tourists' regular experiential encounters with ghosts (Wiseman et al. 2003). This nexus of features allowed the owners of the Vaults to successfully position themselves as an ideal haunted destination. My point here is that while being featured on a paranormal reality program or in a ghost guidebook could positively construct a haunted destination image, the managers of sites themselves also have agency in this process.

While some sites actively capitalized on their newfound haunted celebrity, others adopted more ambiguous stances. For them, such newfound fame could be both a blessing and a curse. The director of one historic home that appeared on the show described what he called "the *Most Haunted* effect." He told me that after his site was featured on *Most Haunted*, the number of visitors nearly tripled for the following months. In this case, he seemed to regret his site's collaboration with *Most Haunted*. He worried that it misrepresented the site to visitors. He explained.

> People come here expecting some sort of ghost experience now. I see them wandering throughout museum. They're not here for the history. I think that they're hoping for a ghost to pop out and scare them. I hate to disappoint them. However, that's really not what our museum is about, and I don't see us changing our focus to accommodate this interest.

His frustration with the "*Most Haunted* effect" is obvious. The disjuncture between touristic expectations and his site's content was deeply troublesome to him. That this group of tourists persisted in their visits, despite the disjuncture also surprised him.

This director's experiences ultimately points to the power of ghost tourists themselves to shape, circumvent, and complicate the representations and engagement with ghosts found at heritage sites. This reveals that ghosts are not always safe, controllable elements of heritage.

Conclusion

Ultimately, the tension between understandings of ghosts as historical figures and experiential beings enables the orthodox heritage industry to tentatively adopt them as productive figures. However, it is significant that this dialogic tension obscures the transgressive elements of the ghostly that trouble commonplace assumptions about nature, history, science, and spirituality. Paranormal reality television programs, encyclopedias of hauntings, as well as anthropologies of ghost stories produce a network of meanings, practices, and expectations for tourists; however, tourists ultimately have the power to configure and reconfigure these meanings and practices to their own ends.

Ghosts are far from a "safe" component of heritage. As I show throughout the rest of this book, recourses to the ghostly empower many ghost tourists to critique orthodox historical and scientific knowledge while repositioning themselves as central stakeholders in the heritage field.

CHAPTER TWO

DISCOURSES AND ENACTMENTS OF BELIEF AND TRANSFORMATION ON GHOST WALKS AND COMMERCIAL GHOST HUNTS

D uring my fieldwork in 2008 and 2009, up to seven ghost walk tours could be found winding their way through the city center in York on any given Friday night. While this was going on, one or two commercial ghost tour companies would have been getting ready to lead participants in ghost hunts or vigils in haunted buildings—also in the city center. At the very same time, paranormal investigation teams might have been preparing to engage in their serious investigations somewhere else in the city. Ghost tours would likely stop at the very sites that would host these ghost hunts, vigils, or investigations. This image of three very different groups of people weaving their way through the same city center, intent on learning about ghosts, is an apt representation of some of the differing ideological and practical engagements with ghosts in England. While the heritage industry seeks to embrace a notion of ghosts as static, playful elements of national heritage, not all ghost tourists share this understanding of the ghostly. Some tourists conceptualize ghosts as matters of faith or belief. Here, I explore two such sets of people, the participants on ghost walks and those on commercial ghost hunts, and their attendant understandings of belief and ghosts.

While ghost walks and commercial ghost hunts are structurally very different, they both embrace belief as a means of reckoning with ghosts. In this, they differ drastically from the deployments of the ghostly at the heritage sites I described in the previous chapter. In this chapter, I argue that these two forms of recreation (ghost walks and commercial ghost hunts) mobilize differing understandings of belief, and yet each embraces belief as a way of knowing. I show that ghost walks constitute belief as a predetermined interior state, while commercial ghost hunts constitute belief as an achievable, desirable state contingent on demonstrated evidence. I argue that commercial ghost hunts provide a context for liminality and the reconfiguration of belief or disbelief, while ghost walks provide narration intended to amuse and support participants' pre-existing belief or disbelief. I argue that the former is a form of secular pilgrimage, while the latter is a mode of tourism.

Haunted Heritage: The Cultural Politics of Ghost Tourism, Populism, and the Past by Michele Hanks, 59–85. © 2015 Left Coast Press, Inc. All rights reserved.

Whereas a ghost walk is readily identifiable because it only takes an hour and is sold as touristic fun, a reader might confuse *commercial ghost hunts* with *paranormal investigations*. I caution that they are different. Despite similarities in the activities found on such events, such as embodied encounters with ghosts and technologically grounded attempts to collect data about the ghosts, *commercial ghost hunts* are not interchangeable with *paranormal investigations*. Individuals who purchase commercial ghost hunts are typically eager to have firsthand, embodied encounters with ghosts. They see such "experiences" as potentially capable of transforming them into "believers." Their understandings of evidence, experience, and belief vary in important ways from paranormal investigators, who view the entire enterprise of commercial ghost hunting with sustained suspicion.

Tourism and Pilgrimage

Acts of tourism and acts of pilgrimage are both forms of travel that generate contact with a designated space. As Victor Turner and Edith Turner note, "a tourist is half a pilgrim, if a pilgrim is half a tourist" ([1978] 1995, 21). Similarly, Ellen Badone and Sharon Roseman wrote more recently that "one has to ask the question of where, within this kaleidoscope of juxtaposed images, now lies the distinction between 'religious' pilgrims and 'secular' tourists" (2004, 9).

Turner and Turner ([1978] 1995) usefully argued in *Image and Pilgrimage in Christian Culture* that pilgrimages should be understood as liminal or "liminoid" experiences, and that this liminoid quality emerges from the voluntary nature of pilgrimage in contemporary industrialized societies. The liminoid, they wrote, appears in secular, voluntary acts of entertainment and leisure, such as sporting events, concerts, or pilgrimages, and it expresses "potentiality" rather than the transitory promise found in the liminality of many rituals.

If Turner and Turner are right, pilgrimages—with their emphasis on the liminoid—share with liminal experiences "not only transition but potentiality, not only 'going to be' but also 'what may be'" (Turner and Turner [1978] 1995, 3). In 1995 Edith Turner further clarified.

> The pilgrim is on an adventure, a quest. Her enlightenment is in the lap of the gods. She is not bound to make the passage to membership in some religious community. Optation—individualism—reigns. What draws her is perhaps some message from the holy spheres, not the dictates of biology as the community, as with puberty initiation

. . . in pilgrimage, it is the journey to the actual place containing the actual objects of the past. (Turner 1995, xv)

Based on Edith Turner's work, I argue that the potentiality for transformation—the core of pilgrimage—is the most defining characteristic of commercial ghost hunts. I also draw upon James Clifford's observation that pilgrimage's "'sacred' meanings tend to predominate—even though people go on pilgrimages for secular, as well as religious reasons" (1992, 110). While all of the pilgrimage sites that Turner and Turner ([1978] 1995) considered were explicitly religious, it was clear to Clifford and it is clear to me that there is nothing inherent in their understanding of liminality and communities that prevents it from being applied more broadly to nonreligious acts of pilgrimage. In her 1995 preface to *Image and Pilgrimage*, Edith Turner embraced this very fact. As Jonathan Z. Smith's (1987) critique of Mircea Eliade's (1987) concept of irruption of the sacred showed, it is human action that generates sacrality (or any particular designation of place) rather than an inherent quality.

While there are other highly productive frameworks for understanding secular pilgrimage—for instance, Morinis's (1992) emphasis on pilgrimage as the pursuit of an embodied ideal—I emphasize the role of transformation in pilgrimage. Drawing on Turner and Turner ([1978] 1995), I explore the idea that intention, transformation, and belief lie at the point of disjuncture between tourism and pilgrimage rather than questions of sacredness, religiosity, or meaningfulness. I argue below that participation in ghost walks and commercial ghost hunts can be distinguished along these three axes and that these differentiations are significant with respect to the placement (and perceived rationality) of the participants in contemporary English society. As these two forms of engagement with ghosts demonstrate, believing or disbelieving in ghosts does not necessarily call one's rationality into question. Such quiet engagements are a part of the status quo. However, passionately believing or disbelieving in ghosts begins to call a dis/believer's rationality into question.

Ghost Walks and Commercial Ghost Hunts

While ghost walks and commercial ghost hunts center on understandings of ghosts, they are very different forms of engagement with ghosts. Ghost walks are a ubiquitous form of tourism found across Britain. They can be found in a broad range of English cities, several Scottish cities, and the capitals of Northern Ireland and Wales (table 2.1). Ghost walks usually occur in

TABLE 2.1 LIST OF UK CITIES WITH A GHOST WALK

Aberdeen	Newcastle
Bath	Newport
Belfast	Norfolk
Brighton	Nottingham
Brixham	Oxford
Burton	Penzance
Cambridge	Peterborough
Cardiff	Plymouth
Chillingham	Sheffield
Derby	St. Ives
Devizes	Stirling
Dorset	Stratford-upon-Avon
Edinburgh	Tenby
Exeter	Warwick
Gloucester	Weymouth
Hull	Whitby
Lincoln	Windsor
Liverpool	Worcester
London	York

the early evening, between 7 and 9 p.m., in the city center. They last between one and two hours and cost between £5 and £10, or roughly $10 to $17. A guide, typically a man dressed in black contemporary clothing or black Victorian costume, leads a group of tourists on a relatively short walk through the historic city center and stops at certain places of either historic or ghostly significance to tell stories about the ghosts found there.

In contrast, commercial ghost hunts are more private affairs. They typically occur inside haunted venues, usually pubs, museums, castles, or estates. Different companies and tourists call these events fright nights, ghost hunts, or investigations. I refer to them as commercial ghost hunts. In addition to the companies that offer these commercial ghost hunts, there are also teams of ghost hunters or paranormal investigators that periodically offer ghost hunts to the public. While they share many features with commercial ghost hunts, the organizational and financial structure of these events differ significantly. I refer to these as non-profit ghost hunts and return to them in the next chapter.

In York, there were seven active companies that offered regular commercial ghost hunts at the time of my research. These ghost hunts typically happened on Friday and Saturday nights. Like regular (and non-profit) investigations, they began around 8 or 9 p.m. and lasted until between 2 and 5 a.m. Unlike non-profit investigations, participating in a ghost hunt costs a significant amount of money, typically between £35 and £100, roughly between $65 and $165. Normally, there are between twenty-five and forty participants on these hunts. Attendees usually come in groups. It is rare to have more than one or two participants who attend alone. Each company hosts ghost hunts at a range of haunted sites.

Knowledge on Ghost Walks and Ghost Hunts

The processes through which consumers become aware of ghost walks and commercial ghost hunts differ. For participants on a commercial ghost hunt, the night of ghost hunting results from weeks or even months of planning and decision making. On the other hand, individuals who purchase ghost walks may have decided to purchase a walk in a much less premeditated fashion. This difference in planning points to the significantly different meanings these activities have in the lives of their consumers.

The companies that produce commercial ghost hunts rarely advertise their events in particularly accessible public places. Their advertisements rarely take the form of public billboards, brochures, or even signs. They make their presence known almost exclusively through various online forms of advertising. In the case of commercial paranormal tour companies, their ads have been known to appear on a range of ghost hunting and paranormal investigating websites, especially directories. Individuals visiting these URLs would likely have a pre-existing interest in ghost hunting and paranormal investigation. Thus, the individuals who purchase these commercial ghost hunts typically are well versed and familiar with websites focusing on the paranormal and ghostly. Many of them noted that they regularly watch television programs such as *Most Haunted* or, increasingly by the end of my fieldwork, the US-based program *Ghost Hunters International*. In fact, their narratives of the trajectories that led them to participate in a commercial ghost hunt often highlight their viewership of such television programs and their readership and possibly participation in Internet forums. They emphasize that consumption of these programs and websites is not incidental. They maintain that it struck a nerve with their long-standing interest in the ghostly or paranormal, often since childhood.

While their trajectories into participating in commercial ghost hunts mirror those of paranormal investigators and ghost hunters in many ways, there is a significant difference. For paranormal investigators, the trajectory culminates (for the time being, at least) in organizing and leading their own investigations in the paranormal. For most participants in commercial ghost hunts, it typically ends in joining in commercial ghost hunts. Strikingly, individuals who traveled significant distances to participate in a particular ghost hunt did not tend to situate these journeys as part of weekend breaks where they remained in the city of the ghost hunt for the rest of the weekend. This was made clear to me when talking to a couple who had traveled from Glasgow to Nottingham for a ghost hunt. I asked them if they planned to stay in Nottingham for the weekend, and they were puzzled by my question. The woman explained, "we've got to get home. I have to work tomorrow night. This isn't a city break for us." She and many other participants on ghost hunts subtly point out to me that they did not see their involvement in ghost hunts as a form of tourism. It is, rather, the culmination of a deliberate and often inconvenient decision to partake in a ghost hunt.

Participants' emphases that their journeys to haunted sites were not part of pleasurable weekend-long excursions is significant. As Turner and Turner ([1978] 1995) observed, the blurring of tourism and pilgrimage often troubles sacred authorities. Such authorities tend to condemn any blurring of these boundaries. While such authorities are not really present in ghost hunts, the participants themselves police these boundaries and stress the seriousness of their pursuit of ghosts by highlighting the absence of pleasure-seeking, touristic behaviors.

The decision to purchase a ghost walk is very different. Unlike ghost hunts, the operators of ghost walks advertise their tours very publicly in the vicinity of their walks. While some ghost walk operators may maintain websites discussing their walks and rates, I have never spoken to any tourist who was aware of, or consulted, these websites prior to purchasing the tour. In the city of York, ghost walks maintain the highest public presence. When walking through the city center of York, it would be difficult for visitors to overlook the abundant street advertisements for competing ghost walks. They are found on trashcans, on billboards, and in shop windows. There are also stacks of flyers in receptacles on trashcans, on checkout counters in stores, in the tourist information center, and in hotels (figures 2.1–2.3).

There are typically between five and ten ghost walks operating in York at any given time, and their advertisements make it difficult to distinguish among them. The advertisements often feature a man illuminated against a dark and foreboding background. They include the name of the walk and the place and time of departure but very few details about the nature or content of the actual walk. Many note that they are acceptable to "older children." Some include notes remarking that there are no "gimmicks."

These tours operate against a backdrop of fairly negligible nightlife in York, which is comprised mainly of the city's many pubs. There are only few non-pub-related activities to pursue in the evening in York. There are also very few other walking tours that compete with the ghost walks. The Association of Voluntary Guides offers daily walking tours of the city; however, unlike the ghost walks, these depart in the daytime, usually at 10:15 a.m. The only non-ghostly, evening walking tour is the Viking walk, a relatively recent addition to York's tourist nightlife.

In many ways, York is a unique case. The sheer number of ghost tours is unusual. Most cities have one tour, at best. I have never visited an English city where the prevalence of advertising of the ghost walk competes with York's ghost walks. Ghosts and ghost walks figure quite centrally in York's "destination image." York's reputation as the "most haunted city" in England, Britain, Europe, or the world factors into its marketing. Deciding to purchase

FIGURE 2.1 Ghost walk advertisements are almost ubiquitous in York. One tour company placed its poster on a trash bin not far from the York Minster. Tours often compete for space to advertise.

FIGURE 2.2 At the Visit York Information Center, pamphlets advertising ghost walks appear alongside announcements about other tourism and heritage sites, as well as upcoming theatrical or cultural performances. While these ghost walk advertisements offer visually evocative depictions of guides, spectral beings, or simply darkened cityscapes, they provide tourists with little information that enables them to differentiate between walks.

a ghost walk occurs against this backdrop of advertising and manufactured destination imagery. While the volume of ghost walks in York is unique, the deliberate marketing of ghosts as part of a touristic experience is not as much so. "The phrase 'most haunted,'" according to historian Owen Davies, "has become part of the English tourist experience, with numerous pubs, villages, and towns laying claim to the title. Ghost tours and walks have become a popular leisure activity" (2007, 62). While Davies does not offer a precise account of when these tours and marketing strategies became so prevalent, he does note that such widespread manifestations are a "largely twentieth-century phenomena" (Davies 2007, 62). As Davies suggests, ghosts truly have become a mainstream and marketable feature of the touristic landscape in England (figure 2.4).

In York, the superabundance of ghost walks and the similarities in their styles of advertising result in difficulties tourists and tourist officials both have in making distinctions between the tours available. For example, when

FIGURE 2.3 Some ghost walk guides go beyond offering posters or pamphlets for their tours and instead take to the streets themselves to attract tourists. This ghost walk guide strategically positioned himself at the intersection of Stonegate and High Petergate, two of the busiest tourist streets in York. Other ghost walk guides took to the streets of York in costume aiming to attract costumers.

I talked to staffers at the York Tourist Information Center about how they describe the different ghost tours to interested tourists, a woman explained to me, "I tell people that there are two styles of ghost walks. There are the funnier ones where the guide is a bit more theatrical. Then, there are the ones with a bit more history. They're both good, of course. It just depends on what you're in the mood for." It is unclear to what degree tourists who purchase these tours are aware of these differences. When I asked participants on the ghost walks how they decided on a particular walk, they commonly expressed ambivalence about the differences between the walks. One tourist, a man from Hartlepool, who was spending the weekend in York with his wife, described their selection process by noting, "we saw the signs for this one. We figured it would be fun, something different. It left from the Minster and we knew how to find the Minster."

Tourists' lack of differentiation between the tours became even more evident when I talked to them a day or more after their tour. For example,

FIGURE 2.4 A large billboard featuring a costumed ghost walk tour guide aims to attract tourists. The billboard also marked the spot where the ghost walk would commence. Different ghost walks started at different spots in the touristic hub of the city. This particular tour started at the Evil Eye Lounge on Stonegate; however, others began at the York Minster, the top of the Shambles (another street in York), and pubs, such as the King's Arms.

when I was talking to the older parents of a ghost hunting friend, they were eager to tell me about their ghost walk experience, since they knew I was generally interested in ghosts. When they tried to tell me which walk they took in York, they were unable to remember either the name or any revealing characteristics of it. Elaine, a woman from Bridlington, observed, "I can't remember which walk it was. They're so similar, really. Well, the man who led it was quite good. He was dressed in black and looked like he was trying to dress historical like. It left from the city center." This description could apply to nearly all of the ghost walks in York (and any ghost walk that I have observed in England). Elaine was not unique in her inability to recall which ghost walk she purchased. I encountered numerous tourists who could not correctly identify which tour they took.

Tourists' inability to identify the ghost walk they purchased says much about the casual nature of this activity. Little planning or forethought goes into the selection process. Tourists assume that they are interchangeable. For tourists, participation in a ghost walk is a casual act; however, the sheer casualness of these acts of consumption points to the undeniably public role ghosts play in contemporary England.

The varying costs of ghost walks and ghost hunts further differentiate ghost walks and commercial ghost hunts. In part, the low cost of ghost walks explains why so many tourists purchase them without prior consideration. For most people who spend a weekend or day touring a town, £5 is not a significant cost. As one recent York ghost walk reviewer commented in *The Guardian*, "£5 is not a large sum to gamble for over an hour's entertainment." Many tourists who purchased ghost walks emphasized that the relatively inexpensive cost encouraged their casual consumption. As one man from Ripon explained, "it's only five quid [pounds]. That's nothing. That's a drink in the pub. We thought, let's see what this is like. It might be interesting. It's something to do at least."

In contrast, participants in commercial ghost hunts tended to see the price of the event as quite costly. For many, the price was very significant. Many participants in commercial ghost hunts remarked that they wished they could participate in ghost hunts more frequently but that the cost was prohibitive. Participants' reactions to my solo status on one ghost hunt demonstrated their understandings of the price of hunting. I had planned to attend a commercial ghost hunt with one of my paranormal investigating friends. Together we had purchased tickets for the event, which was to be held at the York Castle Museum; however, at the last minute, her transportation for the evening fell through, and I was forced to attend the event alone. The host for the night publicly asked where my friend was. After I explained that she would not be coming, several of the other participants befriended me. They voiced shock that my friend did not join us. As one woman noted, "it's so dear [expensive]! I would have walked here if I had to." The cost of commercial ghost hunts led to a more deliberate, careful consumption of these events. In fact, many participants I met would periodically lament the cost of participating. Many of the tourists who purchased a commercial ghost hunt were from working class or middle-class backgrounds. As a result, cost was a significant factor in deciding to purchase such an experience.

The length of time needed for either a ghost hunt or ghost walk also differed greatly and resulted in different modes of consumption. Ghost walks are comparatively brief time commitments. They rarely last more than ninety minutes. Participating in one does little to diminish tourists' capacities to enjoy the rest of their night in York (or any other city). The event typically finishes by 9 p.m. at the latest, which leaves tourists sufficient time to visit one or more of the city's many pubs. Commercial ghost hunts, on the other hand, typically last between five and eight hours. This is not an insignificant amount of time to spend on an activity. Furthermore, these events generally occur between 10 p.m. and 5 a.m. Most participants are not in the habit of routinely staying awake all night. To do so requires significant commitment on the part of consumers. Such engagement is not intended for casual consumption.

The varying costs, time commitments, and public accessibility of ghost walks and commercial ghost hunts demonstrate that these events are produced for very different demographics and are consumed accordingly. The variations in the degrees of deliberateness and intentionality point to one of the major differences between ghost walks and ghost hunts. In commercial ghost hunts, participants explicitly seek out and pursue an encounter with ghosts that is demanding in terms of finances, time, and emotional involvement. They are seeking a meaningful encounter with ghosts. In many cases, participants are seeking the "evidence" or "experience" necessary to transform them or turn them into "believers" or, if not believers, at least into people who are slightly more convinced that ghosts exist. The ghost walk participants, by contrast, are seeking entertainment that corresponds to their already existing belief or disbelief in ghosts. They do not anticipate that the walks will alter their beliefs, and the tour guides make very little effort to do so.

While transformation alone does not distinguish pilgrimage from tourism, I want to consider the possibility that the type of transformation sought by participants on commercial ghost hunts may distinguish it from less transformative forms of tourism. Scholars, such as Bremer (2004), have highlighted the difficulties in attempting to differentiate tourists visiting religious sites from pilgrims visiting those same sites. For the pilgrims, the place in question has always had transformative potential. For some tourists, the encounter may, quite unexpectedly, provide a type of transformation or transcendence, but it comes as a surprise. It is never their goal in visiting the site. In commercial ghost hunts and ghost walks, the casual tourist is differentiated from the ghost pilgrim, in part, by how deliberately they seek transformative encounters with ghosts. While I do not want to underestimate the transformative potential of a ghost walk, I have never met a tourist who found the experience to be profound in any way. They have identified the walks as "fun," "entertaining," and "historically interesting." However, they have not described the walks as transformative. As I discuss later, participants' beliefs tend to stay unchanged on ghost walks. It is this very fixedness that identifies their practice as a form of tourism and enables the other, more complicated enactment of belief. The fixedness and public disclosure of their belief is the most interesting thing to me about ghost walks.

The Presentation of Ghosts

As I argued in chapter one, the term "ghost" has a far less defined or coherent meaning than most people realize. The range in visual, sensory, and rhetorical depictions of ghosts is huge. This inherent ambiguity in the term "ghost" enables one of the sharpest and most meaningful distinctions between ghost walks and commercial ghost hunts. In addition to presenting ghosts remarkably different, commercial ghost hunts and ghost walks conceptualize and enact belief in significantly different ways. Ghost walks center on ghost stories whereas commercial ghost hunts seek to enable participants to experience ghosts. Each activity's organization and structure demonstrates its different understanding of ghosts and how to know and understand them.

Ghost walks traffic in ghost stories similar to those found in ghost guidebooks and in some heritage sites. This is made clear even in some of their advertisements. As I have noted, not all of their advertisements include a description of what the ghost walk entails. Those that do so tend to operate on the notion of storytelling. One ghost walk pamphlet reads, "I am the ghost creeper. Follow me along dark passageways and narrow streets to hear . . . sinister stories of the absurd and the unnatural . . . chilling tales of scandal and death." Another ghost walk flyer reads, "Come! Let me be your guide! Walk with me through the back streets and alleyways of historical York. Let me regale you with stories of mysteries, gruesome ghosts, and the foul deeds once committed in medieval York." In each of these advertisements, the act of storytelling emerges as the primary feature of the ghost walk. Tourists will learn about ghosts through stories.

The format of the walking tours reflects this emphasis on stories. The guides tend not to offer any sort of broad introduction to the tour. Rather, they simply begin the walk and storytelling. For the more serious, historically oriented ghost walks, this tends to include mentioning some safety reminders and then embarking on the route. On one historically oriented walk, the guide introduced the tour by loudly exclaiming "Good evening everyone! Welcome. We're going to walk around a few haunted places tonight. We're not going to walk too far, though. Don't worry. Every ghost story I tell is perfectly true. Some ghost stories are more true [sic] than others." The guide then launched into his first ghost story, which was set at the starting point of the tour. In his introductory comments, the guide himself identified the purpose of the tour to be the dissemination of ghost stories while maintaining an ironic stance vis-à-vis the stories' veracity.

The more theatrical tour guides tinge their introduction with comedy. For example, on one ghost walk, the guide asked tourists to stand in the corner in front of a closed shop. He then proclaimed to the group, "ladies and gentleman, that concludes our ghost walk!" This was met with laughter from the group. He then launched into a discussion of their location, the course of their tour, and its correlation to Victorian York. He commented:

We will head down Swinegate, where in Victorian times you could buy yourself a pig. A nice pink, pork pig. We will cross over Grape Lane where you could have bought yourself a bottle of wine. Now, in Victorian times, Grape Lane had a nickname, 'Grope Lane.' And, ladies, if you had hung around there in Victorian times you could have made yourself a bit of a profit. [The audience laughs.] Well, one or two of you anyway. [The audience laughs again.]

Now very important, you must stay behind me at all times and the man at the back, keep up!! [This tour guide always chose one middle-aged man to pick on and tease through the night. This was the source of significant comedy.] Or you may find yourself grabbed by a goon. [As he mentions goon, the guide eyes the man in the back meaningfully. The crowd finds this highly amusing.] Now, get ready. We are going to go down Swinegate and across Grape Lane. We will end up on Stonegate, where our ghost hunt begins!

The brevity of this introduction demonstrates the degree to which guides and tourists alike assume that the goals of a ghost walk are self-evident. On these walks, it is extremely rare to encounter an explicit overview of what the walk entails or what constitutes a ghost. In the introduction to the more historically oriented tour, ghosts are explicitly referenced in their capacity to be more or less true; however, no definition of ghost is provided, and no explanation of how to gauge the "truth" of these entities is offered (figure 2.5).

After the introductions, the guides lead the group to the first stop on the tour. In York, guides for different walks coordinate with each other to avoid stopping at the same location at the same time, which can be a delicate and challenging task, especially during the busier periods of tourism. Tours stop in front of buildings, and the guides stand with their backs to the building, facing the group of tourists who stand in front of them. The tourists tend to watch the guides closely during the stories and may glance occasionally at the building in front of them. The guides and the tourists do not interact in many significant ways during the tours. Tourists periodically laugh at the intentionally comedic acts of guides, and guides may rely on tourists to act out or participate in scenarios. Tourists very rarely ask questions or interrupt the tours.

Upon arriving at the designated location, the guide launches into a story about the particular site. The story typically lasts five or ten minutes. Sometimes, especially at particularly significant sites, such as the York Minster, a guide will tell two stories at the same place. The stories, which emerge as the central points of the tour, vary somewhat in style and substance (figure 2.6). Some stories are intended to be funny while others remain serious in tone. One of the York guides, who offers a tour he imagines as a comedic and magical encounter as well a ghost walk, often tells the typical stories of York's ghosts in an explicitly funny, dramatic, and sometimes over-the-top fashion. For example, on his first tour stop, this guide stops at a haunted building on

FIGURE 2.5 Ghost walks occur regardless of the weather. Even on rainy nights, they attract a lively, substantial audience. Despite the rainy weather, the ghost walk pictured here stopped at Bedern, the site of a former workhouse or ragged school, to tell the story of an abusive workhouse master who murdered the orphans in his care.

Stonegate, a main shopping street that is fashioned to resemble a medieval street. There he tells a story about the ghost of a young girl. I tell of this story in some detail here to examine his use of comedy and to consider the depiction of ghosts.

On one tour in which I participated, this comedically and magically oriented guide launched into the ghost story after arranging the tour group in front of him. In a very dramatic tone and elongated syllables, he noted,

Okay, the building behind me is haunted by the ghost of a small child. How old are you child? [He turned to a young girl standing at the front of the crowd. She replied that she was nine years old.] She was nine years old when she died in a horrible manner. This used to be the home of a local doctor. He was famous for the parties he would hold down here in his dining room. One night his small daughter had attended one of these parties. When it came to nine o'clock, she was sent up to her attic bedroom. Well, like all children, she wasn't tired. She didn't want to go to bed. And she must have been leaning over the banister trying to look at all the fun and the excitement below when her hand slipped and she fell fifty-five feet down through the stair well to the basement below, where she broke her poor little neck. Fortunately, there was no damage to the staircase. [At this, the crowd laughed heartily.] And I would recommend that all of you enter this building tomorrow. You can go down to the basement where she fell and stare up through the staircase. And you, you can go to the top. [This comment was directed to a man who the guide had humorously been teasing throughout the night. The audience found this comment very funny.] And try leaning over. [The crowd laughed even more.] Now her ghost has only ever been seen on one occasion. But she is more famous for her poltergeist activity.

While it would be easy to portray this as a sad story, the guide's excessive drama and irreverent telling of the story render it more comedic. Interestingly, in his telling of this story, he treats ghosts as self-evident. The young girl died a sudden and untimely death and became a ghost who lingered around the site of her death. Unlike some, this guide makes no claims regarding the truth-value of the story in question.

In this story, as in every ghost story I have heard on a ghost walk, the narrative treats the notion of a ghost as self-explanatory. The narrative styles assume that tourists understand what a ghost is. The guides also rarely put pressure on tourists to accept or reject the truth-value of their stories. These are not tales to be carefully interrogated. Rather, they are flexible, able to support belief or disbelief. In the story of the little girl above, the guide jokes about the details of the story. He fashions the dead girl's age to the age of an audience member. This could be interpreted in several ways. One possible interpretation is that the guide doubts the veracity of the story. Another is that it is a rhetorical flair intended for comedic effect. Notably, that comedic effect is grounded on the untrustworthiness and implausibility of ghost stories. By taking these tours, hearing these stories, and not engaging in ongoing, tortured analyses of them, participants (perhaps unwittingly) locate themselves as believers of a very different order than participants on a commercial ghost hunt.

In contrast to the narrative whole presented on ghost walks, commercial ghost hunts present a more fractured, fleeting conception of ghosts. In fact, the idea of ghosts bleeds seamlessly into a broader category of "paranormal activity." As one commercial ghost hunting company advertises on its website, "We only book locations with recent reports of activity to increase our

FIGURE 2.6 This ghost walk paused very close to the York Minster to tell a ghost story. Many ghost walks pause several times in and around the Minster. It provides a beautiful and atmospheric backdrop for stories.

chances of witnessing something paranormal. Of course, there are no guarantees, however be prepared as our locations have never let us down yet!" As this explanation demonstrates, notions of "activity" and "witnessing" figure prominently in the packaging of ghosts on commercial ghost hunts. Overall, commercial ghost hunts are designed (and purchased) with the intention of enabling encounters between participants and the ghostly or paranormal.

At the beginning of commercial ghost hunts, the hosts and mediums typically welcome the guests and excitedly discuss the possibilities of the evening. Their excitement, in and of itself, is remarkable. For them, as well as for the participants, the night remains an unknown entity replete with encounters that they are not yet sure of. This stands in stark contrast to the guides of ghost walks. For them, each walk is more or less the same. Setting aside unusual circumstances, they typically know and anticipate the geographic and social contours of their night. This is not the case for hosts and mediums. Like the participants, they are on the verge of having a new experience themselves.

During these periods of introduction, it is not uncommon for mediums to comment in passing on the site. They tend to share their excitement about the evening's possibilities. On one commercial ghost hunt, one medium told the group, "I won't spoil anything for you, but I reckon it should be a good night." On another ghost hunt, the medium explained, "I think it's quite an active building. It should be a good night." While the host/investigator often emphasizes that the company cannot ensure paranormal activity on a particular night, the mediums often express a positive outlook on the likelihood of activity. It is common for ghost hunter organizers and consumers, as well as paranormal investigators, to equate a "good night" with an "active night." Participants generally respond in an excited and favorable fashion to these comments from mediums. It is not uncommon for some to exclaim enthusiastically that they hope it is an active night. Already, in these introductory moments, the organizers of commercial ghost hunts construe the participants as active consumers of the paranormal rather than passive recipients of crafted knowledge. Here hosts and mediums cast ghosts as immediate, experiential entities.

In fact, the entire structure of commercial ghost hunts explicitly enables encounters with ghosts. These first-person experiences with ghosts range from the initial "walk-through" with the medium to participants' later direct interactions with the ghosts through divination and *calling out*. The understandings and realizations of ghosts that these styles of engagement produce are distinctly fragmented and partial. The walk-through with the medium, a guided walk through the darkened building led by the medium who narrates the ghostly presence, provides the first glimpse of the ghosts' presence. In each room, the medium quickly walks about and then begins to share mediumistic impressions of the space. S/he generally describes whatever presences are sensed in the room. They typically refer to the presences as either spirits or ghosts. They use the terms somewhat interchangeably. If the medium had the chance to walk through the building prior to the arrival of participants, s/he might share what s/he "picked up on" during the early visit to the building. S/he simply describes it. For example, one medium described something he picked up on prior to the start of the night:

> It was interesting. I had a feeling about a room like this all day and then when I walked in before I got the overwhelming sense of sadness. Something terrible happened here, I think. Before, I was getting a bloke who I think might have hurt himself. He's not here now but we might try calling out for him later.

Some mediums also actively "get things" while they lead the group through the rooms.

For example, during a commercial ghost hunt in a museum, the medium led the group into a room that depicted life in the sixteenth century. She commented that she was "getting" children. She observed, "there are children all around you. Do you feel them? They're reaching toward you . . . they . . . they want to play! They might grab your hand. They're lovely!" Assertions such as these present an image of the building as full of spirits that one might encounter. They also recast the building so that a site housing a museum or a pub "becomes" a site replete with invisible presences that are the object of consumption.

The participants typically stand and face the medium. They do not move around the room as freely as the medium. However (unlike participants in ghost walks), participants are constantly engaged in processes of evaluation and active involvement with the ghost present despite being rendered as the less experienced or more passive party in the encounter. When the medium speaks about a spirit in a particular location, most of the people realign their bodies to face that general direction. Sometimes, participants quietly confirm what the medium says. For example, in the instance above in which the medium described children's spirits, several participants reported feeling children reaching for them and holding their hands.

After the walk-through with the medium, participants break into two groups and set off to "investigate" and look for ghosts either with the host or the medium. When doing so, the host makes sure that they are equipped with technologies that enable their encounters, such as electromagnetic field readers (commonly called EMF readers), dowsing rods, or crystals. Many participants embrace these technologies. They treat changes in temperature or variations in the EMF levels as indications that ghosts are present.

Participants also tend to bring digital or video cameras with them hoping to document ghosts that are present. Participants photograph the area frequently. The host or medium rarely does anything to impede this. Some hosts express extreme interest in seeing photographs that capture anything potentially paranormal. Hosts and mediums encourage participants to alert the group before using flash photography in order to allow them to shield their eyes from the flash. This engagement with visual technologies points to many participants' deep hope that they will capture "visual evidence" of a ghost. As one man who participated on a ghost hunt with his wife explained, "I would love to get a picture of something. [My wife] is convinced there are ghosts. She sees them, you see. But me, I don't know. If I had a picture of one, that would convince me, though. Definitely." This visual engagement acted as another way in which participants sought to experience ghosts during these hunts. As the man's comments suggest, they are also hoping for a technologically mediated transformative encounter. The man aspires to capture evidence. He hopes that this ghost hunt will finally enable him to be firm in his belief in ghosts.

The resulting photographs differ significantly from the images of historical figures or artful photographs of empty rooms or landscapes found at heritage sites and featured in guidebooks. These photographs are often partial and out of focus. Since tourists use their flashes to produce such photographs in the dark, the resulting images often feature small areas of illumination surrounded by looming darkness. The photographs that tourists deem to include evidence of the paranormal—albeit often unsatisfactory evidence—frequently feature what they call an "orb," which I described in chapter one. While individuals might long for photographs of full-bodied ghosts, such images remain rare. That orb's emergence as the most common type of "evidence" highlights the gap in the tourists' engagement with ghosts and the heritage industry's understanding of it.

Tourists' photographs provide a privileged site for understanding their motivation and engagement at a particular site. Urry influentially argued that tourists' photographs are conceptually and practically linked to the practices of tourism. He suggested that "photography is . . . intimately bound up with the tourist gaze. Photographic images organize our anticipation or daydreaming about places we might gaze on. . . . The tourist gaze thus irreducibly involves the rapid circulation of photographic images" (Urry 1990, 140). Examining the "circulation of photographic images" in the case of ghost tourism requires attending to the rupture between heritage understandings of touristic desire and tourists' photographic enactment. Through ghost tourist photographs, it becomes clear that tourists' gazes are centered on the ghosts themselves rather than the heritage site. Tourists aim to photograph and share photographs of ghosts not of the sites that they occupy; such sites are of secondary importance to tourists.

The commercial ghost hunt is largely designed to enable active encounters between participants and ghosts. On those in which I participated, when hosts led the groups into rooms, they generally suggested an interactive activity like calling out. The host typically starts the calling out but encourages participants to join in and redirect it if they want to. Calling out is an activity that ghost hunters and paranormal investigators invoke to try to entice ghosts or spirits into interacting with the humans present. To "call out," hosts (or, in paranormal investigations, investigators) ask in a clear and slightly loud voice if there are any spirits present. Participants often participate or join in eventually. They then pause, and the group waits for some discernible response. The response could take the form of a noise or, ideally, a voice. I have never been present when a group encountered a voice; however, I have observed instances when participants and hosts interpreted knocks and bursts of wind as positive indications that spirit was present. In some instances, the nature of the activity was unclear. For example, in the following excerpt from an investigation held at a museum in York, the host engaged in fairly typical acts of calling out:

Host: Is there anyone there?
(Pause)
Host: Come on, we're here to talk to you. Please make yourself known to us.
(Pause)
Participant 1: Did you feel that?
Participant 2: I felt it on my left hand.
Participant 1: I felt it as well.
Host: If that was you, spirit, can you please do that again!

Here, as in most instances of calling out, a period of silence follows unsuccessful and successful invitations for spirits and ghosts to participate. In instances of calling out that generate positive outcomes, the period of silence is interrupted by participants' descriptions of what they interpret as contact with the spirit. In the instance above, no one ever clearly established what the two participants felt. However, this did not diminish the host's willingness to encourage the spirit based on their encounter.

This activity assumes that ghosts or spirits are able to understand and engage with the humans present. This is a proposition with several implications. First, it suggests that ghosts or spirits are able to hear. This implies that ghosts or spirits maintain a sensory apparatus (rather than simply being able to act upon living humans' sensory apparatuses). It also constructs ghosts or spirits as discursive participants in an ongoing conversation with ghost hunters. Participants and hosts wait with careful and rapt attention during the silence that follows each instance of calling out to see if the ghost or spirit answers or offers some discernible signal of its presence.

The ghosts that emerge in these situations, as well as the methods of contact that they require, lend themselves to the participants' particular images or understandings of ghosts. These are of partial beings and are profoundly fragmented. A ghost's hand touches a person, but the ghost's hand or body never materializes. Participants' visual glimpses of the ghosts are brief and fleeting. Beyond the ghosts' only partial bodies and physical capacities, the narratives that emerge about them are severely fractured. The biographical sketches of the ghosts generated by calling out or sometimes through the use of a Ouija board are tantalizing, brief, and partial. Participants may learn a bit about why the ghosts died and pick up some fragmentary pieces of his or her autobiography, but a complete sketch of who the ghost was and why she or he died is elusive.

This is a far cry from the ghosts of ghost walks, who emerge as complete and fully formed in the tour narratives. Whereas participants in ghost walks can evaluate a complete story about a ghost and decide whether or not they wish to espouse belief in it, participants on commercial ghost hunts face a more complicated situation. Many hope for evidence of the reality of ghosts—to enable participants, as they put it, to "believe in them"—yet what they actually find is profoundly fragmented and partial, which leaves them to grapple indecisively with their encounter.

Haunted Places/Spaces

Place figures very differently in ghost walks and commercial ghost hunts. Ghost walks are entirely outdoor events organized to show tourists the exteriors of haunted buildings. Guides lead visitors from the setting of one story to another, but tourists are never able to access the interior of these sites. The city center of York acts as an atmospheric setting for ghost stories. One website noted, "tales are drawn from the immense History of York and are told against a backdrop of haunting beauty [sic]." In contrast, commercial ghost hunts bring participants into the interior of buildings. This difference corresponds to the different notions of belief and ghosts associated with each form of engagement.

On ghost walks, guides lead tourists to buildings that act as the backdrop of their stories. The guides may gesture to the buildings and, in some cases, even touch the buildings; however, the tourists themselves are never invited to do so. Since the ghost walks occur in the early evening, most of the buildings (which are often commercial or touristic buildings) implicated in the ghost stories are already closed for the day. Even when it is possible to visit the site of the ghost stories in question, guides typically do not stress that possibility. The most notable instance of this in York is the telling of Harry Martindale's ghost story, which I detailed in the Introduction. This story, perhaps most famous ghost story in York, is told on every ghost walk in the city. To tell the story, guides typically stand in front of the closed and locked gates of the Treasurer's House. The house itself stands about twenty feet back from the gate. The crowd looks at the house from this distance and listens as the guide tells the story of the Romans in the basement. They routinely fail to mention that the Treasurer's House is a National Trust property that is open to the public most days and, even more interestingly, that the National Trust sells tickets for an hourly tour to the haunted basement itself.

If they are not aware of this information, tourists remain ignorant of it while on the ghost walks.

When I asked guides why they omitted this information, one man jokingly noted that he would not want to "shill" for the National Trust. Others noted that they did not think the information was relevant to the tour or interesting to the tourists. As one guide explained, "they want to hear ghost stories. That's what they're there for." I suspect that their reluctance to mention the Ghost Cellar is less connected to their desire not to "shill" for the National Trust and more that they do not consider this information interesting or relevant to the ghost walk. Visiting the Ghost Cellar entails a larger degree of commitment than participating on a ghost walk. The same visitors who participate in the walks may not have an interest in visiting the Treasurer's House in general or the Ghost Cellar in particular. There are persistent stereotypes of National Trust visitors as overwhelming older, middle classed, and white. One journalist characterized the typical crowd of National Trust visitors as "a mix of earnest—and overwhelmingly white—middle-class parents wishing to instill in their children such essential English values as the Importance of History and the Appreciation of Beauty and genteel retired couples gagging for a gander at the garden" (Henley 2010). While the National Trust actively seeks to cultivate a more inclusive image (McGinty 2010), the ghost tour guides seemed to assume that there was little overlap between consumers of a ghost tour, an activity with less elite class associations, and National Trust visitors.

The understanding of place is markedly different on commercial ghost hunts. A main feature in the execution and advertising of commercial ghost hunts is access to haunted places. One commercial ghost hunting company explicitly prides itself on access to "haunted and unusual locations" and boasts of this in its ads. Other companies similarly boast of their access to the "best haunted sites" and the "most active haunted sites." Commercial ghost hunting companies and consumers alike conceive of "access" as entry into a space and not just viewing it from outside, as is the case on ghost walks. Interiority, here, signifies haunting.

These events occur entirely indoors, in sites that are supposedly haunted. From the moment participants arrive, they enter the space of the haunting. This positions them very differently. By entering the space responsible for claims of ghosts or hauntings, they enter a murkier and less resolved realm. While remaining outside a haunted building allows participants on ghost walks to stay physically and experientially removed from the haunting, participants in commercial ghost hunts enter a domain of partial, embodied encounters. Theirs is a messier engagement fraught with uncertainty and ambiguity. The haunted space and the event itself become a liminoid space.

Ultimately, ghost walks and commercial ghost hunts offer nearly opposite ideas or encounters with ghosts, experience, and belief. In ghost hunts, the ghosts are less identifiable; however, participants are invited to encounter and experience them, whereas on ghost walks the ghosts are clearly identified and storied, but tourists lack the ability to access them. Participants on commercial ghost hunts, then, encounter ghosts by entering haunted spaces that, in a sense, constitute two overlapping domains featuring elements of liminality. These multilayered spaces constitute a heterotopia (Foucault 1984). Commercial ghost hunters step well outside the domain of their day-to-day lives. They stay awake when others normally sleep; they spend those hours of the night typically confined to the private sphere in profoundly public spaces; they exert ideological control over venues typically under the purview of a museum or private authorities, thus they disrupt established hierarchies. And, most importantly, they enter a space thought to be occupied by ghosts. To understand the layers of quasi-liminality, it is necessary to contend seriously with the ghosts said to occupy such spaces. Taken as literal entities, they too are entering a space of liminality. Ghosts are truly liminal beings. Turner wrote that "liminal entities are neither here nor there; they are betwixt and between the positions assigned and arrayed by law, custom, convention, and ceremony" (1979, 95). Taken literally, this really is the case for ghosts, who are caught between life and death, embodiment and disembodiment. The space of a haunting, then, acts as overlapping domains of liminality intended to bring the living and the ghostly into contact.

The fragmentary, partial nature of this contact contributes to its liminoid status. Turner and Turner ([1978] 1995, 253) indicated that liminoid, or "quasi-liminal," describes the "many genres found in modern industrial society that have features resembling those of liminality [and that] these genres are akin to the ritually liminal, but not identical with it. . . . They are plural, fragmentary, experimental, idiosyncratic, quirky, subversive, utopian, and consumed by identifiable individuals." The partiality of the ghosts and the fragmentary nature of participants' encounters with them further constitute these as liminoid encounters. In turn, these commercial ghost hunt companies capitalize on and commercialize this liminality.

Do You Believe?

Lastly, the structure and narratives inherent in ghost walks and commercial ghost hunts implicate belief in very different ways. While references to belief are found on ghost walks and ghost hunts, their implied (and enacted) understandings and performances diverge greatly.

At the beginning of many ghost walks, guides commonly ask participants the question, "do you believe in ghosts?" They then ask them to raise their hands if they do or they do not believe. Some guides, but not most, ask people to raise their hands if they are unsure of what they believe in. In this presentation of belief, the choices are clear-cut, and the bifurcated (or, in rare cases, trifurcated) possibilities are presented neatly. The act of deciding and declaring belief in this neat fashion positions participants more readily than their belief, disbelief, or agnosticism. Their willingness to raise their hands signals their public assertion of a particular style/mode of belief. This mode of belief is what I refer to as "hard belief," and it is the belief that some paranormal investigators and ghost hunters mock as "blind" belief.

Belief, in this instance, is not based on evaluations of evidence or examinations of personal encounters. It is, rather, an articulation of a stance decided in advance and a position that is definable. When I talked to ghost walk participants about this question, they failed to see why it interested me. To them, answering the question of whether or not they believed in ghosts was straightforward. As one tourist put it, "of course, I don't believe in ghosts." He had no qualms or hesitation in answering me. When I asked why he chose to take a ghost walk, he replied, "I thought it would be fun, different. Just because I don't believe in ghosts doesn't mean I don't want to hear a few ghost stories." Another participant explained, "I suppose I believe in them. I've never seen one or anything, mind you." When I asked if this belief drove her to take the tour, she laughed and said, "to be honest with you, I never considered that. I just thought it would be fun!" Tourists do not see their taking a ghost walk as an implication of their internal beliefs in a meaningful way; however, at the same time, they are prepared and content to perform their identities as believers or disbelievers. Such a public performance does little to alter their social position or internal understanding of the world. Consuming a ghost walk is a casual act for them, in part, I would argue, because of how little or how shallowly belief is implicated.

The enactment of belief on commercial ghost hunts is markedly different. While roughly the same categories are referenced—believer, disbeliever/skeptic, and agnostic/uncertain—in ghost walks and commercial ghost hunts, they are differently understood and enacted. Whereas belief is conceived as predetermined and static on ghost walks, participants and producers of ghost hunts understand belief as a shifting engagement with unfolding evidence. Their association of belief and evidence/experience distinguishes them from casual ghost tourists.

On some commercial ghost hunts, the host may raise the question, "Who believes in ghosts?" Like ghost walks, people will raise their hands to identify themselves as believers or skeptics; however, in contrast to ghost walks, this question generates considerable discussion between the host and the participants. For example, on one ghost hunt, the host raised the question of belief. Out of the group of thirty-five, by a show of hands, seven people identified themselves as "believers," nine people identified themselves as "skeptics," and the remaining nineteen were unsure. This show of hands prompted a dialogue between the host and the participants, as well as among the participants about the status and nature of their belief. At the show of hands, the host replied, "Ah, well, I'm in the same boat as most of you. I'm not sure what to make of a lot of it. I want to believe but I'm not there yet." A woman from Darlington who identified as a believer responded to this, saying "I know what you mean. I mean, I said I believe, and I do in a sense. I think there is something but I'm not sure what it is. So in a sense I'm uncertain." Uncertainty, rather than firm belief, emerged as the dominant posture toward ghosts.

Similarly, when I spoke with participants about their belief, many expressed a high degree of uncertainty. However, this uncertainty was marked by a desire to believe. In fact, many participants saw their participation in the ghost hunt as an act intended to secure their belief (ideally) or disbelief (less ideally). When I asked one participant, a woman who had driven two hours to attend the commercial ghost hunt, if she believed in ghosts, she replied, "I'd like to [believe]. At the moment, though, I don't know. I've seen some things, but I'm not convinced. Maybe I'll get some evidence tonight!" The participant cast her belief in temporal terms. At that moment, she did not believe; however, she hoped that emerging evidence would change that. Participants' engagements with belief demonstrate the degree to which commercial ghost hunts act as a "liminoid" state (Turner and Turner [1978] 1995). Here the host and participants imagine transformation as a key facet based on belief, and they accept that ghost hunts are the sites of these transformations. This engagement with belief seems to me to do the most to identify commercial ghost hunts as a form of pilgrimage.

Turner's idea that liminoid phenomena have a voluntary component is apt here, too. "Liminoid phenomena," he wrote, "tend to be more idiosyncratic, quirky, to be generated by specific named individuals and particular groups—'schools,' circles, and coteries. . . . They have to compete with one another for general recognition and are thought of at first as ludic offerings placed for sale on the 'free market'" (Turner 1979, 208). This precisely describes commercial ghost hunting. Companies sell commercial ghost hunts to willing consumers who consider the variety of available options on the market before selecting one. The explicitly commercial nature of these transactions does not negate their significance for participants.

Ultimately, Turner argues that the liminal is more thoroughly transformative than the liminoid. Pilgrimages, which typically entail the hope for transformation, are examples of the liminoid. Participants on commercial ghost hunts desire a transformation from nonbeliever to believer, which is contingent on the production of evidence; however, the commercial ghost hunts seem unable to yield the transformations they desire.

Conclusion

As anthropologists have demonstrated, attempts to engage people's actual beliefs often lead to a problematic terrain ripe with guesses and suppositions about the interiority of others (Keane 2008b; Luhrmann 1989; Needham 1972). My intention in this chapter has been not to suggest that belief in ghosts differentiates ghost walks from commercial ghost hunts. Rather, what I have tried to demonstrate is that a quest for belief, a desire to believe, distinguishes the two forms. In ghost walks, belief is incidental. Tourists purchase these tours hoping for entertainment and perhaps historical education.

Transformation is absent there. In commercial ghost hunts, many participants explicitly hope for the evidence necessary to transform them from doubting skeptics to believers in ghosts. In a very real sense, their journeys to pubs in Nottingham, museums in York, or castles in Newcastle are secular pilgrimages and, as Turner and Turner ([1978] 1995) have made clear, not all secular pilgrimages in modernity are successful or transformative. This speaks to their very liminoid nature. The differences between ghost walks and commercial ghost hunts demonstrate the perils in assuming that any and all engagements with ghosts traffic in similar notions of the ghostly or belief. The paranormal or ghostly engenders different types of belief and reasoning for different people.

Clearly, belief is a highly variable concept for people interested in ghosts. Belief is seemingly the simplest for ghost walk participants. They either believe or do not believe in ghosts. They seem to know from the start where they fall. For people who buy commercial ghost hunts, it is more complicated. Many of them see these commercial ghost hunts as a chance to foster belief. These events function as a form of pilgrimage, which, they hope, generates the experience or evidence necessary to transform them into believers. In both cases, the status of belief remains unchallenged. For both sets of actors, ghosts are a matter of belief. This is a far cry from investigators' fraught struggles over belief, evidence, and science, and their inability to assert an ontology of ghosts with any degree of certainty.

CHAPTER THREE

STAGING GHOST HUNTS: THE ROLES OF KNOWLEDGE, EXPERTISE, AND SCIENCE IN GHOST TOURISM

Paranormal investigators and ghost hunters are another set of people with active and sustained interest in the paranormal in contemporary England. They see ghosts and the paranormal not as stories or history to learn or entities to believe in but as something to research and know. They aim to objectively understand the paranormal in scientific terms. Their quest to know the paranormal leads them to locate haunted sites that may serve as research sites, to craft experiments intended to understand the unknown, and to refine epistemologies of the paranormal. These practices have necessitated carving out a position for themselves among a populated field of paranormal tourism. While ghost hunters and paranormal investigators might engage in any number of the touristic practices I discussed in chapters one and two, they understand themselves as distinct from casual ghost tourists. They see themselves as serious, dedicated, and ultimately authoritative. In short, they see themselves as experts on the paranormal. In this chapter, I explore the staging of paranormal investigations, or ghost hunts, the performative events that allow ghost hunters and paranormal investigators to refine and instantiate their distinction from casual ghost tourists. Paranormal investigations are the central activity for investigators and ghost hunters. They are typically overnight visits to haunted sites during which investigators perform experiments and chronicle their experiences with the paranormal. Paranormal investigators and ghost hunters look forward to the event, plan for it, and avidly discuss its outcomes in the days and weeks that follow an investigation. Staging such events requires investigators and ghost hunters to navigate a complicated nexus of commercial interests in order to locate viable sites to investigate. Because many haunted sites charge ever-increasing fees for investigation, paranormal investigators stage "public" iterations of their investigations, which they sell to members of the public. In this chapter, I explore these practices and argue that ultimately producing touristic experiences for themselves and others enables paranormal investigators and ghost hunters to successfully perform their expertise.

Haunted Heritage: The Cultural Politics of Ghost Tourism, Populism, and the Past by Michele Hanks, 87–116. © 2015 Left Coast Press, Inc. All rights reserved.

In this chapter, I adopt a performative approach to understanding ghost hunts and paranormal investigations as crucial sites for the production of expertise. E. Summerson Carr has argued persuasively that expertise is performative. She explains that "expertise is something people do rather than something people have or hold" (Carr 2010, 18). This is clearly the case for paranormal investigators who actively work to fashion themselves as experts on the paranormal. For them, paranormal investigations are key sites in which they publicly enact their emergent expertise, which, as Carr argues, is highly "interactional . . . [and] involves the participation of objects, producers, and consumers of knowledge" (2010, 18). For paranormal investigators and ghost hunters, enacting their expertise requires staging investigations. Investigations accomplish three goals: 1) they provide the social, physical, and intellectual space in which they mobilize their theoretical understandings, material technologies, and immaterial presences; 2) they enact the analytic stances necessary to become producers of knowledge; and 3) they perform these understandings for a knowledge consuming public. These practices necessitate that paranormal investigators and ghost hunters carefully negotiate their relationship with forms of ghost tourism. They simultaneously distance themselves from the commercialism, thrill seeking, and unscientific nature of such practices while ultimately staging an intermediate form of ghost tourism that allows them to visit the sites they desire while providing the necessary audience to consume their paranormal expertise. I contend that this careful negotiation ultimately results in successful enactments of their paranormal expertise.

Amateurs and Ideologies of Research

In contemporary England, there is a great range of individuals and groups who actively pursue knowledge of the ghostly or paranormal. This includes paranormal investigators, ghost hunters, mediums, and parapsychologists. While these groups agree that they are in pursuit of knowledge of the paranormal, they do not always share a practical or ideological orientation.

Parapsychology is the professional branch of inquiry into the paranormal. Parapsychology, as a field, is defined by its professionalism. Today, parapsychology is largely a laboratory-based, university-sponsored field of inquiry. There are academic programs that offer qualifications in parapsychology at a master's and doctoral level across the UK. Some of the most noteworthy university programs are housed at Edinburgh, Nottingham, Northampton, and Liverpool Hope Universities, although institutions such as Coventry, York, and Safford also accommodate parapsychological research in their broader psychology departments. While amateur researchers on television or in ghost hunting groups may call themselves parapsychologists, they use the term to signify a skeptical approach to ghost hunting rather than an academically grounded pursuit of parapsychological knowledge. Parapsychologists themselves are very rarely involved in forms of ghost tourism. Therefore, I do not focus on them here.[1]

Rather, I learned that individuals with various educational and professional backgrounds pursue ghost hunting and paranormal investigating. The vast majority of paranormal investigators lack formal training in scientific research and university or academic affiliations. They are, for the most part, self-trained amateurs with serious interest in the paranormal. Their educational backgrounds are not at all uniform. Some have completed university while most have not. They tend to have educated themselves about the paranormal through popular publications, online websites, television programs, online forums, and personal experiences. The information they encounter in these sources is far from uniform, and the intellectual and professional backgrounds of their authors are heterogeneous.

For paranormal investigators and ghost hunters, paranormal research does not constitute a full-time or paid line of work. Their passion for the paranormal alone motivates them. Sociologists have dubbed the type of dedicated, amateur engagement of people like the paranormal investigators as a form of "serious leisure." Robert Stebbins (1982, 2001) influentially defined serious leisure as "the steady pursuit of an amateur, hobbyist, or career volunteer activity that captivates its participants with its complexity and many challenges" (2001, 54). Such serious leisure should be "long lasting," Stebbins argued, and grounded in the development and articulation of "substantial skill, knowledge, or experience, if not all three" (2001, 54).

Stebbins (1982, 2001), and others (Jones and Symon 2001; Weiss 2011), have tied the rise in "serious leisure" to economic and cultural shifts in the North Atlantic world in the latter half of the twentieth century. These changes have resulted in greater amounts of free time, including longer lives, earlier retirements, and shrinking job markets. Hobbyists and amateurs, Stebbins suggested, are able to gain personal fulfillment and meaning through the pursuit of their passion. This is especially important in the economies of late modernity in which individuals are less likely to find meaningful, absorbing forms of employment. This is the case for many of the paranormal investigators and ghost hunters whom I met during my research; many were either underemployed or partially employed. Many identified themselves as working class, and they struggled to find long-term, meaningful employment. While the search for employment was often frustrating, it allowed them ample time to dedicate to their paranormal research. Their identities as paranormal researchers figure prominently in their senses of self. They take great pride in their accomplishments, and their shortcomings in research lead to significant anguish. As Stebbins suggested, their engagement with paranormal research might allow them to craft meaningful identities grounded in emergent expertise.

In his taxonomy of serious leisure, Stebbins distinguishes between hobbyists and amateurs. The former pursue recreation in fields with no professional counterpoint, such as knitting or backpacking. Amateurs, in contrast, operate in fields with corresponding professions. Examples include amateur chemists, astronomers, and ornithologists. In this schema, paranormal investigators and ghost hunters constitute amateurs, since they pursue knowledge in a field with a defined set of professional experts, namely parapsychologists. While Stebbins presents the status of amateurs as unambiguous and unproblematic, for experts as well as amateurs themselves, this is not the case for paranormal investigators. Their status as amateurs is a tacit challenge to them as well as parapsychologists themselves. Paranormal investigators see themselves as the ultimate authorities on the paranormal, a position that parapsychologists passionately contest.

Pursuing knowledge of the paranormal is challenging, even for established parapsychologists (Collins and Pinch 1979; McClenon 1985; Pinch 1979). Part of the problem is the elusive and complex nature of the paranormal itself. As others have noted (Bader, Menken, and Baker 2010), the paranormal is a broad and seemingly inclusive domain that supports inquiry into topics ranging from cryptozoology, to alien abduction, and to ghosts. The paranormal investigators whom I met and worked with in England used the term paranormal in a more qualified manner. They see the paranormal as a wide selection of largely unknown or poorly understood phenomena, especially those connected to ghosts, hauntings, and human's awareness of them. Most of the investigators whom I met were exclusively active in researching hauntings and ghosts; however, their interest lay in mapping the underlying mechanisms of a haunting rather than simply chronicling the presence of ghosts at a given site.

For many, this interest emerged in early experiences with the supernatural. For example, Clara, an investigator from Yarm, explained that she had a "lifelong interest" in the paranormal because of experiences that occurred when she was a girl. She explained:

> I've always been interested in the paranormal like. When I was a little girl, strange things would happen in the house. Things would be moved. Sometimes I would feel someone watching me. I don't know what it was. I'm not saying it was ghosts. It just sparked an interest for me. I've always read books [about the paranormal] and whatnot.

Researching the paranormal, trying to find out what's behind this type of thing is dead interesting.

For others, researching the paranormal acts as a means of contemplating and analyzing questions of life after death. For Ginny, an investigator who had been active in research for about a decade, her father's death and her desire to communicate with him sparked her interest in learning more about the paranormal:

> I got involved in the paranormal when my dad died about ten years ago now. I'd always been interested in spooky things like, but I took it quite hard when he died. We hadn't been close, and I just really wanted a chance to talk to him, to figure things out a bit more. So, I started going to Spiritualist circles and trying to develop myself as a medium. I don't believe in that anymore of course. But, I do wonder what's out there. What happens to us when we die? I don't think it's simple. It's not like we show up as ghosts and just have a chat with who we like. But, I do think it's interesting to think through it a bit more.

By the time I met her, Ginny eschewed mediumship in favor of a more scientific approach to the paranormal; however, these personal experiences of death, loss, and mourning, as well as the ontological questions they raised, spurred her toward active involvement in paranormal research. As indicated in chapter one, for many investigators, paranormal reality shows, such as *Most Haunted*, played an instrumental role in enabling them to transform their passive, longstanding interest in the paranormal into a more active, research-based interest. The show, with its emphasis on watching an investigation unfold—or in Koven's (2007) terms "ostension"—provided useful templates for viewers interested in crafting their own modes of researching the paranormal. As I discuss in greater depth elsewhere (Hanks 2011a), viewing *Most Haunted* first as a fan and then as an anti-fan provided investigators with what Collins has called "interactional expertise," or the ability to engage in expert discourses about paranormal research. For many, watching *Most Haunted* sparked more sustained inquiry into books, websites, and research about the paranormal.

Ginny and Clara's reflections on how their backgrounds led to their involvement in paranormal research highlight a crucial element of investigators' approaches. Ultimately, investigators find the causes and ontological elements of the paranormal—questions of causality, perception, and meaning—the most significant. They are not interested in particular ghosts or ghost stories;

rather, they want to understand the dynamics at work that may cause such phenomena. Their reluctance to identify their project as one of "hunting ghosts" or "seeking out ghosts" is representative of paranormal investigators' general uneasiness with the concept of the ghostly.

While many expect paranormal investigators who seek out and spend the night in reportedly haunted houses to identify the object of their interest as ghosts, this is surprisingly not the case. Investigators tend to be uneasy with the idea of ghosts, in part because of their popular depictions. Early on in my research, I regularly asked investigators if they "believed in ghosts." This, to me, seemed like a straightforward question. Almost invariably, investigators problematized first the term ghost and, then, my use of the verb to believe. For example, Harry, a scientifically oriented paranormal investigator, gently critiqued my use of the term ghost:

> I know what you mean by ghost; Casper or something like that. Some sort of spirit associated with the dead that interacts with the living. It's fine if people are interested in that, but that's not for me. It's putting the horse before the cart, if you know what I mean. . . . I think there are things out there we don't know about, but they're part of nature. There must be laws and whatnot that apply to them. . . . To call them ghosts and talk about them like they have personalities like, that's too far for me. We don't know enough to do that. . . . What I'm after is whether there is any evidence of things outside the normal working at all.

For Harry, the idea of ghosts is overly determined. He suggested that it was more productive to focus on charting and understanding any patterns of unusual events rather than simply assuming they were the work of ghosts. He, like most paranormal investigators, emphasized the naturalness of the paranormal. For example, on many occasions investigators even criticized the term paranormal for its association with mysticism and the occult. As Ginny put it, "we call it the paranormal, but if it's out there, it's normal." By this, she meant that the phenomena they sought to study were part of the natural world, and as such, modes of scientific inquiry could be applied. For both Harry and Ginny, understanding the paranormal was a matter of scientific empiricism rather than faith. Investigators tended to understand paranormal research as a scientific, empirical pursuit, albeit one that broadened the typical boundaries of science by objectively analyzing personal experience with the paranormal, as well as the experiences of mediums. Empiricism and experimentation lay at the heart of this pursuit.

Investigators and ghost hunters recognize an inherent conflict between their desired scientific empiricism and experimentation and the fleeting, ontologically complex nature of ghosts or the paranormal. Investigators' desires to know the paranormal translates into a variety of practices. Unlike academic parapsychology, which is largely a laboratory-based field of inquiry, amateur paranormal investigating fashions itself as a field science. While they explicitly distance themselves from more common ghost tourists found on ghost walks or on commercial ghost hunts, their desire to query, experience, analyze, and experiment upon paranormal forces leads them to seek out haunted sites and stage research events, called investigations, at these places. While paranormal investigators and ghost hunters tend to conceive of the paranormal as something profoundly natural, they nonetheless view it as something exceptional, and this in turn leads to a number of practices that attempt to render it more understandable.

Analyzing Experience and Conditioning the Senses

Like many researchers who engage in various forms of fieldwork, paranormal investigators and ghost hunters worry about the ways in which their subjectivity will impact or impede their attempts at objective, scientific research. The senses play a powerful role in paranormal investigators' and ghost hunters' imagined science. Investigators and ghost hunters aim for objectivity and critically analyze their own embodied encounters with the paranormal as part of their overall research. They conceive of the paranormal as a natural, external force operating around them in the world. As such, it has the power to impact them like other natural forces; however, the nature of this impact is less than clear to them.

There are two ways in which paranormal researchers conceive of paranormal forces acting upon them or impacting them: external and internal. Externally, they believe that paranormal forces can lead to changes in temperature and lighting discernable to observers' senses. They also believe that paranormal forces may be able to touch, push, or physically manipulate people. The internal elements of paranormal contact are even more troubling for paranormal researchers. They hypothesize that paranormal forces have the capacity to alter the thoughts, moods, and consciousness of nearby people. While they do not conceive of this as a form of mediumship, it shares many similarities with it. Ultimately, they understand themselves in particular, and people in general, to be susceptible to the paranormal. Paranormal researchers see, and naturalize, a markedly different sense and understanding of self. In Charles Taylor's terms, they see human bodies and consciousness as "porous" rather than "buffered" (2007). Charles Taylor writes that one of the significant differences between modernity and pre-modernity is the constitution of the self, and that the pre-modern world—what he calls the *enchanted world*—is characterized by porous minds. To him, "the line between personal agency and impersonal force was not all at all clearly drawn" in pre-modern times (Taylor 2007, 32). A porous self, he wrote, was open to influences, possession, and encounters with external others. Taylor argues that, with the disenchantment of the North Atlantic world, buffered selves became the normative senses of self. Taylor notes that "for the modern, buffered self, the possibility exists of taking a distance from, disengaging from everything outside the mind . . . things beyond [the buffer] don't need to 'get to me'" (2007, 38). To embrace the porous self is to position one's self as a believer at best or potentially irrational at worst. For paranormal researchers, such associations pose a serious ideological problem. Their aim is to be scientific, not simple believers.

Translating such personal experience, which arise grounded in this porous sense of self, requires ideological work and practical discipline. Ellen, a paranormal investigator from Sunderland, described this to me in an interview:

> A big part of investigating is thinking about your own experiences with the paranormal . . . but treating them objectively. If we want to move forward with this [paranormal investigating] it's important to be objective like, scientific. We can't just say, 'oh I felt something on my shoulder. It must be a ghost.' We've got to think about what those experiences mean, about how we perceive them. Our mind and our senses both play a big role.

Ellen's concern with critically evaluating her perceptions of the paranormal is shared by many investigators. Researchers propose various ways of addressing this. During my research, one of the main ways that some paranormal researchers aimed to address the unreliability of their own senses, perceptions, and mind was to engage in what people jokingly call *training the senses*.

The practice of training the senses requires researchers to familiarize themselves with their own emotional, physical, and sensory responses to unusual places and sensations as a means of better understanding them. Molly, a paranormal investigator, explained, "your senses are like anything else, I reckon. The more you use them, the better you are at it. That's why we do this [train the senses]. We want to be as objective about it as we can." This training typically entails individuals visiting unusual places with the intention of charting and reflecting on their own reactions to the experience. Jack, who did not engage in the practice himself, but applauded those who did, explained it further to me. He remarked that "I worry about observer bias . . . the sense that we're in an unusual place, and so we might blame ghosts or the paranormal for things we oughtn't to. When Rose or Ginny are out doing that [training the senses], they're trying to offset it. Now I don't know if it works, but it's an idea." Many, like Jack, suspect that if they could understand how they respond to unusual stimuli, they would have a better chance of objectively analyzing their experiences.

To train their senses, investigators would organize evening walks with some of their closer friends in the paranormal research community. They would embark on their walks after the sun had fully set and darkness had fallen. Investigators tended to walk in out-of-the-way, deserted areas as a means of learning to become comfortable and sensually aware while on their own in out-of-the-way, possible "spooky" places. This could take the form of such natural places as wooded areas or beaches; it could also take the form of walking around or near abandoned buildings or ruins. Ellen explained the logic of it to me by observing that "on an investigation, you're out of your element. It's dark. You're in a new place. When we do these walks, that's what we aim for. We go to a new place and just sort of see how we feel." Training the senses, then, required seeking out the unknown. It was an experience grounded, in part, at least on difference. Their experiences of and reactions to the paranormal, they believe, are grounded in a sense of unusualness. As such, they need to seek out other unusual experiences as a means of disciplining their minds and bodies to objectively respond to such events.

While investigators tend to frame these walks in terms of their educational and research benefit, the walks also clearly constitute a form of thrilling fun for investigators. They look forward to them intensely and enjoyed sharing humorous stories about them. When I met up with my interlocutors, they almost invariably told me stories about recent, exciting walks that they had taken. For example, during the course of a rainy afternoon that I spent in a pub with Jack, Rose, and Jen, stories of walks came up many times. Jen and Rose told me about a recent walking adventure, and it is interesting to note the balance that they strike between pleasure and research.

Jen: So, we're out on one of these walks we do. We're traipsing through some woods outside Yarm. We've left my car by the side of the road about a mile back. It's pitch black.
Rose: We'd found quite a good spot. It was quiet and dark. We were going to stand there for a bit to see what we sensed and felt. Good practice, you know.

Jen: It's spooky as hell. You hear leaves crunching. . . . You can't tell what kind of animals are nearby.

Rose: It was a dead good spot. . . . So, we're stood there and all of a sudden there's this loud crunch or crash or I don't know what. [laughing] Before I know what's happening, Jen's swinging her torch around like some sort of madwoman. She's using it like a sword.

Jen: I wish you'd let me bring my bat!

Rose: You'll get us arrested.

By the end of this brief exchange, Jen, Rose, Jack, and I were all laughing. Their recounting demonstrates a key tension that shapes these walks and much of paranormal investigation, namely a tension between *serious* research and *pleasurable* exploration. At the start of the narrative, Rose framed the walk in terms of its research impact, emphasizing that it was part of their practice as dedicated paranormal investigators. She and Jen ultimately reveled in the absurd and humorous components of the walk; however, this insistence on the seriousness of the project legitimized the walk.

During the course of my fieldwork, I joined several of these walks. Each walk contained multiple instances of navigating the tension between uncanny pleasures and rational responses. Consider a walk that I took with Jen and Rose in early October 2009. On a brisk night, Jen picked up Rose and me from Rose's home in Middlesborough at around 8 p.m. As we drove across the North Yorkshire Moors toward Whitby, Jen and Rose reminisced about previous nighttime walks. Unlike previous discussions in pubs and during interviews, they no longer emphasized the research components of the walks; instead they lingered on the pleasurable or humorous elements of the walks.

After arriving and parking just outside of Whitby at around 9 p.m., we began our walk by silently hiking up to some cliffs overlooking a beach. It seemed quite empty as we silently maneuvered along the trail. After walking for ten or fifteen minutes, we came to a stop. Jen and Rose took some deep breaths and seemed to settle into their positions. We stood there silently for a few minutes with our backs to the cliffs, facing out toward the sea. The near silence was interrupted by distant laughter, which seemed to unnerve Jen. She anxiously asked what it was. Rose held up a finger, indicating that we should listen. In the distance, there were some roaming lights. Jen seemed increasingly anxious. After a moment, Rose declared that she knew what it was. It was the October school holidays, and she imagined that it was some teenagers having a party off in the woods or on the beach. This knowledge immediately calmed Jen. Considering the nearby presence of the teenagers, Rose proposed that we move. As she explained it, "we won't get any quiet here. They'll [the presumed teenagers] be out there all night for all we know." Jen agreed and we began to hike back down to the car. Rose's complaint that the cliffs wouldn't be quiet (and Jen's assent) reveal a significant element of what compels these nighttime walks. Investigators are in search of remote, unpeopled areas. The obvious presence of others detracts from their enjoyment. It also diminishes their potential to enact their experiential ideal, which will lack obvious human intervention.

Jen's response to the unknown sounds and lights is worth considering. Her immediate reaction seemed to be fear. Of course, it quickly dissipated when Rose offered a plausible explanation for it. When I asked her about that moment the next day, Jen explained that "I guess I was a bit scared. But not bad scared, you know? That's part of the fun of it. But it's important to move past it . . . to understand it a bit." Here, the fear posed an implicit challenge for Jen. Jen's experience of fear had a paradoxical role. On the one hand, it generated pleasure. On the other hand, it is the sensation of fear that they seek to minimize and objectively engage. The tension between the thrill of being scared and the need to rationally manage that fear compel investigators and pose one of the central tensions in their practice. While they are never fully sure that they have mastered the discipline necessary to make sense of their personal experiences, investigators consider such ventures proof of their more serious, analytic approach.

The Investigation

While practices such as these nighttime walks helped investigators and ghost hunters understand and operationalize their own sensory engagements, they only served as preparation for paranormal investigations, which were the core of their enterprise. The investigation took two forms: the group-only investigation and the public investigation. Both occurred overnight, typically between 9 p.m. and 5 a.m. at haunted sites. The former was only for members of the particular investigation group or team and sometimes their close friends or colleagues from other teams. The latter included a larger group, typically between fifteen and twenty-five additional people. The tension between group-only and public investigations is key in investigators' performative enactment of their expertise.

Group-only Investigations

Group-only investigations tended to be small gatherings of no more than ten people. They typically occurred at sites that did not charge the group a fee for investigating. In cases where there was a fee, attendees split the fee accordingly. Examples included a private home, whose residents approached a team about a potential haunting, a factory where one team member worked, and a pub that a group approached about investigating. In most cases, the team was (to their knowledge) the first group to investigate a particular site. Investigators and ghost hunters conceived of private investigations as ideal sites to conduct research. These investigations constituted a challenge to participants. Investigators and ghost hunters needed to manage their identity as *researchers* rather than *tourists* or *experiencers*. Being a researcher required disciplined passion and careful engagement with personal experience. It was a category explicitly contrasted with tourists.

Typically, such investigations began with "baseline" tests around the site, an important symbolic demonstration of the seriousness of the night. During such tests, one or two members of the team visited each room and recorded the temperature throughout the room with their digital thermometer, a measure of the ambient electromagnetic fields with their reader, as well as a written general physical description. Commercial ghost hunts did not include such baseline recordings. The inclusion of them on non-profit investigations signaled the seriousness of paranormal investigators' and ghost hunters' approaches. Ghost hunters and paranormal investigators considered temperature and electromagnetic fields to be highly significant domains. When people reported paranormal or ghostly activity, it often corresponded to changes in temperature. Because of this, investigators and ghost hunters reasoned that changes in temperature might be significant in the paranormal, although they were careful not to specify *how* or *why*. As Rose explained "when temperatures suddenly drop few degrees, it's important. People are more likely to report paranormal activity. I'm not saying the drop in temperature is a ghost materializing or anything, although maybe it is. What do I know? It could also be that when the temperature drops, people are more likely to *think* they're experiencing something paranormal like."

In discussions leading up to investigations, paranormal investigators and ghost hunters avidly debated the tension between these explanations and possible ways of reconciling them. Likewise, investigators acknowledged that some people understood electromagnetic energy as direct evidence of a ghost's presence, while others understood that higher-than-normal levels of electromagnetic energy might simply correspond with people's sense that something paranormal was occurring. Indeed, investigators and ghost hunters often pointed to academic parapsychological findings (Wiseman et al. 2003) to support it.

While investigators like Rose remained genuinely open minded about various interpretations of changes in electromagnetic energy or temperature, others viewed the straightforward association of temperature or electromagnetic energy changes with ghost to be overly simplistic. It was an intellectual position they associated with dilettantes and individuals likely to purchase a commercial ghost hunt. As Jack explained:

> I've seen people assume that EMF changes are ghosts. Some people even call EMF readers 'ghost boxes.' That's fine, I suppose. I think it's a bit . . . simplistic, but the thing is if you're only out for an experience, then it's fine. You want a scary night out, a ghost hunt like on TV, and you'll get one. The thing is that they're not out looking for evidence, so it's fine. We want evidence though. That's what I'm after.

Jack's dichotomization of paranormal investigators who seek evidence and casual ghost enthusiasts who want experience was common, and it often entailed a tacit critique or dismissal of the motives of casual tourists.[2] These casual consumers of the paranormal, investigators suggested, were interested only in experience, not in crafting new knowledge out of that experience.

Conducting baseline tests, then, was a way of demonstrating and enacting the seriousness of ghost hunters' and paranormal investigators' approaches. It showed that paranormal investigators did not just care about experiences with the unknown during the course of the night, but rather they were committed to a serious, scientific approach. Perhaps members of paranormal research groups did not entirely enjoy conducting the baseline. They tended to treat it as a necessary chore, but not something that they relished.

After the baseline tests, which typically lasted about fifteen minutes, the main component of the investigation would begin. The team would divide the site up into rooms or areas and then break into small groups of two or three members. They then would schedule when each group should visit each room. They aimed to allow the smaller groups at least forty-five minutes to an hour in each room. Breaks for discussion and snacks in well-lit rooms interrupted these investigative sessions. Structurally, these investigations strongly resembled those found on commercial ghost hunts, as I described in the previous chapter. Both events took at least partial inspiration from popular paranormal reality television shows like *Most Haunted*. Unlike commercial ghost hunts, these group-only investigations were entirely self-directed; the team members who participated in these investigations organized and executed their activities entirely of their own accord.[3] This element of self-determination figured prominently in investigators' sense of themselves as experts.

Investigators and ghost hunters engaged in a broad range of activities during the course of the night. Despite their nuanced and complex ideas about the role and validity of experience as a form of evidence, investigators and ghost hunters typically allowed ample time for team members to acquire varied experiences. Groups typically devoted time to amassing experiential encounters. Groups would sit silently in dark rooms to see if anything paranormal would happen. When members began to feel, think, or sense something out of the ordinary, they typically described it aloud for those present. These descriptions varied from detailed, evocative descriptions to fairly brief declarations. For example, during an investigation at a library in the Middlesborough area, I was sitting in a darkened reading room with Rose and Jen on a team-only investigation. We had been sitting in silence and relying on our senses to indicate any paranormal presences. Rose interrupted the silence and asked "is anyone starting to feel a bit weird?" Neither Jen nor I felt anything. Rose paused and, then, began to slowly describe her sensations: "In my mind, it's like I'm stood outside myself. I'm stood watching things around me. . . . I feel like I want to walk in a pattern on the beach [there were beaches nearby]. The pattern's significant like . . . maybe a ritual or something. I don't know. . . . I feel like there's a power to walking it." After describing this sensation for about three minutes, Rose began to speak in her everyday tones. She remarked that it was "interesting." Jen agreed and wrote some brief notes on Rose's experience. Then, we returned to our silent sitting. Such episodes were very common during investigations. As this reveals, private investigations differed from commercial ghost hunts in their treatment of the identity of ghosts. While the mediums, leaders, and participants on commercial ghost hunts placed great significance on amassing details and crafting identities of ghosts, many investigators remained less concerned. After this experience, Rose did not seek to craft a coherent historical narrative that rendered her experiences sensible. She did not, for example, propose that her experiences signified the historical presence of a cult or particular religious activity near the library; rather, she simply remarked that it was an interesting experience. Of course, such encounters and narratives gave rise to implicit historical narratives, a topic that I return to in the next chapter.

This is not to say that mediums were absent from these group-only investigations or that investigators were uninterested in their findings. Investigators and ghost hunters typically included one or two people who identified themselves as mediums in their teams or research groups. Paranormal investigators' and ghost hunters' views of the mediums tended to be complex though. On the one hand, mediums were members of the group and could help with planning experiments, locating sites, and conducting research. On the other hand, mediums' purported skill set distinguished them. Most investigators were intrigued by the idea that some people might have a better-developed set of senses for the paranormal. Investigators remained unsure, however, of how to address these differences. Investigators and ghost hunters tended to refer to mediums as an additional type of investigative tool or technology. Jen explained that "mediums are a tool. They're like EMF readers or thermometers or whatever. They can get things that are different and interesting. But it's not straightforward. You've got to interpret what it means."Jen, like many, viewed the findings and experiences of mediums as fascinating; however, she emphasized that they were not a type of straightforward evidence that demonstrated the presence of ghosts. Significantly, investigators interpreted the act of a medium as a less straightforward revelation of paranormal reality and more of a complicated piece of evidence to interpret. For example, during a paranormal investigation at Castle Keep, Jen, Rose, and I were in a small group with Rachel, a medium who was working with the team. We stood silently along a darkened corridor at the top of the Castle overlooking its atrium. Rachel began to vocalize her experiences. In a slow, halting voice that slowly became louder and more panicked she declared:

> There's a man stood over there. He doesn't like us. He wants us out. Out. Out. Out. . . . I don't like him. He's not nice like. He's done things . . . bad things. Scary. Out. Get out, he's saying. I don't think he wants us here. . . . Get out! I can see him. He scares me. I think he wants to hurt us.

Rachel's performance as a medium was not atypical among the mediums I observed. She was dramatic and oscillated between perspectives while narrating her experience. At times, she spoke at herself. At other times, she seemed to speak as the man. After she finished sharing this, Rose and Jen said it was interesting. Jen took some brief notes, which described the episode succinctly "Rachel picked up a man. Said he seemed angry. She found it upsetting." The shortness of these notes is significant. While both Jen and Rose genuinely found Rachel's experience "interesting," they remained uncertain of how to manage it analytically.

Experiments and the Production of Paranormal Knowledge

While commercial ghost hunts and group-only investigations included mediums and emphasized the amassing of experiences with the paranormal or ghostly, investigators and ghost hunters primarily included experiments on their group-only investigations. This highlighted the research-based nature of the event. These experiments typically aimed to render the experiential elements of the paranormal in objective terms.

Many investigators and ghost hunters devoted significant time and energy between investigations to crafting and perfecting experiments. For investigators, the process of developing and enacting experiments is at once a serious act intended to establish new (and hopefully meaningful) knowledge and a pleasurable form of tinkering. The vast majority of paranormal experiments attempt to differentiate the mundane from the extraordinary by focusing either on differences in the natural environment or on individuals' experiences of their environment. They run a gambit in terms of complexity. Some are exceedingly simple and form a standard part of almost all levels of paranormal investigation, while others are complex and difficult to stage.

One of the most common types of experiments involves observing stationary objects to see if any paranormal force acted upon them and moved them. I have seen this take the form of placing coins on a flat surface and marking their location in some way, such as covering the surface in flour. If the coin has moved, its trail will appear in the flour. Another popular method entails placing the coin on a piece of paper and drawing a circle around the coin (figures 3.1 and 3.2). Here, again, investigators would be able to assess if the coin had moved. Such experiments aim to visually reveal any movement; however, there is always the risk of human interference. If a coin moved, it would engender debate over how it was moved. Did an investigator accidentally, or even deliberately move the coin?[4] Investigators and ghost hunters struggled to devise mechanisms for distinguishing their own (conscious or unconscious) agency from that of a paranormal forces or presences. One paranormal research group, North East Paranormal Investigating (NEPI), constructed a number of tools that sought to render traditional divinatory tools into more objective devices. For example, many New Agers and faith-based ghost tourists used dowsing rods and crystals to indicate the presence of ghosts. Members of NEPI would devise systems of communication with paranormal forces that resembled the use of the Ouija board. For example, a person might dangle a crystal on a chain from his or her hand. If the crystal began to swing back and forth, it indicated a ghostly presence. Then, he or she might devise a communicative system with the crystal and invite the ghost to communicate by moving the crystal to the right or left to indicate yes or no. To investigators and ghost hunters, unsurprisingly, this suggested a lack of scientific rigor and a willingness to embrace belief as a means of knowing. Some investigators, though, did not want to "toss the baby out with the bathwater," as Kevin, the leader of NEPI, explained. The group NEPI

FIGURE 3.1 Some paranormal researchers craft devices intended to diminish the potential for human interference. In this photograph, researchers crafted a free-standing device that would hold crystals. Some ghost tourists believe that crystals are especially sensitive to paranormal energies, and crystals held by a person may register paranormal energies by swinging. Of course, skeptics suggest that the ghost researcher may be knowingly or unconsciously moving the crystal. Ghost tourists use devices, such as this one, to avoid such problems and doubts.

considered Kevin to be their best scientific mind, and they praised him for his innovations in investigating. To eliminate the potential for what he called "human intervention," Kevin designed a freestanding structure that would hold a crystal or dowsing rod, such as the one depicted in Figure 3.1. He argues that this would "stop anyone from directing the course of the crystal [or dowsing rod]. I'm not saying people do it on purpose. It could be subconscious or accidental. But there's always that risk when people are involved." His innovations were applauded for their ability to render the experiential elements of paranormal research into seemingly objective terms.

Investigators and ghost hunters rely on these various means of knowledge production on their investigations; however, they are often unsure of how to translate their findings into authoritative knowledge following an investigation. Investigators and ghost hunters often criticized their own investigations

FIGURE 3.2 Ghost researchers and tourists often leave coins in places where a ghost may move them. They aim to trace this movement by drawing a circle around the coin, as in the picture here, or by placing the coin in the center of flour or sugar. The goal is to produce evidence of ghosts' interference in the physical world.

and considered them wasted opportunities to investigate. Following their investigations, they typically produced "investigation reports." These are narrative accounts of the night that summarize people's experiences with the paranormal, the results of any experiments, and the baseline findings. Groups typically organized the reports into a section on the baseline findings and then sections that integrated the experiences of participants in a particular room. For example, in one report, EGR included the following details in their baseline report: investigation type (team only or public), EGR members present, guests present, investigation date, investigation start time, investigation end time, moon phase, cloud cover, precipitation, year site built, building material, and possible environmental factors.[5] The reports for each room or area in a site were descriptive accounts of individuals' experiences and any environmental factors. For example, in describing their investigation at a Whitby pub, EGR reported the time they spent in the shed outside the pub and that "there was nothing noted within this location that could affect the investigation." The report stated:

Jack, Rose, and Peter visited the Shed for their first location for the night. It was dark in there—almost pitch black other than a few shafts of light shining in through holes in the walls and roof and a little light from the adjoining dog pen. One of the first things that Jack noticed was a dark figure of a man in a top hat who was standing in the corner glowering at them!!! But, upon investigation, it was discovered that it was just Frosty the Snowman, keeping cool in the shed until it was time for him to appear to the world again at Xmas! Although there were a few flashes of light from inside the [pub] from people's camera flashes—Jack commented on, as a separate thing, little balls of light that could be seen in the shed. Not just stationary balls, but balls that would shoot across the shed itself from one side [to] the other. These lights were faint—just above the level of noticeable—and which left a tail behind them as they moved.

Rose thought that this effect could possibly be caused by Jack seeing raindrops being lit up at certain points, which were coming in through the slats in the roof, as when she saw little moving, disappearing lights this is what they were. Rose's description of them did not match Jack's exactly though, so possible they were describing different things as Jack says he saw the lights before it started to rain as well as during. When [she was] sat on the stool, Rose felt the right side of her leg and lower torso go freezing cold. Temperatures were taken but no difference was noted.

This report was fairly typical. Its author provided a narrative of what individuals felt and saw, as well how they made sense of it. Such reports typically sought to include explanations that discounted the potentially paranormal, such as when Jack perceived Frosty the Snowman to be a potentially paranormal figure. They also typically included but did not laud less inconclusive evidence, such as Rose's cold leg that could not be explained with the external temperature taken with the digital thermometer. These reports rarely offered any conclusive findings. They never stated that a site was paranormally "active" or "haunted." They simply stated what the group encountered.

Significantly, these reports did not reflect the explicitly nuanced understandings of paranormal causality that investigations debated and discussed in the preparation for investigations. These reports offered little in the way of interpretation. This, in part, may reflect the nature of paranormal investigators' amateur expertise. While investigators and ghost hunters passionately develop, study, and discuss theories of the paranormal, they remain, for the most part, untrained in the research methods of science, social science, or parapsychology. While their understandings of the nature of paranormal phenomena are complex, they cannot translate the complexity into analytic strategies for dealing with their data. They embody what Harry Collins (2004) called *interactional expertise*. He described this as "the ability to converse expertly about a practical skill or expertise, but without being able to practice it, learned through linguistic—socialisation among the practitioners" (2004, 125). While investigators and ghost hunters can debate the causalities of paranormal experience, they cannot ultimately mobilize their investigative technologies or theories to empirically verify them.

Investigators and ghost hunters found this limit to their expertise and analytic capacity highly frustrating. In the aftermath of investigations, they tended to dismiss their experiences, encounters, and ideas as well as the entirety of the investigation. They were aware of their own analytic shortcomings and judged themselves harshly for it. After the night at the Whitby pub that I mentioned above, Rose was highly critical of her experiences and the work of the team. "I get frustrated," she complained. "What we did wasn't investigating. It was a waste. We're sat around having experiences and that's the end of it. What's the point? We're nothing more than ghost hunters." Rose deployed the term ghost hunter here in a derogatory sense to mean one who was not serious about one's endeavors and did not engage in the more analytic elements of investigating. Rose was not alone in recognizing the limits of these investigations. Jack also commented on his experiences that night in Whitby. While he felt and saw several things that he thought might be paranormal, he remained unconvinced. He explained that "we don't know what they were. I mean, they might be paranormal. They might not be. We didn't investigate properly." Unlike participants on commercial ghost hunts, his experiences lacked the power to act as evidence. He saw them as problematic and understudied. Jack was frustrated by what he saw as the team's investigative failures; however, such failures were not limited to that night in Whitby. Jack, Rose, and other investigators typically found their inability to translate their critical and careful thinking about the paranormal into research and analysis—what ultimately surmounted to their interactional expertise—deeply unsatisfactory.

Investigators' and ghost hunters' inabilities to translate theory into knowledge does not imply that they have no expertise, but rather a particular kind of expertise. While Collins emphasized the role of interactional expertise in allowing science and technology studies scholars or anthropologists to interact with members of the expert community they study, I contend this is significant for amateur researchers as well. While these amateur ghost hunters and paranormal investigators rarely have cause to interact with parapsychologists or elite psychical researchers, their ability to mobilize expert discourses persuades a particular public of their legitimacy as experts. Paradoxically, they perform their expertise not through interacting with elite parapsychologists but through engaging an interested public through ghost tourism.

Public Investigations

While investigators and ghost hunters embraced private, group-only investigations as ideal research opportunities, they viewed "public investigations" with greater skepticism and trepidation. These engagements with the public were motivated primarily by financial concerns and obligations. As ghost hunting in particular and ghost tourism in general became increasingly popular past times, sites increasingly sought to profit from their haunted heritage.

This issue of commercialization was a delicate one for investigators and ghost hunters. As amateurs, they lacked (for the most part) either the research grants of academic parapsychologists or the commercial profit of ghost hunting tour companies. No paranormal investigator whom I met was able to translate this amateur engagement into a full-time, paid career. This lack of financial support constrained their opportunities and means of investigating.

As a way of responding to this, teams of investigators and ghost hunters would stage public investigations. Public investigations included this core group of team members and close colleagues, as well as "members of the public," as investigators described it. These outsiders were members of a very specific public, mainly the online communities associated with particular investigation groups. During 2008 and 2009, most of the groups that I worked with maintained group websites that featured information about their research, approach, and online forums.[6] Many groups divided their forums into a public area, where anyone could contribute, and a team-only area. The public area often housed lively, engaged discussions from individuals who were interested in the paranormal but were not formally associated with a paranormal research group or team.[7] These enthusiasts would pay roughly £25 (roughly $40) to participate in the events.

Economies of Investigation

The economics of investigating were a major concern for investigators and ghost hunters. As ghost hunting and paranormal investigating became increasingly popular pastimes in the UK, properties with a reputation for hauntedness began to seek profit from their encounters with ghost tourists. When teams wanted to investigate sites that were better known, they often had to pay a fee to do so. In some cases, it was roughly £100 (the equivalent of $165), but some venues charged up to £500 (the equivalent of $820). Investigators often claimed commercial ghost tourism and casual, thrill-seeking tourists drove the fees up at well-known haunted venues. They viewed participants on commercial ghost hunts with some skepticism for their embrace of belief as a means of engaging the ghostly and their willingness to pay to participate in such an event. Hailey Stevens, a prominent paranormal researcher and blogger, reflected on the financial restructuring of haunted sites between 2005 and 2013. When she and some ghost hunting associates sought one of the venues that they had once frequented, they encountered financial difficulties:

> It never happened though because all of the locations that we visited between 2005 and 2008 as curious-yet-naive ghost hunters suddenly wanted us to pay over £300 or had such a long line of ghost hunting teams already visiting that they couldn't fit us in. We thought perhaps the first venue this happened with was an unfortunate one off, but then the second venue did the same, and the third, the fourth. . . . Then we realized that the traditional approach to ghost hunting that we had so loved has been skinned alive, and instead of allowing it to rest in peace, a more modern version is parading around wearing its flesh. The modern version is adventure tourism with the lights turned off; copying those cool looking people off the television who have action-filled nights in the most haunted of venues across the world.

Stevens's reflection on the changing economy of paranormal investigation, as well as its association with what she calls "adventure tourism" is revealing. She is concerned by the changes that make investigating financially untenable and the quality of pursuit undertaken by newer ghost hunters.

While Stevens's critique is grounded in the political economy of 2013, I encountered similar criticisms in 2008 and 2009. For example, during one conversation in late 2008, Jack, a leader of EGR, commented on the increased difficulties associated with paranormal investigating.

> It's getting harder. We need to keep an eye out for new venues. So many people are interested in investigating now because of *Most Haunted* and shows like that. All these ghost-hunting companies [commercial ghost hunting tours] are competing with little non-

profit groups like us for space. Of course, they'll win. They can pay. The thing is, people want an experience like that. They want to go out and have the "*Most Haunted* experience." And that's fine. There's room for everyone, I think. But, it makes it harder for groups like ours.

While Jack aimed to adopt a tolerant approach to more causal ghost hunters, he worried that the growing number of casual ghost hunters hurt his group's ability to enact the investigations they wanted.

Other paranormal investigators and ghost hunters worry about the consequences of investigating the same sites as commercial ghost hunting companies. For example, one EGR team member questioned the financial practices of the Golden Fleece, a well-known and well liked haunted site. On his blog, he observed that "to the paranormal community, the Golden Fleece raises mixed reactions. Some believe it is haunted, others believe is it just an old pub with a nice and unique atmosphere that plays on its 'ghostly' reputation to draw in the punters." His skepticism about the financial practices of the Golden Fleece is clear. Referring to people who visit the site as "punters," which is slang for customers, highlighted the financial nature of the transaction. He questions whether investigators will be able to have a genuine experience there and if the popularity of the Golden Fleece is not simply a result of marketing.

Ironically, the concerns of amateur paranormal investigators and ghost hunters like Stevens and Jack echo the concerns of more professional researchers, mainly parapsychologists and psychical researchers. Many of these researchers, especially those who relied upon spontaneous cases of paranormal activity for their research, observe the increasing popularity of the paranormal and its corresponding touristic developments, including ghost walks, commercial ghost hunts, and paranormal investigating groups, with marked alarm. For example, in a compelling 2008 presentation at the joint meeting of the Society for Psychical Research and the Parapsychological Association, Ann Winsper, Steve Parsons, Ciarán O'Keeffe, academic parapsychologists, argued that the growth of this tourism sector led to a decline in the spontaneous cases reported to more established, academic groups. They reported that between 1995 and 2001, they received two to three reports of spontaneous cases a week. By 2008, they received only two to three a year (Winsper, Parsons, and O'Keeffe 2008).

From the perspective of many investigators, paying for access to a site, or at least paying a significant amount, delegitimizes the scientific component of their investigation. They believe that since their endeavor is a research-based one rather than a thrill-seeking, touristic one, they should be able to freely access sites; paying for the privilege of doing so positions them as "nothing more than tourists," in Jack's words. In a sense, Jack was correct. The commercialization of sites propelled teams like his to become de facto tour companies.

Staging Public Investigations

Conducting public investigations complicates the position, activities, and status of ghost hunters and paranormal investigators. They tend to view it as a denigration of their research, and it paradoxically provides them with a forum in which to effectively and persuasively stage their expertise. While their private investigations rarely yield the knowledge or expert status they desire, staging and selling access to public investigations—in short, producing another form of ghost tourism—presents team members as experts and allows them a forum to share that expertise. As Gregory Matoesian has argued, expert actors may "finesse reality and animate evidence through mastery of verbal performance" (1999, 518), as well as the mobilization of material objects. Investigators and ghost hunters mobilize linguistic and material resources, including jargon, technologies, and self-presentation to successfully persuade the members of the public of their expertise. Ultimately, these public ghost hunts, I argue, are the sites that allow for investigators and ghost hunters to most successfully enact their expertise.

Selling Expertise on Public Investigations

Public investigations are more rigidly structured and include a slightly different range of activities than group-only investigations. While team members mutually construct the organization and structure of private investigations, this is not the case in public investigations. Typically, the team who organizes the public investigation divides up the attendees into groups of eight or so and pairs them with investigators. Sometimes this is done arbitrarily. Other times, the team might have concerns about a particular attendee and, as a result, pair that person with more experienced team members. The team members act as guides through the night's activities. The organization times and orders the smaller groups' visits to particular rooms or areas of the haunted sites. This aspect of the evening highlights the role of the team as coordinators and leaders of the investigation. Mapping and guiding non-members' movements positions the team as experts capable of exerting and enacting their judgment and power on a lay population.

Team members also have more explicit opportunities to perform their knowledge and expertise throughout the night. The first and most important of these opportunities occurs at the very start of the night when all of the guests have arrived. The team and guests typically gather in a central room. Two or three of the more outspoken and central team members welcome the guests, explain the plans for the nights, and address any known ghosts associated with the site. Then, the team typically spends between fifteen to twenty minutes introducing and explaining the various tools and devices that they plan to use for the night, like the EMF reader, digital thermometer, and any divinatory tools, such as dowsing rods or crystals. Then they pass the items around the group. These displays are fascinating performances worthy of closer examination. Groups who advertise events on their website often emphasize that guests have the opportunity to use and learn about these tools. As one group advertised "use of ghost hunting equipment, including Dowsing Rods and EMF Meters" is a core component of the event. The tools on display are widely available, and most guests are familiar with them from paranormal reality television shows. During the time of my research, one could acquire them either online or at retail stores for as little as £10. Ghost hunting and paranormal investigation groups tend not to bring any particularly rare or valuable technology to such events because everyone at the event has access to them. What, then, made these displays of common technologies so compelling to the public? That the tools were introduced and used by apparent experts increased their interest and value significantly. Guests sat with apparent rapt interest as these demonstrations unfolded and then passed the sample equipment around with a sense of reverence, which is commonly found in lay responses to scientific expertise (Traweek 1988). Jamie, a guest on an investigation, praised these demonstrations. She explained, "it's interesting to learn how to use them. I've read books about them, but they actually know how to do it." This introduction and explanation of technology was key because it enabled team members to demonstrate their knowledge and, in essence, teach the guests the ways of investigating.

That the public tended to perceive these events as authentic investigations was very important. The groups who organized these public investigations did not present them as "tours" or "ghost experiences," like the commercial ghost hunting companies. When they advertised upcoming events, they did not guarantee or promise encounters with the ghostly, like commercial ghost hunting groups. Their claims were far more circumspect. For example, Ghost Seekers, a small ghost hunting group, sold fifteen additional places on an upcoming investigation for £10 each. In advertising their event they simply described the site, an abandon outdoor well in a small village:

In the early 1920s a farmer . . . built [the site] as a get-rich-quick scheme. He even went so far as to label it the 'magic' well. He sold the water and called it 'Medicinal Water.' The well was shut down around the mid 1920s due to water contamination, perhaps because of a tuberculosis sanatorium that opened in 1927, which was on higher ground to the well. The farmer died [soon thereafter] and the well was sold. Even though the haunted history is very vague, some believe that an old poacher called Dave roams the site. We've heard rustling and footsteps around the well.

While Ghost Seekers noted the potential activity at the sight, they acknowledge the "vague[ness]" of the haunted history. Even the discussion of potential paranormal activity was quite mild. Similarly, in advertising an upcoming investigation, NEPI emphasized the differences between their events and what tourists may expect based on television shows. On their website, Kevin wrote "this is real life—it's NOT *Most Haunted*, and even if you're really interested in the paranormal, it's not going off every two minutes like what you see on *Most Haunted* or *Ghost Hunters*." Ghost hunting groups were very careful not to promise regular paranormal activity. Doing so would have associated them with the commercial companies.

Many of the individuals who purchase one of these public ghost hunts do so because of the perceived authenticity of the experience and the seeming expertise of the team in question. When I spoke to Joe, a long-time reader of and participant in EGR's online forum, about his decision to dispatch £20 to spend the night at the Golden Fleece, he explained his motivations for participating.

> EGR's a good group. They're professional. They know what they're doing. I respect their approach. They've been doing this awhile, and I think they're sensible. . . . I'm interested. I'll read a book about [the paranormal], but I haven't got the time to join a group like that. I can just do a one off like this. . . . I know that they won't mess about it. They won't fake anything.

Many echoed Joe's appreciation for the presumed seriousness of the team and their expertise in the area. When I spoke to Lydia, a long-time reader of EGR's forum who commented very rarely, she emphasized her desire for an "authentic" experience. In response to my question about why she chose EGR's public night rather than one of the commercially operated tours, she explained that she had "been reading their forum for ages. It's quite good. It seems nice, welcoming. They also take it seriously. I don't just want to go out and call out for spirits. I'm interested in the investigating side, and that's what they're about too. I wanted an authentic investigation, not some nonsense based on *Most Haunted*." Lydia's decision to join these public investigations was grounded in an appreciation for the established sense of community and the perception that the team was knowledgeable. Lydia and Joe also appreciated the team's emphasis on scientific research and analysis rather than simply amassing paranormal experience. Both were interested in acquiring such experiences, and it was important to them that it be coupled with a more analytic approach.

By 2010, some groups had begun to include guests' comments about their experiences on their websites as a way of marketing their public experiences. They also tended to emphasize the teams' knowledge, accessibility, and friendliness. Consider the following two reviews of Ghost Seekers.

Review No.1:

A friendly, experienced, and knowledgeable team

I have attended several ghost hunts with this small and professional ghost hunting team. . . . These are professionally run events, which have achieved some amazing results during the evening. A friendly, experienced, and knowledgeable team who always make you feel welcome. A good selection of gadgets and gizmos are provided for the hunts including EMF meters, heat detectors (thermometers), voice records, cameras etc. Always an entertaining evening, you never know what is going to happen next! Can't wait for my next one!

Review No. 2:

I felt like I'd known the team all my life

I would like to tell you about the event I attended recently, I'm old to the paranormal scene having been doing it some years now, but we attended [this event] with [Ghost Seekers], we got there the first time in the lashing rain, but as luck would have it, it stopped as soon as we set off, it was cold! Wet! And muddy! But the guys were very welcoming and accommodating having never met us before. We walked into the woods, and I felt like I'd known the team all my life, a very welcoming, professional bunch of guys! Very knowledgeable about their subject area and answered all mine and our questions with professionalism and gusto! They made the night—which just happened to be a bloody eventful one with non stop activity the whole night—worthwhile! I've returned to the same location with the team since then and again, we came away a happy group of people :) highly recommendable.

It is clear that potential guests appreciate the knowledge of the group, the group's sense of warmth and friendliness, technological expertise, and the potential to have paranormal *experiences*. These reviews, taken together, suggest a tension that emerges between guests' goals and those of the group. While the public who purchases these public investigations or ghost hunts crave more authenticity, intimacy, and rigor than those offered by commercial ghost companies, they also desire experiences with the paranormal. This, in turn, pressures team members to cater to these demands. Paranormal investigators and ghost hunters were especially uncomfortable with this experiential element of the paranormal.

Providing Experience

In structuring their public events, ghost hunting and investigative teams were acutely aware of the experiential desires of participants. In describing such events, Jack remarked that he thought the public wanted a "bit of a *Most Haunted* experience. They want a walk-through with a medium, that sort of thing." Jack and other investigators questioned the scientific legitimacy of such practices, but they felt that they needed to offer them to cater to the expectations of the public. As a result, investigators and ghost hunters included events like a walk-through with the team's medium and vigils, which are activities typically included on commercial ghost hunts. The walk-through with the medium was nearly identical to those I observed on commercial ghost hunts. The medium or mediums led the group from room to room sharing their impressions of the spirits present and history associated with the site.

The perceived value of the medium differed significantly between private and public ghost hunts and investigations. While research teams were often wary about or uncertain of how to incorporate mediums, members of the public looked to them as supreme authority figures and expected them to facilitate experiences for them. Many mediums seemed to relish this heightened role. Katie, a medium who had a somewhat troubled working relationship with her ghost hunting team, described the differences between team-only and public events:

> I prefer the public ones to be honest. People are interested in what I have to say, which is the point to me. I'm interested in sharing what I get, and they want to hear it. In the past . . . you know I've had some issues like with the team. [One team member] was starting rumors about me, saying I was faking and the like. It's just petty. I can't be

bothered with that kind of politics. I know what I get is real. If the team wants to question it or whatever, that's their business but I can't be bothered. They want me at these public events, and I'm happy with that. I love them.

Katie's sense that the public found her interactions and impressions of spirits interesting was accurate. The public's understanding of what constitutes paranormal knowledge differed from investigators' and ghost hunters' ideas. For the guests, experiential contact with a spirit could be a satisfactory type of evidence. They looked to investigators to offer more nuanced analyses and validation of their interpretations. While they shared some of the team's complex feelings about the role of mediums, they embraced the mediums on these ghost hunts because they presumed the ghost hunting or paranormal investigating team had scientifically vetted and accepted the legitimacy of the mediums. While this was rarely the case, the illusion powerfully enabled guests to embrace mediums and the experiences that they facilitated as legitimate, useful forms of knowledge.

Ultimately, guests tended to leave these public ghost hunts with a sense of accomplishment. They had experienced the paranormal, engaged in science, and worked with experts. These nights tended to meet their expectations. As Joe, a guest on an EGR public event, reflected on his experience: "it was a good night. I think I learned a lot. I also had some experiences, which was great. Dead interesting night." For guests combining their paranormal experiences with the presence of experts legitimized the experiences. They were not thrill seekers; rather, they were engaged in a legitimate pursuit of knowledge. Of course, the team members were less satisfied by these nights, which they saw as misplaced attempts at research that yielded little knowledge.

Conclusion

Being publicly recognized as a paranormal expert paradoxically required embracing acts of divination, mediumship, and experience that investigators and ghost hunters saw as the signs of amateurs or dilettantes. While investigators viewed their public events with a fair amount of skepticism, these events ultimately enabled them to perform their expertise to a public who embraced and recognized them as experts. For the guests who purchased these public ghost hunts, encountering such expertise enabled and substantiated their own interest in and experiences with the paranormal. While guests shared investigators' perception of commercial ghost hunts as unrefined sites of simplistic thrill-seeking, these guests desired such experiences when experts, such as the investigators, were nearby to corroborate and authorize them. For ghost hunters and paranormal investigators, their uneasy association with the paranormal was a culturally, if not financially, advantageous one. Through staging tours, they legitimized their expertise at least in the eyes of their guests.

ENCOUNTERING THE GHOSTLY: MEDIUMSHIP, POPULISM, AND THE ARTICULATION OF AMATEUR EXPERTISE

Public understandings of the past, such as those found at museums and heritage sites, are typically grounded in the expert research of historians, archaeologists, folklorists, or anthropologists. Mediumship, based on people's encounters with spirits of the dead, constitutes a very different way of knowing the past. In this chapter, I examine the ideologies and practices that define contemporary English mediumship. By focusing on these practices, I reveal how they challenge the orthodox production of historical knowledge, how they produce canons of history that challenge current thought, and, finally, how the practices of mediumship ultimately displace established historical knowledge. As I show, ghost tourists conceive of mediumship as a radically democratic phenomenon open to anyone. The practices of mediumship allow a cross-section of ghost tourists, including ghost hunters, paranormal investigators, and mediums themselves to destabilize orthodox ways of knowing the past while ultimately repositioning themselves as experts. Mediumship, then, acts an emergent embodied epistemology of the past.

While their methods are markedly unconventional, ghost hunters and paranormal investigators are part of a broader trend of amateur researchers who seek to produce their own understanding of the past. In England, there has been a broad range of popular engagements with the past. Societies dedicated to local history have flourished since the end of World War II (Edwards 1998, 2000; Hewison 1987; Hoskins 1959; Wright [1985] 2009). Individuals and local societies actively work to better understand the local past through access to public records and regional archives. More recently, many people have turned toward family histories as a way of engaging the past (Edwards 2012). Scholars have debated the cultural significance of this turn to the past. Some (Hewison 1987; Hoskins 1959; Wright [1985] 2009) argue that this realignment represents an attempt to grapple with the complexity and pace of change found in the contemporary world. The past, they say, offers a sense of stability, control, and identity for the masses. Others (Edwards 2000, 2012) have cautioned against adopting such explanations wholesale. Thus, Jeanette

Haunted Heritage: The Cultural Politics of Ghost Tourism, Populism, and the Past by Michele Hanks, 117–140. © 2015 Left Coast Press, Inc. All rights reserved.

Edwards, drawing on her ethnography of engagements with the past and kinship in North West England, warns that "nostalgia does not capture [the entirety of the] preoccupation with the past, nor does it adequately describe the endeavors of local historians" (2000, 42). Ultimately, she concludes that the "past is a forum in which relatedness is put to work" (2000, 75). Following Edwards, I see ghost tourists' and mediums' embodied encounters with ghosts as more than just nostalgia for the past, although it certainly includes nostalgic elements. Their encounters, rather, constitute a way of challenging, disrupting, and destabilizing knowledge of the past and provide a means for positioning ghost tourists as knowledge producers.

Mediumship in England

Mediumship is a very broad term that encompasses a range of sometimes-divergent cultural practices.[1] Historians and psychologists, as well as para-psychologists and practitioners, have generally argued that there are two forms of mediumship prevalent in England: physical mediumship and mental mediumship. Physical mediumship seeks to produce physical manifestations of spirit. It was most popular during the Spiritualist movement of the nine-teenth century. Wooffitt recently described it as a process wherein "the spirits offered visible, audible, and sometimes tangible evidence of their presence" (2006, 5). Janet Oppenheim described the varieties of psychical mediumship in nineteenth-century séances by writing that some mediums,

> specialized in particular effects, whereas others offered a broad rep-ertoire of manifestations. That repertoire might include the materi-alization of entire spirit bodies . . . in addition to more commonplace rapping, table tilting, and the emergence of spirits' heads. Reports of séances also told of furniture cavorting around the room, objects floating in the air, mediums levitating, musical instruments playing tunes by themselves, bells ringing, [and] tambourines jangling. . . . From the bodies of some mediums a strange foamy, frothy or filmy substance, dubbed ectoplasm, might be seen to condense. (1985, 8)

In contrast, she noted that mental mediumship tends to involve the medium experiencing a range of senses in consciousness and, then, verbally articu-lating them to the audience. While parapsychologists, historians, and other scholars have found this to be a useful demarcation of modes of medium-ship, most of the mediums I met do not use this language to describe their practice. Rather, they simply identify as mediums and explain that their mediumship manifests itself in a variety of ways. While I agree with Robin Wooffitt (2006), a sociologist who studied the linguistic practices of mediums in England, that contemporary modes of mediumship tend more toward mental mediumship, rather than physical mediumship, elements of physical mediumship still appear in mediums' performances on paranormal investigations. For example, elements of physical mediumship, such as raps and sounds, emerge upon mediums' invitation. Mediums also come to embody the spirits in question.

Self-identified mediums in England today experience and understand their mediumship in a variety of ways; however, sensory perception is a foundational facet of it. Some mediums use the terms clairvoyance, clairsentience, clairaudience, clairalience, and clairgustance to refer to modes of extrasensory perception grounded in vision, touch, sound, scent, and taste respectively. There is another category of perception, claircognizance, which is not so easily tied to a particular sense; rather, it includes the acquisition of knowledge of the unknown, dead, or paranormal gained through unspecified extrasensory channels.

Mediumship has played an important role in the religion of Spiritualism (in its past and present incarnations), as well as in forms of New Age spirituality such as channeling (Brown 1999).[2] In these contexts, an individual medium's encounter with a spirit entity—be it the spirit of a dead family member or an alien from a different dimension—serves to reveal a religious or spiritual truth. For example, contemporary Spiritualists tend to interpret mediumistic encounters with spirits as demonstrations of survival of the spirit after death (Meintel 2007; Porter 1995).

Mediumship emerges as a way of knowing in less spiritually charged contexts as well. Wooffitt suggested that stage demonstrations, psychic fairs, private one-to-one sittings, Spiritualist services, telephone psychics, and popularly published books by psychics are the main ways in which the public interacts with mediums, psychics, or what Wooffitt refers to broadly as *psychic practitioners* (2006, 8–11). Mediumship has emerged as a way of knowing the obscure information about the present and the past—albeit contested in many spheres.[3] I would add to this list the important setting of paranormal investigations and ghost hunts. In recent years, some scholars have begun attending more closely to the discursive strategies deployed by mediums in their performances of stage mediumship and one-on-one sittings (Wales 2009; Wooffitt 2006, 2007). But there has been little attention devoted to mediums' activities in the context of popular paranormal investigation. While mediums often financially profit from their engagement in commercial one-on-one sittings or acts of stage mediumship, their participation in ghost hunts or paranormal investigations brings them little in the way of financial compensation.[4] Increasingly, mediums came to be seen as agents capable of producing knowledge about obscured parts of the past or present.

Democratizing and Naturalizing Ideologies of Mediumship

There are diverse contemporary ideologies of mediumship, and there is little consensus regarding the distribution, development, or practices of mediumship. There are, however, several dominant ways that members of the paranormal community conceive of mediumship and paranormal experience. Many individuals who engage in paranormal research or investigation believe that everyone has the capacity to experience the paranormal or to pick up on something paranormal. They tend to conceive of this as a passive sensory capacity akin to hearing or seeing. If any person, regardless of prior experience or belief in the paranormal, visits a haunted site, they have the potential to experience something. This capacity is tied directly to their understanding of the paranormal itself. Investigators and enthusiasts understand the paranormal as a fundamentally natural phenomenon. One investigator, Joanna, liked the paranormal to a range of other natural phenomena, observing that "it's just as much a part of the world as electricity or gravity." Her point was that if the paranormal existed, it was part of the natural world and, as such, was likely subject to similar laws and patterns as other natural phenomena, such as gravity.

Many mediums, particularly those who trained or regularly attended Spiritualist church, saw mediumship as something that could be learned and refined. Spiritualist churches, such as the one in York, held weekly development circles where participants learned to better channel spirits and energy for either communication of healing.

Again, there was a strong tendency among ghost tourists to conceive of mediumship, like paranormal experience, in naturalized terms. Alice, a medium from York, described the development of mediumship:

> Well, everyone has the capacity for it, don't they? It's one of those things we're born with. You see it with babies and children all the time. They see things we don't. They talk to people we can't see. We chalk it up to their imaginations, but it's more than that. We socialize them out of it. Train them to shut down those senses. But we should be developing them. Helping them embrace it. So, we all have that part of ourselves. We just need to focus on it and train it. I'm not

saying everyone's set to be a crack [exceptional] medium. It's like any-thing else. Some people are better at some things than others. Some kids are smarter. Some are better at sport. You know what I mean? It's like any other gift. . . . But we all have the capacity for it, if you know what I mean.

Alice's articulation of mediumship is a fairly standard perspective. Alice, like Joanna, emphasized the naturalness of mediumship. By likening it to traits such as intelligence and sports, Alice emphasized the connection between innate talent or capacity and training. Her point, I believe, was that while someone might have an innate sense of intelligence, they develop their intel-ligence through training as a means of crafting it into something more useful.

Some people, particularly self-identified mediums, qualify such optimis-tic statements of distribution. They assert that mediumship is a less demo-cratically distributed trait. They see it, rather, as something that is passed down along kin lines. For example, Joe, a medium from Bradford, explained how he understood mediumship:

It runs in the family. My Gran had it. Her mum had it. I have it. It doesn't come in every generation though. My mum doesn't have any of it. Or, if she does, she's never shown a sign of it. Now, Alice [his wife] is pregnant and the little one clearly has it. I can hear her loud and clear. What's really interesting, though, is that Alice, who's never had a touch of it, has been suddenly picking up on things left and right. It's like having the little one in her has changed her.

As Joe's explanation of his family's legacy of mediumship shows, it is pos-sible to explain the presence of mediumship through reference to family histories. In Joe's account, he seemed to offer an almost biomedical interpre-tation of mediumship, casting it as a genetic trait passed along a particular genetic trajectory. Despite rendering mediumship as an almost elite genetic pedigree, Joe nonetheless also allowed for the presence of a more democrati-cally distributed mediumship. He conceded to me that "while [he] might be especially blessed, everyone has some degree of it." He went on to offer a similar argument for the role of socialization in curtailing mediumship that Alice's provided.

Ultimately, these ideologies of mediumship reveal something key, namely, that many people conceive of mediumship as a democratically distributed and naturally occurring phenomenon. This democratic ideology is crucial to the project of mediumship in particular and ghost hunting in general.

Because mediumship is understood as a natural reality and a window into the past, this democratic distribution of mediumship translates into an implicit belief that anyone can produce new, important understandings of the past. Practices of mediumship, then, actively redistribute the epistemological authority traditionally limited to established experts, such as historians. This belief manifests itself in the practices of touring museums and heritage sites, as well as in the ensuing historical narratives that investigators and mediums produce and circulate.

Re-interpreting the Past at the Museum and in the Country House

Investigators, ghost hunters, and mediums all have a deep-seated interest in visiting historical places and a strong interest in the past itself. They enjoy visiting historical sites or museums even when not actively participating in organized paranormal investigations. This interest in history and commitment to mediumship often combine in fascinating ways during these visits. In this section, I consider the collision of paranormalists with authoritative sites of English history.

Disrupting the Image of the Polite Tourist

Ghost tourists are broadly interested in historical and heritage sites Their passion brings them to country houses, stately homes, and local museums, places that abound in England. But their engagement with these places disrupts the usual profile of tourists

Scholars and touristic literature have often presented the stately home as a quintessentially English tourist site. Stately homes have gradually been opening to the public since the early nineteenth century. This opening process has accelerated since the end of World War II when the aristocracy lost much of its political and economic clout, and stately homes became increasingly dependent on public support and tourism for survival (Mandler 1997; Tinniswood 1989). Historian Peter Mandler suggested that the "clichés of the present day" maintain an image of the stately home as "epitomiz[ing] the English love of domesticity of the countryside, of hierarchy, continuity and tradition" (1997, 1). Scholars have suggested that such sites attract visitors interested in art, history, architecture, and the aristocracy (Mandler 1997; Tinniswood 1989). Period films and television series, or what some call "heritage cinema and television" (Higson 2001), also play a crucial role in constructing such sites as destination images (Higson 2001, 2003; Sargent 1998; Tooke and Baker 1996). Historian Adrian Tinniswood acerbically notes that "the country house's appeal as a monument to a way of life 'no longer possible' has become its most potent attraction" (1989, 191). Ghost tourists visit such sites because of an interest in a different "way of life;" however, it may not be precisely the one that Tinniswood expects.

With their commitment to an ideology of mediumship and inspiration from guidebooks that cast such sites as experientially rich domains, ghost tourists visit stately homes and country houses with radically altered expectations and forms of engagement. Many ghost tourists tend to rely on their own senses and impressions of a site rather than official signage or guides. For example, as I have accompanied ghosts tourists on commercial ghost hunts, privately organized paranormal investigations, and casual visits to museums, I have observed them avoid signage and museum personnel and rely on their own sense of the ghostly to guide their interpretation. Ghost tourists, including paranormal investigators, ghost hunters, and mediums, disrupt popular images of the passive, adoring heritage pilgrim-tourist.

Textual Authority

This active disregard for the textual interpretations present in a museum is especially evident in commercial ghost hunts, which are often held at museums. A central premise of commercial ghost hunts is that participants *will* experience the paranormal during the course of their visits. Ghost tourists purchase such experiences because they want or hope to encounter some component of the paranormal firsthand. During the course of such hunts, guests and mediums alike experience a range of sensations associated with encountering a ghost. There is significantly less emphasis on collecting data—other than photographic evidence—than there is on paranormal investigations.

Most standard tourist visits to museums occur during the day and include attentive examination of artifacts and close readings of the descriptions and interpretations of them. This is not the case on ghost hunts, which begin in the evening and last through the dark and atmospheric night; clearly these visitors are not focused on the visual and textual script of the material record curated in these places. Whether day or night, throughout the course of their museum ghost hunts, ghost-focused guests and mediums avoid reading or engaging the descriptions and analyses of museum objects throughout the site. Instead, they focus on their own impressions grounded in their personal mediumship or paranormal experience.

For example, The National Railway Museum in York focuses on the history of train travel, engineering, and rail nationalization in the UK (figure 4.1). It is housed in a massive building near the York rail station that is filled

FIGURE 4.1 The National Railway Museum in York features this cast-iron foot-bridge from 1891. During the daytime, it provides an interesting glimpse into the design and structure of earlier rail stations. Children and their parents often enthusiastically climb it. During the course of an overnight, commercial ghost hunt, however, the bridge takes on a darker, spookier character.

with many rail cars from various historical eras including Queen Victoria's royal train carriage, among others. A thorough and accessible interpretation accompanies each displayed train or train artifact. This museum served as the site of a commercial ghost hunt in early 2009. On the night of the ghost hunt, guests and mediums moved easily between the trains and artifacts; however, I never observed any of them reading or attempting to examine the textual analyses of the artifacts. Throughout the night, they eschewed the authoritative vision of the museum in favor of producing their own understanding through mediumship and paranormal experience. Guests and mediums wandered through the museum, experiencing a range of paranormal thoughts and sensations and vocalizing these thoughts to the group. They also engaged in a variety of divinatory practices, including glass divinations and calling out, which were intended to bring them into close contact with spirits.

The narrative that emerges in the National Railway Museum provided a standard history of British railways (figure 4.2). This narrative, and the ghostly narrative that emerged during the course of the ghost hunt, did not

FIGURE 4.2 Opened in 1975, the National Railway Museum in York is the largest rail museum in the world and attracts almost one million visitors annually. While many commercial ghost hunts occur at sites that look either old or spooky, this is not always the case. The National Railway Museum is housed in a modern building behind the York Rail Station that does not appear to signal ghosts or hauntings in anyway. Despite this, commercial ghost companies successfully stage ghost hunts there.

overlap at all. One remarkable divergence from the Museum's narrative occurred very late in the night at a cast-iron footbridge from 1891, a large artifact on display in the museum. Its placard explained that "a notable feature of many North Eastern Railway Stations was the cast iron footbridge connecting adjacent platforms of ordinary double track stations" (National Rail Museum 2012). It further elaborated on the construction, history of use, and location where this particular bridge had once stood. When Jeff, the medium, and the group of ghost hunters approached the bridge, however, they ignored this simple description and, through their engagement with the spirit world, crafted a far more complicated narrative of the bridge's history. Jeff began the process of recontextualizing the bridge by sharing what he was "picking up" on. He explained:

> There's sadness and anger here. Something important happened. Something important. I'm stood here, and there's a man on there [the

bridge]. He's angry and scared. . . . He's been caught out. He's done some awful things and he's scared now. . . . He doesn't want to face it. I . . . . He's so angry. I think he's . . . he's done terrible things to women. He's stood up there thinking about that and he's not sorry. He's glad that . . . glad that he raped them. Not sorry. But the . . . the police are coming and he wants no part of it. I think . . . . I think he killed himself here. Like, I'm getting that he threw himself off this bridge.

As Jeff narrated this encounter, the guests wandered around, photographed the bridge and its vicinity, tried to pick up on energies, and quietly vocalized what they picked up. Others further fleshed out the narrative. One guest, Louise, a woman who had traveled to York with a friend for the ghost hunt, picked up quite a bit about the rapist and his victims. She elaborated to the group: "I can see him. He's dressed like it's [the] 20s, I think. He's so angry. He's got cold, dead eyes. Cold, dead eyes. I feel the sadness of his victims around them. I think he killed one of them. I'm glad he's dead." Others shared similar elaborations. Collectively, the group constructed a bleak picture of a deranged serial rapist who had raped and possibly killed women and eventually committed suicide by jumping off the bridge. This vision of the past was very much at odds with the historical narrative of the museum.

That nothing in the Museum supported the factual existence of a rapist did little to deter guests and mediums from accepting it as a historical reality. Following that night, several of the guests on the ghost hunt, with whom I kept in touch, referred to the historical existence of the rapist and his presence in the museum as historical givens. More than one attendee took to referring to the bridge as the "rape bridge." The enactment and acceptance of such acts of mediumship and paranormal experience implicitly displace the authority of museums to provide authoritative, singular explanations of the past. By the end of the night, a museum dedicated to celebrating technological triumph had been recast as a repository for forgotten, upsetting, and often violent histories. Such reconstitutions of the museum space actualize the promise of democratization implicit in their ideologies of mediumship. The medium and guests collaboratively emerged as experts on the past, and their form of knowledge displaced that of the museum in producing an authoritative understanding of the past.

Peopling the Past: A Critique

In addition to re-imagining the nature of epistemic authority in knowing the past, ghost hunters and mediums are also engaged in a process of repositioning the narrative emphasis in museums. Through their mediumship and embodied encounters with spirits, ghost hunters are especially interested in encountering and making sense of individual ghosts and spirits.

Many ghost tourists explicitly articulate a class-based critique of the representations of the past found in museums and heritage sites. They argued that museums, castles, and other sites failed to represent *their* ancestors or historical equivalents. Alice, a working class ghost hunter explained.

> When you go to those grand houses and castles, you don't see any evidence of people like me. That's always bothered me. When we [her group] go to a place, we tend to get the spirits of people like us, not the fancy people who lived here, but the ones who worked for them. We're more likely to get them because of who we are ourselves.

She explicitly points to the role of omission in existing narratives. She and many other ghost tourists position their project as a reclaiming of public space for the non-elite members of society.

It many ways, their project is analogous to the work of social historians (Thompson 1966), as well as feminist historians (Scott [1987] 1999), who have demonstrated and brought light to the role of women, the working class, and other disenfranchised groups throughout history. While the project of including working class histories, as well as women's histories, in museums is of paramount importance, I think that ghost tourists are often overly general in their critiques. While it is undeniably true that stately homes and castles privilege the perspective of the elites (Higson 2001; Mandler 1997; Tinniswood 1989), there are many other museums that do not. There is an established history of museums focusing on components of folk life and non-elite populations, especially in the North of England (Bailkin 2002; Grek 2009; Watson 2011). There are many museums throughout the North East that highlight histories of the working class along with broader social histories of the region, such as the National Coal Mining Museum for England in Overton or the York Castle Museum in York. While the reality of depictions of the past found in museums may be more nuanced than ghost tourists allow, their critique is nonetheless important. It speaks not only to a perceived deficit but also ghost tourists' concerns regarding their own social position and social exclusion, a theme I return to in chapter five. While contemporary museums almost invariably include some component of social history in their representations of the past, ghost hunters and mediums seem to challenge them to include even more.

Consider the ghost hunt at the National Railway Museum. Throughout the course of the night, the professional mediums, as well as the guests, were dedicated to encountering a cast of spirits associated with the train. They varied from the rapist to train conductors and soldiers returning home on the trains. In each case, the group collectively sought to construct a biography of a spirit complete with personality and temperament. This emphasis on the intimate details of the lives of these mundane figures reconfigures the narrative of the railway museum. While the museum effectively includes elements of social history, such as a discussion of railway workers' lives and the social impact of the rails upon the public, the predominant narrative focuses on the history, science, and engineering of the rails. The mediums and ghost tourists seemed to challenge this distribution.

Feeling the Past

The built environment is of great significance for ghost tourists and mediums. Like historians, mediums see the built environment as existing in the present and offering a window (of sorts) into the past; however, the nature of the window and the nature of their interpretation is significantly different. Unlike historians, they do not foreground the necessity of contextualizing buildings or artifacts within a historical record. Rather, they compress or simplify the act of history-building in significant ways. Namely, their mediumship offers a direct experiential window into the emotional, physical, and chronological events of the past. This is a recourse immediately available to them through the psychical deployment of their senses. It is an instant, sensual knowledge at odds with Western modernity's orthodox renderings of history.

For example, Rob was a core member of CPI, a paranormal investigation team. During the course of a night's investigation with his team and me at the Golden Fleece, a York pub that was popular with paranormal investigators, he produced and sustained intimate, sensual understandings of the past that exemplify the common approach found in ghost tourism. Throughout the night, he and the team moved from room to room in the pub. As he moved through the rooms, he picked up on different spirits. In one of the bedrooms on the uppermost level of the building, he began to describe a ghost:

> I'm getting a little girl here. . . . She's dressed in an old dress. It's to the floor. Yes . . . Yes . . . Thank you for that. . . . She's sad. She's been here for a while. She likes to sit in that chair. She has some attachment . . . some um interest in it. She's a pretty little thing. I think she's quite sweet. She likes it when people are in here with her. I think she gets lonely a bit . . . when she's on her own. She feels a bit sad to me . . . . Come on sweetheart, can you tell me why you're sad? Come on. . . . Alright . . . Thank you for that. . . . I think she's sad. I can feel the sad-

ness coming off her. Something happened to her here. I think she was left here. I think she came with her mum and something happened to her mum, and she was left here. I'm trying . . . I'm trying to figure out what but I'm not sure. Maybe some kind of illness. Maybe she was a maid? A cleaner? Something like that.

This example of Rob's performance of mediumship was typical in many ways. Throughout the event, he shifts his "footing" (Goffman 1981) many times, particularly regarding to whom he is addressing his speech. At times he speaks directly to the investigators who are gathered with him in the room and describes what he is learning about the girl. At other times he speaks directly to the girl (and perhaps his spirit guide).

The content of this encounter is also fairly representative of many mediums' performances. Rob attuned himself to the emotional and personal components of the girl. When he poses questions to her, he aims to tease apart her personal biography rather than contextualize her with a broader historical context. He seems to focus very little on the particulars of the historical context that produced the girl. For example, at the start of this instance of mediumship, he noted that the girl was wearing an old-fashioned, floor-length dress. He did not attempt to specify the era of this dress. In his exchanges with the girl, he did not question her about the historical era from which she came. When I asked him about this the next day, he explained that he "followed the leads" the girl was giving him. He privileged understanding the emotional experience of the little girl over attempting to produce a historical narrative that would meet the requirements of an "objective" history.

Rob's performance of mediumship was book-ended by other investigators picking up on similar emotions in the room. Joe, an investigator, vocalized his own sensations and remarked that "wow. All of a sudden, this feeling of sadness has just come over me. I feel like I've not got a friend in the world. So sad." Lucy echoed this further. "I'm feeling very maternal like. Like I want to comfort a little one." They saw these sensations as directly connected to the young girl that Rob had encountered. In Joe's case, investigators saw his sudden feelings of sadness as emerging from the girl. Joe was, in essence, feeling her sadness itself. Lucy, on the other hand, felt herself being drawn into an almost kin relation with the girl. Rob, Lucy, and Joe, as well as the investigators present, considered these reactions to be fascinating and revealing glimpses of the haunting. When I talked to investigators about the absence of historical facts or specifics from the account, they were unconcerned. Joe explained to me "maybe that will come with time. For now, we know something about one of the Fleece's ghosts and that, in and of itself, it is dead exciting."

Emotions associated with anguish and suffering are among the most common that mediums and ghost tourists pick up. In the example above, Rob picked up on the sadness of the little girl. Other mediums picked up a range of similar emotions at other venues. For example, on a commercial ghost hunt at the York Castle Museum, the medium felt the presence of hungry, scared Workhouse children who longed for their parents. During the course of a casual walk around a stately home, a medium began to pick up the presence of a maid who was sexually harassed by her employer and eventually committed suicide. Other examples of ghostly emotions include the fear of a falsely persecuted woman, the confusion of an abandoned child, and the pain of a starving pauper. These emotions are portrayed in vivid terms. Tourists often experience them to some degree. Such encounters act to produce a strong sense of empathy in participants. Claire, who I met at a commercial ghost hunt in Nottingham, was a ghost tourist who regularly purchased tours. She praised the historical insights such events generated. She remarked that "you get to know a lot of history doing this. Certainly more than I learned at school. You really feel for them too . . . knowing how they felt and what they went through." Of course, Claire did not mean that she learned or even read the historical narrative presented by the Museum; rather, she came to know a particular vision of the past grounded in empathic, embodied experiences with ghosts. Others shared Claire's sense that these encounters engendered enhanced empathy.

The emotions of anguish and suffering are not the only sentiments present; mediums and ghost tourists also focus on the vengeful elements of the past. They fixate on ghosts filled with rage, anger, and hatred. These are the ghosts of rapists, murders, and villains. This thematic focus on individuals who either violently disrupted the past or victims of such disruptions is not accidental. I shall return to this theme in the next chapter. A focus on the emotions of the dead acts as an implicit critique of the structural inequality present throughout much of English history.

The Emergence of a Localized Canon

Acts of mediumship, such as Rob's encounter with the little girl at the Golden Fleece, produce particular group-specific understandings of the past. Individual paranormal investigation groups or networks of paranormal investigators develop specific and, often unshared, understandings of the past and the ghosts of particular sites.

Consider the status of the "sad little girl" ghost that Rob encountered at the Golden Fleece. Following their visit, members of CPI did not forget about the "sad little girl," as they came to call this particular ghost. Rob and the other members' experiences with her were discussed further. They were also chronicled on the group's forum. The "sad little girl" began to figure prominently in their understanding of the history of the Golden Fleece and, by extension, York. Several months after my first visit to the Golden Fleece with CPI, they returned to re-investigate. Once again, I joined them.[5] In approaching the history and ghosts of the pub, they accepted the "sad little girl" as an established part of the site's history. During the course of that investigation, they sought her out explicitly in the room where they first encountered her. Eventually, Rob and another medium working with the group made contact with her.

The emergence of particular, group-specific ghosts at venues was not at all unusual. I observed it repeatedly in my interactions with paranormal investigation groups. Interestingly, groups did not necessarily adopt or seek out the same ghosts as others groups even at the same venue. For example, EGR, another investigation group, routinely investigated the Golden Fleece. Much like CPI, they developed a specialized and seemingly group-specific canon of ghosts and paranormal entities that they sought out at the Fleece. Their specific canon included ghosts, such as "an evil strangler" and an entity they called "an evil black hole" or demon located in the fireplace of an upper bedroom. These ghosts, like the ghost of the "sad little girl," were not part of the recognized ghost lore of York nor did they factor into official histories of the Golden Fleece.

Despite the lack of "official" recognition of these ghosts and despite their historical inchoateness, EGR, like Central Paranormal Investigators (CPI), looked forward to encounters with these particular spirits. Central Paranormal Investigators and EGR were not groups that personally knew each other, and neither group knew of or sought out the others' ghosts. What their mediums' work ultimately produced was localized and fragmented visions of the past. In a sense, these specific and unshared visions of the past destabilized existing metanarratives of the past or touristic images of particular cities or sites. They replaced such visions with particularistic accounts that did not always amount to a coherent narrative. Mediums' encounters had little to do with the chronological unfolding of the past and more to do with sensual, intimate, and particularistic encounters with spirits. This proliferation of particular, non-generalized canons disrupts the type of coherent, national narrative that heritage sites tend to promote.

At times though, ghost tourists' localized canons seemed to spread in interesting and unpredictable ways. For example, several other groups echoed EGR's assertion that there was an evil black hole in one of the rooms at the Golden Fleece. I observed participants on commercial ghost hunts, who were completely unaffiliated with EGR, seek out and experience roughly similar haunting symptoms associated with the "black hole" or "evil void." When I approached them about how they came to know about this occurrence, they were unsure. I found that tracing how groups came to share perceptions of the ghostly canon of a site was extremely difficult.

The Perils of a Canon

While ghost tourists' and mediums' encounters produce an emerging canon of ghosts that displaces more official histories, this emerging canon poses problems for ghost tourists themselves. An implicit assumption associated with much of ghost hunting is that encounters should produce *new* knowledge. That they displace or run counter to orthodox narratives of places and their histories is to be expected. They were uneasy when their mediumistic encounters replicated known events in either the orthodox or paranormal canon. Ghost tourists' complicated relationship with historical canons is made explicitly clear during an episode from my fieldwork involving a young medium, her encounters with a known ghost, and the status of that ghost in the historical and paranormal canons.

Ruth, who worked closely with EGR, was a self-developed medium who avoided Spiritualist development circles in favor of working on her own. She could be a bit shy with groups she didn't know well. During the course of her collaboration with EGR, she had come to know Ginny and Harry. Eventually, they invited her to join them on one of their weekend-long paranormal investigations.

Harry and Ginny, along with their paranormal investigation team from DNR, had organized an investigation at Chillingham Castle near Alnwick that would last for three nights and four days. Chillingham Castle has a strong reputation with ghost tourists. It has appeared on *Most Haunted,* and it is featured in many ghost guidebooks. Unlike many other stately homes or castles, Chillingham markets itself directly to potential ghost tourists, boasting of its ghostly population on its website. It also offers regular Chillingham Castle ghost walks. Groups, such as DNR, were often eager to spend a period of time there because it was considered a prime investigative site. Like others, Ruth was eager to experience the ghosts there and share her insights with the group.

During the first night we spent at the Castle, several of us gathered in the courtyard of the Castle around 11 p.m. It was very dark, and hoping to pick up on some spirit or sense, investigators used their flashlights to illuminate their pathways as they wandered around the courtyard. Ruth, Ginny, and I stood near the central staircase in the courtyard. Ginny and I were quietly chatting about the gentleman who owned the Castle while Ruth stood silently nearby. She seemed to be deep in thought. After a spell, Ginny turned to Ruth and asked her, "How's it going? Are you picking up on anything?"

Ginny's question signaled the beginning a public enactment of Ruth's mediumship. While Ginny and I had been talking, Ruth had been picking up on a series of things. In a faraway voice, Ruth haltingly told us, "I'm getting a bit. I'm picking up on something. The word Sage is in my head. I don't know where it's come from though. It's just there. Sage. What do you think it means?" Ginny did not directly answer her question. She just slightly shook her head and asked what else Ruth was getting. Ruth continued:

> Sage is still in my head. I'm not sure what it means . . . [long pause] At first I thought, sage like the herb. But, now, I think it's a name. A man's name. He lived here for a while. He was a bad man. A cruel man. I think he did terrible things. He would be stood there [gesturing toward the current location of the torture chamber] hurting people like and loving it.

Ruth paused briefly and looked to Ginny for confirmation or reassurance. Ginny nodded at her and told her that "it was quite interesting. Can you pick up any more?" After another few moments of silence, Ruth continued.

> He did terrible things to loads of people. This man, Sage. Like torturing them and killing them. Throwing them down a pit and just leaving them there to die. Hundreds of them. It was a long time ago. Maybe 800 or 900 years ago. I can't tell. He wore a metal thing on his chest, like knights sometimes do in movies. He did terrible things, but then he got his in the end. I think he was killed here as well. I feel like he was hung [hanged]. [long silence] I'm sorry. That's all I'm getting. Was any of that useful, do you think?

Ruth's delivery was more tentative than some other mediums. At times, she felt uncertain of herself because of her lack of training, as well as her comparative youth in the group. This act of mediumship, her description of Sage, and the group's response to it reveal key components of the complicated relationship between mediumship and orthodox forms of historical authority.

It was only the next day that people began to discuss and analyze Ruth's contributions. Her comments about the figure "Sage," who was a cruel man who eventually died at the Castle, generated significant interest because they conformed quite closely to known information about the ghostly record at the Castle. There were two distinct camps with regard to her contributions.

The next day, in the car, Ginny and Harry were eager to discuss Ruth's mediumship. They began by asking what Rose and I "made of" Ruth during the previous night. Rose, seeming to sense where the conversation was headed, offered a noncommittal answer, observing that she found it to be an interesting night. She asked what Harry and Ginny thought. Ginny replied that she couldn't believe it when Ruth "came out with" Sage. I asked why this was so remarkable.

Harry explained that John Sage was the "most famous ghost" associated with Chillingham Castle. According to Harry, Sage was the former executioner and torturer who was eventually executed himself at the Castle. For Ginny, the public nature of this information was troubling. She commented with agitation, "he's the most Google-able ghost there!" She paused and then noted, "I think Ruth researched this beforehand. She must have." Rose, who was often careful not to become embroiled in gossip of this nature, remarked that it was interesting. Harry agreed with Ginny and noted that he thought it was "suspicious." Ultimately, for Harry and Ginny, the close correspondence between known knowledge of John Sage and Ruth's insights was deeply troubling.

Harry and Ginny's reaction reveals an unspoken, but persistent assumption about the nature of mediumship. Many believe that it should be used to generate *new* knowledge, to alter existing knowledge, or augment known histories. Ultimately, they saw mediumship as something that should be transgressive and disruptive to existing canons in some way. When Ruth offered insights that did none of these things, they subtly questioned her legitimacy as a medium.

Ruth's mediumship is a fascinating glimpse of the paradoxical relationship between mediumship and (semi-)authoritative forms of knowledge. In this case, that she provided information that fairly precisely confirmed public information regarding John Sage was cause for concern and delight. In conforming so closely to the known public record, Ruth's credibility was bolstered for some and diminished for others. As David put it, "it would be quite nice if she had gotten a bit more though. Something new about him [Sage]." Here, again, they echo Ginny and Harry's implicit assumption that ideal or good acts of mediumship contribute something inherently new. To reaffirm known records is not adequate; rather, good mediumship requires new information.

The Ghost of John Sage

It is worth considering the nature of historical record surrounding John Sage that produced so much conversation and contestation following Ruth's act of mediumship. Despite the tenor of Harry, Ginny, David, Matt, and Chris's comments, the historical reality of the ghost known as John Sage is far from certain. In many cases, tracing the historical origin of particular ghost stories is fruitless. Since John Sage appears to be a recently emerged ghost, attending to how and when his story counts as part of the established haunted heritage of the Castle provides some insight into what counts as established knowledge.

Leonora Tankerville, a former resident of Chillingham Castle, published what many take to be an authoritative list of Chillingham's ghosts in 1925 in her brief pamphlet *The Ghosts of Chillingham Castle*. She cited the ghost of a small boy ("Radiant Boy") and Lady Mary Berkeley as the key ghosts in the Castle. It did not include any information about John Sage. Many other ghost guidebooks, such as *The Good Ghost Guide* (Brooks 1994), include no reference to Sage either. Echoing Tankerville, Brooks cited "Radiant Boy" and Lady Mary as the key ghosts of the Castle (1994, 203–4). Likewise, in Tony Liddell's very interesting *Otherworld North East: Ghosts and Hauntings Explored* (2004), no mention is made of Sage. Liddell's text is especially interesting because it is, in part, a series of case studies of recent paranormal investigations at well-known North East sites. In Liddell's discussion of his group's research at Chillingham in 2004, there is no mention of Sage (2004, 26–33). The same can be said of television depictions of Chillingham's ghosts, which was included on episodes of *Most Haunted* and *Famous and Frightened*.

There is also no discussion of John Sage on the ghost section of Chillingham Castle's website.[6] The website boasts of the many ghosts who haunt the Castle, and it is written that "the Blue Boy [another name for Radiant Boy], poor, wandering, Lady Mary, a tortured child, the Royal procession and so many other famous stories. Chillingham retains them all because the Castle stays calm and unaltered ever since ancient battling days" (Chillingham Castle 2013). The absence of Sage in this list of ghosts is intriguing. While there are quite a few ghosts that the Castle seems to accept as official residents or ghosts, such as Lady Mary and the Blue Boy, Sage remains curiously absent. Interestingly, the website points to the fact that the family "lived exciting and romantic lives" and states

no less than eight famous, well recorded, executions. Some were hanged, drawn and quartered. While alive, they were cut down from the Gallows, to have their entrails removed. Still living, the failing body was cut into quarters. The head was displayed on city gates, as a warning. Other members of the family, more fortunate, simply had their heads chopped off. ("Ghosts" 2013)

Certainly, this depiction of the dark history of the Castle corresponds to the imagery abundant in Ruth's mediumship.

Despite this, there are a great number of accounts in recent books and websites detailing John Sage. An account of John Sage can be found on the Real British Ghosts website, a site popular with the public and investigators that offers a catalogue of ghosts. They describe Sage.

> This cruel and sadistic torturer, who died about 1200, has often been seen wandering around the castle. He used to take great pleasure in his grisly work, even devising new and 'improved' methods of inflicting pain on his victims. During the three years he held the job, he is said to have tortured to death over 7,500 people and killed several hundred others in various ways. At the end of the war with the Scots, wanting to rid the castle of the prisoners, he rounded up the Scottish adults and older children being held and burnt them to death in the courtyard. He then took an axe, which can still be seen, and hacked to death the smaller children in the Edward room. . . . John Sage's undoing was when he accidentally strangling his girlfriend as they made love on the 'torture rack' in the castle dungeon. Unfortunately for John Sage, his girlfriend's father was a Border Reiver who said that he would gather a great army and attack the castle if Sage was not put to death. John Sage was publicly hanged from a tree in the castle grounds in front of a very large and enthusiastic crowd. And as he slowly died, people cut off pieces of him as 'souvenirs'. So ended the life of a truly detestable man. (Real British Ghosts 2013)

This description of Sage corresponds with others found online (Ghost Story 2013; Ghost Northeast 2013), as well as in more recent ghost guidebooks (Kirkup 2008, 31–34). Such lurid description of Sage epitomizes what many investigators know about him. Ruth's description of Sage fits nicely within Real British Ghosts' description of him.

The historical status of Sage and investigators' perception of him is significant. Despite the fact that Sage appears on no known history of the Castle and that the Castle itself, which proudly boasts of its haunted heritage, doesn't embrace Sage, investigators perceive Sage as an established historical figure. The historical imaginings found in recent websites and publications trumps his absence from the orthodox historical record or even the more established ghostly record. Ruth's mediumship was questioned for its overly strict adherence to the known historical record. This reveals the degree to which investigators imbue ghost websites and popular publications with historical authority. Ultimately, such acts displace orthodox forms of historical authority. They also demonstrate that, at its core, the embodied, mediumistic encounters that are central to ghost tourism disrupt and critique known understandings of the past.

Consequences for Heritage Industry: Contestations and Collaborations

These mediumistic engagements with the past certainly pose both challenges and questions for heritage sites. In an era in which funding for heritage sites is often sparse and stately homes are increasingly dependent on the public for survival, how should sites respond to the interest of ghost tourists? As I showed in chapter one, heritage sites that were inclined to include the ghostly did so in modest ways that positioned ghosts as established figures in the historical record. While a few stately homes, such as Chillingham Castle, have incorporated ghosts into their advertisements and destination image, most have not. Reflecting on the situation in Scotland, Inglis and Holmes (2003, 60) remark that stately homes "would probably only mention hauntings in passing" if at all. This is also the case in England. For many sites, a reputation of hauntedness would be "off brand."

Heritage sites may become disenchanted with the presence of ghost tourists. Consider Glamis Castle's engagements with its ghost tourists. At one time, Glamis Castle, which is the childhood home of the Queen Mother, willingly marketed itself as one of Britain's "most haunted" castles. Shows such as ITV's *All Fright on the Night,* a ghost hunt presented by Uri Geller, were filmed at the castle. The Scottish Tourist Board boasted of the many ghosts associated with the castle in an attempt to draw tourists to the region. However, the Bowes-Lyon family, which has historically held Glamis, stated its opposition to the castle's haunted reputation and marketing. Cameron Brooks, a journalist for *The Daily Mail,* reported on the small controversy in 1999. Brooks observed that the Bowes-Lyon family, the Queen Mother's relatives, were "angered by a Scottish Tourist Board marketing ploy that seeks to lure travel journalists north" to the castle (Brooks 1999). Brooks quotes Glamis spokesman Gill Crawford who claimed that:

> We never, ever, in any of our literature, draw attention to the stories to attract visitors. We concentrate on the three most historic facts about the castle. The Bowes-Lyon family wishes the castle to be presented to the public as a place connected with the Queen Mother, Princess Margaret, who was born there, and Shakespeare's Macbeth, who held the title Thane of Glamis. (Crawford in Brooks 1999)

The aspiration for such historical associations is not surprising. They are illustrious and worthy of royal associations. Interestingly, the ghost stories that the Bowes-Lyon family and the castle management were allegedly displeased by included what Crawford described as "lurid ghost stories," such as "headless coach drivers, the Grey Lady of Glamis who stalks the halls, a little African Boy who can be seen crying in various rooms, and an apparition called Evil Beardie" (Crawford in Brooks 1999). These ghosts do not seem to be entirely distinct from the types of spirits that the mediums I observed contacted. That castle management cast these particular ghosts as "lurid" is, perhaps, unsurprising. They are a far cry from Macbeth and the Queen Mother.

In 2009, the castle's management began to distance itself from the world of ghost tourism even more actively. David Adams, the new manager explained this to the press.

> We don't encourage ghost-hunters, we don't encourage ghost-hunting TV programmes and we certainly don't encourage people who want to come in and do overnight stays to try to locate ghosts. We don't want anything to do with that. If you happen to believe that stuff, that's fine, but we don't. There are various myths and legends surrounding the castle but they are just that. There is absolutely no evidence whatsoever that there are any supernatural beings in the castle. (Adams in STV News 2009)

Adams's frustration with some ghost tourists is evident here. His statement seems to indicate that he believes the Castle is not a place for ghost tourists. His use of the language of evidence is striking. He is not annoyed simply by ghost tourists' presence, but by the epistemological significance of their claims. He repositions their claims as supernatural *beliefs* rather than historical *evidence* about the past of the castle. This approach effectively allows him to ignore the politics of access and democratization that I have argued are evident in mediums' and ghost hunters' engagement with the past.

Historically, many fields have worried about the presence and practice of amateur researchers. For example, archaeologists have long been concerned about the ways in which hobbyists' attempts at archaeological research may undermine, illegitimate, or destroy their own investigations (Kelley 1963).[7] The rise of such amateur experts in science and history has a range of sociopolitical and epistemological consequences that are not fully understood. This has been most thoroughly explored in the domain of science and technology studies. Harry Collins and Robert Evans (2002) have suggested that by attempting to include the public in technical decision making as a means of democratizing science, we have troublingly blurred the boundary between expert and amateur, which has chilling consequences in contemporary engagements with vaccinations, global climate change, and more.

The relationship between amateurs and experts, however, need not always be fraught with tensions over authority and epistemology. Some fields of science, such as astronomy and ecology, have fostered productive collaborations with interested members of the public and amateur scientists. In such fields, non-specialists have provided localized, longitudinal data about environmental changes that experts have found to be complementary to more hypothesis-driven inquiries (Dickinson, Zuckerberg, and Bonter 2010). Is there any way to bridge the expert/amateur gap—or from the perspective of mediums and ghost hunters, the bridge between multiple forms of expertise—in ghost tourists' engagements with the heritage industry?

Certainly erasing ghostly presences and distancing their sites from ghost tourists is not the only recourse available to museums, heritage sites, and stately homes. Consider two productive collaborations. The Peterborough Museum, a museum dedicated to the city's cultural, historical, and geologic past, forged productive relations with ghost tourists. The Museum ran its own ghosts walk in which it seamlessly combines an emphasis on experiential knowledge generated by local people, including mediums, with the orthodox historical narrative. It also hosted commercial ghost hunts, and the museums' interpretation manager, Stuart Orme, often attended these events. During these events, he productively acted as link between paradigms of paranormal and mediumstically grounded knowledge and orthodox historical claims about the building. He was so effective in this capacity because of his seemingly genuine embrace of the value of each world.[8]

Similarly, the town of Swindon granted Swindon Paranormal Site Investigators (PSI) a Lotto Grant to research the town's haunted heritage. The public presentation of this collaboration is worth considering. In an article in *The Swindon Advertiser,* PSI spokes woman Nicky Sewell explained: "we have had a meeting with the council's head of economic development and discussed potentially raising Swindon's profile with the investigations. . . . Interest in the paranormal has never been as high as it is today, and the council hopes it will bring tourism into the town" (Sewell in Walker 2007). That Sewell, an investigator, cast the future investigations as a matter of touristic significance is perhaps unsurprising. That the local Council's Cabinet Member for leisure, Justin Tomlinson, embraced the investigators' interventions in terms of heritage is possibly more surprising. Tomlinson explained the collaboration by explaining that "most people who live in Swindon are proud of our heritage. Interest in this area is at an all-time high and I think most of us know enough people who have had experiences to know we should not rule out this sort of enquiry (Tomlinson in Walker 2007). Tomlinson understood ghosts and spirits in much the same way that ghost tourists, including mediums and ghost hunters, did. While such positive collaborations were somewhat uncommon, they offer a window into the possibility of a productive engagement with ghost tourists that can work with rather than against their understandings of heritage and knowledge.

Conclusion

Ultimately, mediums, ghost hunters, and paranormal investigators have somewhat successfully positioned themselves as epistemological authorities on matters of heritage. Their mechanisms for understanding the past are increasingly embraced by cultural authorities, such as local councils. The implicit critiques of the nature and organization of orthodox historical knowledge may well guide heritage professionals' understandings of touristic motivation. Ultimately, heritage professionals ignore the interests and implicit critiques of ghost tourists at their own peril. While mediums' and ghost hunters' visions of the past may lean toward the lurid, the politicized critique of existing epistemologies and practices of inclusion is worth considering.

CHAPTER FIVE

"THIS IS THE REAL ENGLAND": DISCOURSES OF AUTHENTICITY, NATIONAL BELONGING, AND DIFFERENCE

Toward the end of my fieldwork in late 2009, I went on a late night walk through possibly haunted locations with three of my closest friends and informants. We walked through an empty cemetery, a deserted wood, and a seaside village. When these sites failed to hold my friends' attention, we drove to the seemingly abandoned ruins of a castle near Gateshead. After parking at the end of a road and walking for about a mile into the darkened woods, we came upon a crumbling castle. My friends pulled back the wooden boards blocking the door and led us into the now open center of the castle. From the discarded bottles of beer, drug paraphernalia, and human and animal waste, it was clear that the castle was not regularly tended or visited by anyone other than perhaps the homeless, drug users, and now us. As we trespassed about the remains of the castle, my investigator friends commented on the likelihood of paranormal presences at the Castle and their desire to conduct a proper investigation there. As we prepared to leave, Sadie, one of the investigators, gleefully held her arms out, gesturing to the night sky, the looming forest threatening to reclaim the castle, and the decrepit remains of the once stately home, and declared to me "this is the real England!"

While this was among the most explicitly stated incarnations of that sentiment that I encountered, the underlying understanding of England and its relationship to hauntedness permeated many of my encounters with ghost tourists, particularly paranormal investigators and ghost hunters. In addition to being a pursuit of experiential and objective knowledge of ghosts and spirits, paranormal investigation also acts as an embodied means of encountering Englishness and contesting notions of the nation. In this chapter, I explore practices of seeking out and evaluating haunted places and the attending aesthetic judgments. I demonstrate that the pursuit of ghosts and haunted spaces overlaps with and corresponds to a discourse of authenticity and Englishness that lie at the core of ghost tourism. By pursuing haunted sites, investigators reveal their longing for an authentic English past while critiquing the perceived inauthenticity of the present. This discourse of

---

Haunted Heritage: The Cultural Politics of Ghost Tourism, Populism, and the Past by Michele Hanks, 141–168. © 2015 Left Coast Press, Inc. All rights reserved.

access to haunted social space is a conversation of access to current social space in England. It is dialogue with marked political significance in contemporary England.

Site Selection: "I Would Love to Investigate This"

I observed that selecting sites to investigate is an integral facet of ghost tourism, including paranormal investigating and ghost hunting. Investigators asserted, as a relatively straightforward concept, that a "reputation for hauntedness" is the chief characteristic that an investigation site should possess. Many investigators reported that they found sites to investigate through conversation with pub or hotel owners who reported unexplained, spooky occurrences. Guidebooks, ghost publications, and television programs also offered important resources for more casual tourists. However, this was not always the case.

On many occasions, investigators stated a desire to investigate a site without a known history of hauntings. Hauntedness alone does not recommend a site as an ideal space for investigation. They often pointed to the site's architecture, interior furnishings, and overall management as indicators of its desirability.

For example, during the spring and summer of 2009, a group of my paranormal investigator friends became fixated on a particular pub in York called the Royal Oak (figures 5.1a, 5.1b, and 5.1c). When in York, they would invariably ask to meet at this pub, which was only one of a great many pubs in the city. At first, my investigator friends simply applauded the "realness" of the pub. It was dark and not entirely well kept. It was relatively quiet, and the clientele typically did not include obvious tourists.[1] My interlocutors favorably compared this pub with a variety of other possibilities. Molly, an investigator, contrasted the pub with comparable establishments in her hometown of Yarm. She lamented the fact that in Yarm many pubs that were once "lovely and real like this one" had been converted into "trendy wine bars for footballers." Rose, an investigator, applauded the pub for not being a chain pub. Here, Rose and Molly presented the apparent authenticity of the pub as a rare commodity in the contemporary world.

On several occasions, investigators noted that they would "love to investigate" this pub. It is worth highlighting that at this point, they knew of absolutely no hauntings associated with the pub. The atmosphere, or rather, the aura of the pub served as the primary form of attraction. During that summer, they began a subtle campaign for that very thing. Investigators made it a point to wear their "team jackets"—fleece coats that sported the name of

FIGURE 5.1 a (above), b (page 143 top), c (page 143, bottom) The Royal Oak pub was very popular with paranormal investigators and ghost tourists. While at the time of my research, the pub itself did not advertise its association with the ghostly, tourists and paranormal investigators praised the pub's aesthetic authenticity. They enjoyed its dark wood, small rooms, and comfortable atmosphere. Photographs by Mary Tressider.

their paranormal investigation group—when visiting the pub. Molly stated often that she hoped it would attract the landlord's attention. When this did not come to pass, Molly and Rose approached the landlord after we had spent an afternoon there. He was amused but receptive. He warned them that he knew of no ghosts who haunted the pub.

Undeterred by this, Molly and Rose's paranormal investigation group eventually conducted an investigation at the pub. When I asked Molly about why this was such a desirable site, given its lack of known ghosts, she observed that "it's so real. I'll bet it's loaded with ghosts. There's so much history here, you can just feel it." It's worth noting that Molly never considered herself to be a medium. This was not meant as a mystical claim; rather, it was intended as a characterization of the atmosphere of the pub.

Constituting Hauntedness

That a reputation for hauntedness is not the determining characteristic for paranormal investigators and ghost hunters is revealing. Rose's and Molly's

appreciation for and desire to investigate the Royal Oak was grounded in an admiration of its features and atmosphere rather than explicit ghost stories or sightings associated with the site. This reveals that an *aura* of hauntedness is more than simply an association with known ghost stories.

Investigators tend to interpret visible signs of decay or aging as indications of hauntedness and authenticity, which are tightly entangled for them. While investigators and ghost hunters regularly noted that a house constructed in the twentieth century was just as likely to be haunted as a structure built in the seventeenth century, they showed marked preference for structures with traces of the latter. Since they were not historians and rarely dedicated time to seriously researching the history of particular buildings, their perceptions and impressions of the built environment heavily guided their understanding of its historicity.

Obvious decay or disrepair constituted a major indicator of historicity for investigators. For example, many ghost hunters or investigators urged me to visit Seaton Delaval Hall in Seaton Delaval, Northumberland, as it was somewhere they would love to investigate. To my knowledge, no paranormal investigation or ghost hunting group had investigated the site at that time. When I visited the Hall with two investigators, Jen and Trevor, during an open day, the investigators were delighted by the state of the Hall.[2] In particular, the basement entranced them. Visitors were free to wander in and out of the basement of the Hall. It was a dark, stony area lit only by the sunlight filtering in from outside. Grass and weeds grew freely around the dirt floor. As we walked through the basement, Jen nodded appreciatively at the surroundings. She remarked, "You can just feel the history here." When I pressed her to explain what she meant, she expanded, "look around. You can just tell that this place has a history." Her assertion that it was clear that the Hall had a history seemed to relate to the obvious elements of disrepair present in the basement. Jen, unlike Molly, did identify herself as a medium. Her aesthetically grounded assertion that there was a lot of history present translated into a claim to the building's hauntedness. As we wandered through the basement, she would periodically move in and out of the world of spirits. Her comments regarding the physical structure of the building were interspersed with mediumistic claims regarding the presence of spirits.

Jen was far from alone in equating obvious signs of aging, the presence of the past, and ghosts. Ghost hunters and investigators did not limit their historical praise to sites that had not yet sustained investigation. They often lauded many of their favorite and most visited sites for exhibiting similar properties. For example, they often praised Castle Keep in Newcastle, which regularly permitted ghost groups to visit it (while also allowing commercial companies to host investigations [figures 5.2a and 5.2b]). Rose observed, "You can see that it's been through a lot. It's aged. It's not all made up like. You can tell it has a history." While walking through the Castle with me, she applauded the relatively sparse furnishings present.

Even elements of Castle Keep that might typically diminish investigators' interest appealed to them. In addition to accepting that the castle housed a number of ghosts, they also believed that two of the castle's museum's displays had their own ghosts. In one case, it was a large wooden box in one of

FIGURE 5.2 a (above), b (page 147) Henry II originally founded Castle Keep between 1168 and 1178. It is one of the remaining Norman Keeps in England. Today, it is one of the most popular haunted sites in the North East of England. Commercial ghost hunts are staged at the Keep, and non-profit ghost hunting and paranormal investigation groups regularly visit the site. Tourists and investigators alike enjoy its open spaces and claim that it is very paranormally active.

the galleries. Ascribing a haunting to the box was less surprising since it fit well into the overall appearance of the castle. It is unclear if ghost hunters realized that the inclusion of the box was a curatorial decision. They seemed simply to accept the box as part of the castle. However, this is not the case with the mannequins. The mannequins depicted prior royal occupants of the castle in a domestic scene. They served a clear narrative and pedagogical function, and included as a means of interpreting the castle. Typically, this type of display did not interest investigators, but in this case, the age of the displays had a particular intrigue. The mannequins were clearly old. Their clothing was often visibly worn and dusty. They seemed anchored in another era. While it was not quite the era of the castle's construction, it appeared to be prior to the present. Rose commented that, "even the displays have a sense of history. I mean, some people think they're just as haunted as the castle." Ghost hunters regularly visited one of these mannequins since they believed there was a spirit who inhabited it. Their understanding of historicity and hauntedness was tied closely to visual anachronisms like the presence of aging mannequins in an aged castle. This appreciation, I argue, stems from their desire to see, experience, and value the past and their resistance to what they perceive as attempts to render it invisible or inaccessible.

Ironically, it did not seem to matter to investigators if these signs of decay or earlier use were intentionally included and produced by heritage officials. For example, many ghost hunters embraced the Peterborough Museum as an ideal investigation site. It regularly hosted commercial ghost hunts and even had a live online feed of its basement, one of its reportedly most haunted areas. The Peterborough Museum is an exceptionally well-run and accessible local museum with sections dedicated to local cultural and environmental history, fine arts, and the medical history of the building. Rooms that were once part of the hospital, ca. 1800, now house environmental or historical displays, and ghost hunters are untroubled by this because traces of the building's earlier purposes remain visibly evident to them. For example, today, one of the upper floors features an operating theater from the 1800s complete with a looping audio track that plays the somewhat gruesome sounds of a surgery. When I asked a ghost hunter from Cambridge about what she liked best about the museum, she pointed to the presence of its past. She observed that "you can really see that the building has a past. It's obvious. You can really feel it. I mean, look at the surgery. You can just tell what it was used for it the past. It's a fascinating building."

There were also marked limitations to investigators appreciation of decay or disuse. Ghost Doctors, a North Eastern ghost hunting group, had long hoped to investigate a local pub near Middlesborough. They lauded the pub's authenticity, pointing to the presence of underground tunnels, which they believed dated back to the 1700s, as well as boarded-over, secret passageways as particularly compelling features. During the night of their ghost hunt, they were free to access all areas of the pub, including the kitchen. During their visits to the kitchen, they were profoundly distressed by the obvious presence of dirt, animal hair, and waste on the cooking surfaces. Away from the pub's landlord, the ghost hunters voiced their concern. As one woman explained, "It's just so dirty. I've eaten chips here!" So, while they are willing to embrace some signs of decay—such as faded or peeling wallpaper or grass covered basements—as indications of the past, there are limits. They seem to aspire to limit the dirtiness of the past to the past.

Ghost hunters and investigators tended to praise venues with particular management styles or a marked willingness to work with them. Sites such as Castle Keep in Newcastle and the Golden Fleece in York were perennial favorites among investigators and ghost hunters alike.[3] This stemmed, in no small part, from the venues explicit willingness to work with investigators and ghost hunters and their willingness to identify themselves as haunted venues. Each venue broadcasts its hauntedness in various ways. As I noted earlier, the Golden Fleece proclaims itself "York's Most Haunted Pub" on its website and a placard in front of the pub. It also proudly displays components of its haunted past on its walls; photographs of the *Most Haunted* crew visiting the pub, as well as ghost stories decorate the pub. Similarly, Castle Keep features the cards of investigation or ghost hunting teams who have visited the Castle on a prominent board near the entryway.

While some may interpret this as no more than a simple display of affection for the venues that are willing to cater to them, I think that there are glimpses of a particular ideology of the past present as well. Castle Keep and the Golden Fleece explicitly embrace their association with the paranormal, and they allow investigators and ghost hunters a particular sense of freedom while participating in their investigations. Most importantly, neither venue explicitly seeks to impede the freedom of ghost hunters during the course of their investigations.

At these favored venues, such as the Golden Fleece or Castle Keep, ghost hunters and investigators relished the freedom to move at will between rooms. It was rare that a representative of the management of either facility joins in or observes investigators. I never observed pub management scrutinize, monitor, or restrict ghost hunters in any meaningful way at the Golden Fleece. Most typically, a representative of the pub stayed in the bar area either reading or napping during the course of the investigation. Similarly, in Castle Keep, a management representative stayed on site for the investigation but did not interfere with the ghost hunt in any meaningful way. Rather, they would turn the lights off for the group when they wanted and otherwise stay out of their hair.[4] Ghost hunters invariably praised this "hands off" approach. Joanne, a ghost hunter from the North East, explained her group's preference for Castle Keep to me. She remarked, "it's my favorite place to investigate. I like that it's very open. Places aren't restricted. You can wander where you want. It's dead good." Joanne stressed the significance of free access to the site. At both sites, visitors were free to touch whatever they chose and were able to wander at will. This seemingly limitless access appealed greatly to them.

In contrast, ghost hunters regularly complained about sites that restricted some element of their investigation. For example Paul, a member of Spooks, a team of paranormal investigators from the North East, told me a story about a time when they were invited to participate in a large, publicity oriented ghost hunt at an English Heritage property.[5] During the course of the night, representatives of English Heritage were present for all elements of their investigation. Paul explained their frustrations to me. He reflected that:

When we went to investigate [the English Heritage site], it was a mess. We've wanted to research there for ages. We were dead excited. Now, from the start, they were with us the whole time. One of them followed us from room to room, interfering like. Steve wanted to have the lights off for a bit so Lucy [their medium] could see what's what. They wouldn't let us. They said they couldn't because of insurance. Then, when Lucy wanted to go into a different room because she was getting a sense of something, they wouldn't let her. Said it wasn't part of the plan for the night. It was frustrating, I'll tell you that much. We should have been able to really investigate. Why have us there if you don't want us to actually do our investigation?

The reason for Paul's evident frustration is twofold. He believes that investigators should have unmitigated access to sites. This frustration is compounded by the ways in which he perceived English Heritage officials as curtailing their investigation. Paul's story and his tone of frustration are not uncommon. Investigators and ghost hunters often lamented sites that were either unwilling to or limited in their capacity for collaboration with ghost groups. Sites such as English Heritage and National Trust were especially likely to be cited in such discussions. For example, Molly once critiqued the Treasurer's House, a well known haunted site in York, for its unwillingness to allow groups to investigate. She explained that "it's great that they're proud of their ghosts and all but why won't they let us in? It's elitist if you ask me. We want a chance to explore our history just the same as them." Here, again, Molly reiterated her perceived right to access the haunted spaces of history and her frustration at being denied access.

In addition to celebrating physical and spatial access to haunted sites, ghost hunters also especially appreciated sites that did not actively contest or debate their findings. For example, venues such as Castle Keep, the Golden Fleece, or the North East Aircraft Museum, as well as many less well known pubs, were unlikely to contest ghost hunters' and mediums' claims about the history of the venue or its ghostly occupants. I am not sure if this was due to complete acceptance of the claims, indifference, or a combination of the two. It was clear that some owners or managers of venues genuinely welcomed their insights though. For example, one pub's landlord explained why he allowed a ghost hunting group access. He told me that , "I'm dead interested. I can't wait to find out what's here." For investigators and ghost hunters, such acceptance (regardless of whether it was active or passive) served as an important reiteration of their epistemic authority as knowledge producers, as well their underlying right to access the seemingly restricted areas of the past. Paul commented on sites that collaborated with ghost hunters. He said, "it's how it should be, yeah. We should all be interested in our past. It's all of ours."

Investigators' and ghost hunters' explicit and implicit celebration of freedom of access reiterates their ideology of democratic access to the past. Their access to such sites affirms their sense that "the past belongs to everyone." That they feel the need to celebrate such access and actively remark on its presence reveals a persistent belief they are denied access to the past, both in terms of its spaces and its narratives. Regardless of whether their desired levels of access to historical sites are realistic or viable from a heritage conservation standpoint, their understanding of such spaces reveal that they perceive themselves as denied the kind of access they require.

The Politics of Authenticity

Ghost hunters and paranormal investigators ultimately engage in a type of political critique not only of heritage management but also of perceived and real cultural and economic transformations in contemporary England. The emergence of a multicultural Britain, the decline of public space, and the shifting politics of belonging are among their chief targets. While most of the ghost hunters and paranormal investigators I met were not active in political struggles, they nonetheless passionately commented on and critiqued patterns and transformations they observed. That these concerns emerged in discussions and practices involving trips to the pub, visits to heritage sites, and journeys to abandoned buildings may seem like an odd or superficial manifestation of these concerns; however, each of these sites acts as a nodal point between tradition and transformation and allows ghost tourists to critique the practices of transformation at work.

That nostalgia figures prominently in producing a sense of Englishness is not surprising. Many scholars have highlighted the role of the past in configuring the "imagined communities" (Anderson 1983) of modern nations, especially Britain (Wright 1985). Patrick Wright, in *On Living in an Old Country* (1985) emphasized the role of nostalgia and "vagueness" in many imaginations of Englishness. He suggests that class position is an especially important component in determining the configuration of this engagement with the past.

Deep England can indeed be deeply moving to those whose particular experience is most directly in line with its privileged imagination. People of an upper middle-class formation can recognize not just their own totems and togetherness in these essential experiences, but also the philistinism of the urban working class as it stumbles out, blind and unknowing, into that countryside at weekends (Wright 1985, 86).

For ghost hunters and investigators, many of whom are working class, "deep England" also plays a powerful role in reflecting on the contemporary world; however, the points of nostalgia differed. Rather than bucolic countryside and elite ways of life, their nostalgia was grounded in images of the community pub and thriving local industry. As others have noted (Byrne 2007), this nostalgia is often tied to a sense of loss and mourning. For ghost hunters and investigators, this mourning provided a means of critique and reflection.

Pubs

For ghost tourists, pubs are especially significant sites for conversations regarding hauntings and authenticity, as well as pursuing encounters with the ghostly. The significance of pubs is twofold. In practical terms, they are among the most accommodating sites for ghost hunts. Pub landlords are often far more willing to allow groups of ghost hunters to spend the night in their pub than museum staff. However, there is also a symbolic significance to pubs that warrants closer examination. For ghost tourists and members of the English public, pubs are an important but endangered site. Understanding pubs' cultural and historical role is necessary to contextualize ghost tourists' fixation with them.

Pubs constitute important social spaces in England. Historically, their role has undergone a number of changes. While at one time, pub attendance was limited to the working class, historical, ideological, political, and architectural transformations reconfigured the pub as a "popular haunt" of the middle, as well as working, classes by the 1960s, according to historian David Gutzke (2005,5). Similarly, Geoffrey Hunt and Saundra Satterlee (1987) have argued that pubs constituted one of the primary centers of social life for working class women in England. In contemporary England, pubs come in many forms and remain a focal point of local culture and entertainment. To return to Rose's and Molly's interest in the Royal Oak, such marked and sustained interest in a pub was not unusual among paranormal investigators and ghost hunters. A significant number of ghost hunts and paranormal investigations occurred at pubs, and ghost hunters and investigators spent a substantive amount of time discussing, debating, and analyzing what constituted "a good pub."

Despite their historical and cultural centrality, a series of economic and social shifts have impacted pubs in recent years; however, investigators and ghost hunters' sense that "good" pubs are difficult to find is neither rare nor an entirely new development. For example, in 1946, George Orwell published an essay called "The Moon under Water" in the *Evening Standard* describing his ideal pub. He described a range of physical features. In particular, he highlighted elements of its architecture and design:

> To begin with, its whole architecture and fittings are uncompromisingly Victorian. It has no glass-topped tables or other modern miseries, and, on the other hand, no sham roof-beams, ingle-nooks or plastic panels masquerading as oak. The grained woodwork, the ornamental mirrors behind the bar, the cast-iron fireplaces, the florid ceiling stained dark yellow by tobacco-smoke, the stuffed bull's head over the mantelpiece—everything has the solid, comfortable ugliness of the nineteenth century. (Orwell 1946)

In many ways, his aesthetic preferences mirror those of investigators and ghost hunters with respect to pubs but also to heritage sites more broadly. Ultimately, however, Rose's and Molly's comments echoed Orwell. Molly concluded that the "thing that most appeals to me . . . is what people call its 'atmosphere.'"

Importantly, Orwell's ideal pub does not exist. He concludes his essay by revealing that "there is no such place as" the pub he described. His essay demonstrates the degree to which ideal imaginings of pubs are constituted in British public culture. However, Rose, Molly, and other ghost hunters' longing for "authentic," "real," or "good" pubs are grounded in more than simply the nostalgia or idealism that Orwell described. Socioeconomic changes in Britain since the time Orwell wrote "The Moon under Water" have radically transformed the pub landscape. Among the most significant was the emergence of pub-chains, such as Wetherspoon's, in particular, and *pubcos* in general. The term pubcos refers to a company that owns a chain or group of pubs, such as Wetherspoon's or Walkabout. In 1979, Tim Martin opened the first pub in what would eventually become Wetherspoon's chain. Today it includes roughly 650 pubs. Since then, pubcos have emerged as significant players in English nightlife and hospitality. There are roughly seventy such pubcos, which own at least thirty pubs, in the UK today (Chatterton and Hollands 2003, 372). Such companies own a significant number of English pubs. For example, various pubcos, which owned 16,000 pubs by 1989, had expanded their holdings to roughly 49,000 pubs, or 80% of the market, by 2003 (Chatterton and Hollands 2003). This growth has led to homogenization in the management, style, and offerings of pubs. Paul Kingsnorth, a cultural critic and activist, wrote in *Real England: The Battle of the Bland*, that "today, a combination of corporate power, soaring property prices and often absurd over-regulation is hoovering up colour and character and spitting out conglomeration and control" (2008, 42). Many other cultural critics echo Kingsnorth's critique of the homogenization.

Pubcos also have had disastrous effects on locally owned pubs. As Chatterton and Hollands observe, the presence of such corporately owned pubs "spatially squeeze [s] out independent entrepreneurs and dominate [s] the urban landscape" (2003, 274). By the twenty-first century, pub closings were a common occurrence across England. According to the British Beer and Pub Association, roughly 4,000 village pubs have closed since 1980. More recently, in 2008, 1,973 pubs closed, which was roughly 40% more than the 1,409 pub closures reported in 2007. A widely cited statistic originating with the Campaign for Real Ale (CAMRA) holds that two village pubs close each day in England.

Members of the English press and media have frequently remarked upon the changing landscape of pubs in England. As Michael Moran wrote in *The Guardian*, "it'd be nice to think that there's still room somewhere for the past. Pubs where locals are attuned to the peculiar non-Euclidian tricks of the pool table cushions and know which punters like to be left in peace with their pint" (2013). On a more local level, local newspapers often cover the closures of nearby pubs in a concerned, mournful tone. For example, in 2008, the *York Press*, the local daily newspaper based in York, reported on the closure of several local York pubs. The article speculates that "cheap supermarket beer and the smoking ban coupled with lousy weather and the credit crunch could spell the death of more pubs in York, landlords have warned" (*The York Press* 2008). The use of the term "death" is revealing. The language of death and mourning permeates popular discussion and coverage of the decline of the local or community pub. In the 2010 Christmas edition, the obituaries editor of *The Economist* published an article called "Time, Gentleman," with the subtitle "an elegy on the British pub."[6]

Popular coverage regularly suggests that pub closures constitute the death of a central English tradition. This emphasis on pubs as a core component of English cultural heritage is another crucially important component of the public discourse on pub closures. Members of the media position pubs as key cultural sites in Britain. The closure of pubs is tantamount to a decline in English culture and social cohesion. As *The Economist* mourned "communal imbibing with neighbors and passers-by is fading, in favor of the glass of wine by the television alone" (*The Economist* 2010). Here, pub closures are tied to great social isolation. Further, news coverage emphasizes the role community pubs play in local celebrations and regional culture. The 2008 *York Press* article reported that "publicans in the city have told how the industry was facing huge problems behind the scenes which could see 'the great British pub become a relic in the Yorkshire Museum'" (*The York Press* 2008). The reference to the Yorkshire Museum is revealing, as it is the local museum that specializes in the archaeological past rather than the recent sociocultural past (as is the case of the York Castle Museum).

Ultimately, such popular discourse reveals the degree to which pubs signify Englishness to (at least some) members of the English public. Scholars have long noted that English pubs are powerful indicators of Englishness to foreign travelers. For example, Jonathan Culler, writing in 1990, observed that tourists traveling to England might interpret pubs as a quintessential sign of Englishness. He argued that

> all over the world the unsung semiotics, the tourists, are fanning out in search of signs of Frenchness, typical Italian behavior, exemplary Oriental scenes, typical American thruways, traditional English pubs; and, deaf to the natives' explanations that thruways just are the most efficient way to get from one place to another or that pubs are simply convenient places to meet your friends and have a drink." (Culler 1990, 2)

Culler's observation remains apt. Pubs are still an important index of Englishness for international tourists traveling to the UK.[7] As the media coverage focusing on pub closures demonstrates, pubs remain important signifiers of Englishness to nationals as well. These popular debates constitute a key backdrop for understanding and contextualizing ghost hunters' and paranormal investigators' engagement with and interest in pubs. While they rarely cited such explicit political concerns regarding pub closures, ghost hunters' and paranormal investigators' discursive engagement with pubs mirrored them in several key ways.

Defining a Good Pub

Investigators and ghost hunters praised intimacy, community, and a sense of historicity. They often simply referred to these ideas as "atmosphere." To some extent, each of these interrelated traits encompassed physical and social dimensions of the pub. For example, when investigators spoke of "intimacy," it referred to the nature of the physical layout and design of the pub, as well as the quality of social interactions present within it. Consider Ginny's description of a The Black Swan Inn in York that was well praised among investigators (figure 5.3a). Describing what she liked about the pub, she explained "it's got a lovely atmosphere. You can really feel its history. Each room is so cozy. It gets a lovely crowd. Everyone's nice and friendly. It's welcoming to all sorts." Her allusion to its welcoming atmosphere indexed a number of interesting things. First, it signaled that she and her friends often felt welcomed there. This was due, in part, to the presence of a group of colorful characters who often frequented the pub, such as a tour guide who frequently dressed in ostentatious clothing resembling a Cavalier soldier. Ginny and her partner, as well as their friends, often visited the pub in nearly identical fleece jackets advertising their membership in a paranormal research group. To my knowledge, no one ever mocked or commented on this in a way that made them uncomfortable. Ginny also appreciated that the pub was divided up into many smaller rooms, rather than one large room (figures 5.3b and 5.3c). She noted that this afforded groups a "bit of privacy if you want to have a quiet chat" with someone. In essence, she praised the pub for providing a social space capable of fostering positive interactions with others while allowing for quiet and intimacy when needed. She echoes media coverage that imagines the pub as a multipurpose site.

Ginny's reference to the pub's history is a fascinating component of her description. When I asked her to expand on this, she found it difficult. She knew little of the actual history of the pub, beyond what was advertised on a panel in front of the pub. As we sat in the pub, she gestured to the architectural traits, such as exposed beams, the large fireplace with a small, decorative stove in front of it, and a bar with access points to different rooms in the pub. To her, these characteristics signaled its historicity. Ginny's inability to explicitly articulate what signaled the historicity of a site was not unusual. As I show, for many investigators and ghost hunters, a complex web of physical and social traits signify historicity.

Such discussions of "good pubs" were not limited to investigators or ghost hunters. When the topic of a "good pub" came up in conversation with English friends who were not involved in the paranormal scene, they also reiterated many of ghost hunters' and investigators' points. They pointed to *atmosphere*, an elusive quality. As a means of explaining a good pub to me, Al, an English friend, pointed to the Wetherspoon's chain of pubs as the antithesis of a good pub. He explained that "they embody everything wrong with pubs. There's no atmosphere. It's just one giant room that almost seems designed for [jerks] to fight in." He compared this with his favorite pub, The Golden Slipper, a small independent pub in York. There, in contrast, "there's a good atmosphere. People are friendly. It's cozy."[8] The dichotomy that Al drew between good, local pubs and bad, pubco-run pubs mirrors much of the concern regarding pub closures found in broader public culture. He saw the homogenization of pubs as a danger to the good, local pubs he cherished and enjoyed. While he certainly did not allege that his favorite pub was haunted, the way in which he praised it mirrored many of the ways in which paranormal investigators praised potentially haunted pubs.

The traits that constituted a good pub often translated into traits that recommended a pub as possibly haunted. As I noted earlier, sometimes the atmosphere or physical appearance of a site was enough to recommend it as potentially haunted. There were uncanny parallels in the traits of a *good pub* and a *haunted pub*. For example, Emma, a paranormal investigator, once commented to me that she would "love to investigate" a particular pub in her hometown of Saltburn. When I asked her why, she explained that "it's a lovely old building. The same family's run it for ages. It's got a real sense of atmosphere, of history like." Her reference to the presence of history caught my attention, and I asked if she knew much of the building's history. She replied that "it's been there since I was quite young. It seems almost unchanged." She made no reference to its construction or complicity in important regional events, which one might expect as typical markers of "history." Instead, she

FIGURE 5.3 a (above), b (page 158), c (page 159) The Black Swan Inn, in York, was another popular pub among ghost tourists and paranormal researchers. They praised its exterior and interior décor and often claimed that it had a good atmosphere that seemed full of history.

cast the building as significant in her own personal history. This conversation unfolded when we were not in that particular pub. At a later point, I did visit the pub with Emma and ask her about her affection for it again. Then, she emphasized elements of its built environment and layout, like Ginny.

Emma's answer reveals another important insight into the social nature of how investigators and ghost hunters come to praise particular sites as good, authentic, or, in this case, potentially haunted. For Emma, the famil- iarity of the pub was essential. That she presented its significance as part of her own biography is crucial. Its presence resonated with her own sense of belonging in her community. That the pub was part of the community was central to Emma's designation of it as potentially haunted. Emma expanded

on its virtue as a potentially haunted site. She remarked that "it gets a real local crowd, which is lovely. You feel more at ease with that." Like Molly, who I mentioned earlier, who disliked and distrusted the presence of footballers at upscale, converted wine bars in Yarm, Emma also implicitly divided pub clientele into locals and outsiders. Emma and Molly positioned such local pubs as sites where they belonged. That they suspected such sites were haunted reveals the interconnectedness of perceptions of hauntedness and anxiety about social inclusion.

In a similar vein, investigators and ghost hunters avoided approaching chain pubs or upscale wine bars as investigative sites. During the course of my research, I never heard anyone express a longing or desire to pursue such a site. Emma and Ginny, like many ghost hunters or investigators, viewed wine bars or pubs catering to rowdy youth as foreign, and such venues failed to offer the same sense of comfort, familiarity, and community as their preferred pubs. That ghost hunters rarely suggested that these venues were haunted may mean that with gentrification and urbanization, forces of modernization have displaced the ghosts of their people.

Some ghost hunters and investigators are aware that there is some interesting ideological work at play in such designations. For example, Rose, at one point, commented on this idiosyncratic approach. She remarked to me that she and her friends in the paranormal investigation world "always want to investigate these great old pubs and the like. . . . But it's shortsighted like. If we're being objective, ghosts could be anywhere, right? They could be at a McDonald's or a Starbuck's or Wetherspoon's. But that's not what we look for." Despite this self-awareness, Rose never proposed approaching or pursuing such investigation sites.

Breaking into Sites

Ghost hunters' and paranormal investigators' longing for authentic sites extends even further. Investigators and ghost hunters, as I have noted, were always on the lookout for new sites to investigative. A surprising number of these potential sites were disused, abandoned, or unavailable in some way to the public. Stories of trespassing into abandoned hospitals, private castles, and old factories circulated frequently in the paranormal community. Ghost hunters and investigators often recounted them in a humorous light; however, the underlying sentiment and practice of transgression and claiming access to unavailable sites constitutes a vitally important component of their touristic practice.

I first encountered this practice in the context of an interview with Louise, a ghost hunter from Bradford. As I sat in a coffee shop with Louise and her husband Al, Louise explained her passion and dedication to ghost hunting. After outlining its intellectual challenges, she began to describe the pleasure that she and other members of Spooks, her ghost hunting team, take in their experiences. To demonstrate this, she pointed to a recent "adventure" that they had in the woods near Bradford. Louise, Al, Edward, and Angie, the key members of the group, headed into the woods after dark; Edward had told them that there was "an abandoned asylum" nearby that would be a good investigative site. According to Louise, the group walked about half a mile into the woods before they came upon an old abandoned structure that they believed was once the asylum. Louise was visibly excited as she described how the group walked through the old building and began to call out to any spirits who might be present. She recalled that "it was dead spooky in there. You could just feel these heavy presences. Probably the former patients. Ed works with the disabled now, and you know they weren't always very kind to them back then. . . . That kind of thing doesn't get enough attention." While neither Louise nor Edward knew the specific details of the building's past, they feared that it was once the site of patient abuse. Louise's suggestion that such components of the past may appear obscured was a critique of what constituted a "white washing" of darker moments in history.

As the members of Spooks called out to the former patients of the asylum, the potentially illegal and certainly transgressive element of their activity became clear. Louise paused, laughed, and then she continued.

> I call out and then, suddenly, I start to think that I hear something. Being the ace ghost hunter I am, I start to get a bit spooked. I think I hear footsteps. They're faint, but it sounds a bit like they're coming towards us. I turn to Ed, and I whisper, 'd'you hear that?' Thinking it's a ghost like. But, to be honest, I'm a bit scared. It sounds so real and so close. He looks at me like I'm mental so I get back to calling out. 'Is there anyone there?' 'Let us know you're here.' I still think I can hear the footsteps. Suddenly, Al pauses like and looks over his shoulder. He turns to us and goes 'someone's coming! Leg it!' And we legged it out of there! Turns out that there were some security people patrolling about. We run through the woods and I end up falling into the mud! Can you imagine! At my age! If someone could see us.

Louise and Al have both dissolved into laughter at her dramatic telling of story. To Louise, much of the humor in the situation stemmed from their uncertainty regarding the origin of the footsteps and their response to it. This humorous conflation of ghosts and security personnel is worth considering. That the ghostly presences they sought were replaced by the presence of security forces designed to keep the ghost hunters out reveals a tension between ghost hunters' desired access to space and their ability to actualize this access. While they sought remnants of a past they feared forgotten or obscured, private security forces were present to remove them from the site and curtail their access.

It is worth considering Louise's motives in visiting the asylum. When I asked Louise why they decided to pursue this asylum, she said, "it's there. Why not have a look around?" To Louise, it was simple. When I asked if she had been nervous about getting in trouble for entering the site, she laughed.

She referred to a common line of argument found among investigators. "It's there. It's our history. We should be able to go have a look if we want," she explained. A democratic sense of access to the past and to restricted sites informed her visit to the asylum.

Louise was far from alone in engaging in such visits. In addition to the numerous, often funny, stories I heard about such illicit investigations, I also observed some impromptu visits to restricted sites. During the course of their nighttime treks through the countryside, ghost hunters often came face-to-face with the crumbling remains of former institutions, stately homes, and castles. They greeted such sites with excitement and enthusiasm and often did not hesitate to enter them, regardless of the legality of their visits.

For example, one night I joined Molly and Rose on their evening treks through the countryside, and we ended up wandering the streets of Whitby. We had started the trek with no destination in mind; however, eventually, we made our way up the Whitby Hill and found ourselves looking at the remains of Whitby Abbey (figure 5.4), which appear quite striking at night with dramatic illumination. The ruins stand on a hill overlooking the town of Whitby and the North Sea. Whitby Abbey has a long history as a significant religious site that dates back to 657. It was a Benedictine Abbey until it was destroyed in 1540 during the Reformation and the dissolution of the monasteries. Today, the ruins of the Abbey are an English Heritage property that acts as a museum and historic site. Only a picturesque wall separates the remains of the Abbey from the street (figure 5.5).

As Molly and Rose looked at the ruins of the Abbey, they began to describe their desire to investigate it. While neither investigator knew specific details of the site's past, they both suspected it would be a productive investigation site because "it's got so much history," as Molly put it. Rose agreed, but remorsefully explained "they [meaning English Heritage] would never let us in to do that though." Molly noted that it was a shame. After standing there for a few minutes looking at the ruins, Rose noted that we could climb over the wall and "have a look around." While Molly was slightly hesitant at first, she eventually agreed.

After climbing over the wall, we wandered around the Abbey. Neither Rose nor Molly did much in the way of investigating. They did not call out to spirits nor did they use any of the technology investigators value. They slowly wandered through the grounds. Molly would periodically stretch her arms out, seeking the presence of a spirit. They commented on how exciting it was to be in the Abbey, especially at night. We only stayed on the Abbey's grounds about twenty minutes; however, Molly and Rose spent that time in a deeply

FIGURE 5.4 Photograph of St. Mary's Graveyard and Whitby Abbey, 2009
The ruins of Whitby Abbey, the Church of St. Mary's, and its graveyard stand
at the top of a cliff facing the River Esk in Whitby. The Abbey's ruins and the
graveyard, pictured here, both featured significantly in Bram Stoker's Dracula.
The area is very atmospheric, and many ghost hunters believe the site to be
haunted.

reverential state. They remarked on the feeling of the past. As I walked with
Molly to the wall to leave, she took a look back at the illuminated ruins and
remarked, "This is something to see. This, this is the real England."

Molly's exclamation echoes Sadie's earlier statement almost perfectly. In
part, my presence as an American and as an anthropologist provided a convenient recipient for such explicit statements. I am not certain that either Sadie
or Molly would have declared such a thing if an outsider had not been present. However, I believe that this sentiment underlies much of ghost hunters'
engagement with space and, as such, demands analysis.

There are significant parallels in the sites onto which investigators and
ghost hunters trespass. The three I have mentioned in this chapter—an abandoned asylum, a crumbling castle, and a ruined abbey—share some important traits. Most significantly, these sites are all in a state of obvious decay or
ruin. In the case of the asylum or Ravenworth Castle, the decay is seemingly

FIGURE 5.5 The ruins of the Abbey are owned and managed by English Heritage; however, given the open air nature of the ruins, some ghost enthusiasts (as well as other Whitby tourists) trespass into the site after the site has closed for the day in hopes of encountering a ghost. Photograph by Paul Carr.

unintentional. The buildings have simply fallen into a state of disrepair and await their inevitable destruction, preservation, or reimagining. They appear frozen in the past. This aesthetic preference corresponds to ghost hunters' and investigators' senses that there are forgotten elements of history that they should pursue. As Jack, an investigator, once eloquently put it "they're sort of forgotten. They were built in the past. Their prime was in the past. And, now, they're done. I think that's what makes them so appealing [to investigate]." As Jack described it, such sites emerged as the almost forgotten casualties of social and economic change.

Investigators' and ghost hunters' practices do not unfold in a vacuum. They bear striking similarities to some other key ways in which the public has begun to engage abandoned and neglected public spaces, particularly urban exploration, which has emerged as a popular pastime for some in the recent years. Bradley Garrett, a geographer who studies this practice, explains that "urban explorers recreationally trespass into derelict industrial sites, closed mental hospitals, abandoned military installations, sewer and drain networks, transportation and utility tunnels, shuttered businesses, foreclosed estates, mines, construction sites, cranes, bridges and bunkers, among other places" (2013, 1). Urban explorers, like ghost hunters, express an appreciation for the aesthetics and atmosphere of old, neglected buildings; they photograph and praise the beauty of such sites. For example, in 2013, a group of urban explorers visited the former Terry's Factory in York, which is now an abandoned structure slated to be redeveloped into new homes, stores, and hotels. Mike Laycock, a *York Press* reporter, said that one of the people who entered the factory lauded the experience. He noted that

> The explore was a good one, the site itself was easy to look around. The buildings are very interesting, they had lots of original fittings and features still in place, such as the toilets and all the glazed brick. . . . The clock tower was very fun to go up, the stairs were still all there, and we got to the top and had a very grand view of the whole of York. It's a pity York is losing the factory, as it looks generally beautiful. (An urban explorer cited in Laycock 2013)

The explorer's comments reveal several key components of the practice: an appreciation for the past and a sense of regret or nostalgia for the erosion of the past through forms of gentrification. Their practices mirror those of ghost hunters in many crucial ways.

Urban explorers foreground and render explicit elements of political and economic critique through their practice. For example, the urban explorer who entered the former Terry's Factory in York explicitly alluded to the impending transformation of the factory space. Urban exploration, Garrett argues, is a "deeply political practice" that "can be read as a reactionary practice working to take place back from exclusionary private and government forces, to redemocratise spaces urban inhabitants have lost control over" (2013, 3–4). While ghost hunters are less explicit in articulating the politics of their enterprise, they are nonetheless engaged in a particular form of critique.

The Politics of Decay

Ghost hunters and paranormal investigators, like urban explorers, fixate on industrial spaces that have fallen into disuse. Many of these spaces might once have promised community employment. But now, with the forces of de-industrialization, they have become derelicts. Such interests might rightly be read as an explicitly classed critique of the localized forces of neoliberalism in England; that is certainly a component of their practice. However, ghost hunters' reverent visits to abandoned sites can also be interpreted as a lament of displacement and disorientation.

That they label such abandoned or decayed sites as the "real England" suggests a degree of alienation from the present. For them, the real England lived and died in the past. Much like their uneasiness with new pubs or wine bars stemmed in part from a distrust of outsiders, their preference for abandoned, decaying buildings highlights the degree to which they saw their own presence erased from the cultural landscape. Much like the ghosts they seek, ghost hunters and investigators are displaced by historical change and uncertain of how to position themselves in the emerging world. The tentative illegality of the acts further emphasizes their degree of alienation. They see themselves as structurally isolated from the spaces that are important to them. They must transgress political bounds to access important spaces. I interpret their knowing trespass into an English Heritage site as an act of disruption and critique that resonates with much of their ideological stance toward the past. Their acts of trespassing indicate a sense that they are actively barred from access to a past, that their knowledge is undervalued, and their contributions are unrealized.

Their practices and pursuits actualize their persistent sense that they are denied access to valuable elements of their cultural patrimony. Their forays into seemingly abandoned buildings and into closed heritage sites reveal their deep-seated belief that they should have access to these sites. To deny them access is to deny them a fundamental element of their cultural past. It also demonstrates the slightly transgressive nature of ghost hunting. The act of seeking out spiritual presences enables them to disrupt a political ordering of space that they not do approve of.

Investigators' desperate pursuit of hauntedness and authenticity bears fascinating parallels with various practices engendered by "occult economies" (Comaroff and Comaroff 1999) elsewhere in the world. Jean Comaroff and John Comaroff, writing in 1999, argued that in occult economies, people rely on "spiritual means for material ends" (1999, 279). The "not-quite-fathomable mechanisms" of such complex phenomena as global capitalism and post colonialism—"precisely because they are inscrutable, occult"—they argue, "have become the object of jealousy and envy and evil dealings." This results in the fear "that arcane forces are in the production of value, diverting its flow for selfish purposes" (Comaroff and Comaroff 1999, 284). Some anthropologists have mapped the ways in which people turn to spirits and spiritual means to make sense of complex changes wrought by colonialism or global capitalism (Mantz 2007; Sanders 2003; Shaw 1997).

The identification of threatened, dilapidated sites as haunted, and thereby designating them as belonging to their imagined collectivity, forms a response to the "not-quite-fathomable mechanisms" of international capitalism. However, it is not my contention that paranormal investigations and ghost hunts are something like a British cargo cult. The ghosts they seek have no capacity to protect them in the present or to protect the sites themselves. I contend, rather, that they provide investigators with a means of critiquing sociopolitical changes they sense, but may not completely understand in contemporary England.

Ghost hunters' and paranormal investigators' claims to belonging, their anxiety regarding the decline of *their* spaces, and their deployment of us/them distinctions all resonate with broader political anxieties pertaining to a threatened sense of Englishness. That Englishness is a complex, threatened identity is not a new insight (Cohen, 1994; Crick 1991; Gilroy [1982] 2013, 1991; Hall 1997; Kumar 2003; Modood 2005; Young 1995). Historians and sociologists have masterfully traced the historical origins and varying manifestations of this "threatened" identity. During the period of my research, in 2008 and 2009, there were several key political developments that mirrored investigators' and ghost hunters' sense of a threatened Englishness. Previously fringe political parties that advocated forms of British isolationism, anti-immigration sentiment, or Euro-skepticism, such as the British National Party (BNP) and the UK Independence Party (UKIP), drew growing public support and made significant victories in the European Elections in 2009.[9]

Such political changes are significant. Both parties espouse forms of cultural nationalism and nativism. Anthropologist Gillian Evans (2012) examined the rhetoric of the political far right in Britain, as well as the BNP, particularly its nativism. She argued that the far right and the BNP mobilize rhetoric of British indigeneity to underscore the threatened status and culture of white Britons. Other scholars have traced this ideology in contemporary England, arguing that the English often position Englishness in opposition to multiculturalism (Byrne 2007; Gilroy 1991).[10]

Conclusion

The emerging discourse of a threatened, indigenous people resonates with ghost hunters' and investigators' touristic practices. By seeking out the threatened, ever dwindling sites they consider both authentic and haunted, they highlight their own marginalization in the contemporary nation. In a sense, they align themselves with the ghosts that they seek out. Like the ghosts of the past, ghost hunters and paranormal investigators see themselves as an invisible, marginal presence in the nation. A history with which they align themselves is vanishing and falling into ruin. The sites, like the pubs they value, are disappearing or radically transforming. Accessing the sites they value requires illicit or illegal special transgressions.

Ultimately, ghost hunters' discourses of haunted spaces maps onto a politically charged dialogue of authenticity and belonging. Their practice extends beyond mere discourse. Their dedication to finding, visiting, and investigating these sites constitutes an occult resistance to the erasure and marginalization that they experience. While they fear that they are becoming ghosts in the multicultural domain of the nation, their commitment to seeking out the forgotten ghosts found in forgotten, undervalued sites can be seen as a means of remembering and asserting their Englishness. They are positioning themselves as both the indexes of national heritage, as well as its curators.

CONCLUSION

THE POPULIST LOGIC OF HAUNTED HERITAGE AND ITS CONSEQUENCES

Throughout this book, I have charted the ways in which the practices of ghost tourism constitute a haunted heritage. This heritage is messy, fraught with historical inaccuracies, overlapping narratives of the past, and contested forms of expertise. I have traced the various understandings of ghosts, their attending touristic practices, and their epistemological consequences. As chapter one revealed, even the idea of a ghost is not consistent or coherent. Heritage officials embrace an idea of ghosts as historical figures who can fit into existing stories of the past, while paranormal reality television shows offer a vision of ghosts as an emergent phenomena with the potential to reveal new facets of the past. These different understandings of ghosts correspond to different ways of knowing and believing, as I showed in chapter two. Chapter three considered how accommodating various modes of belief and knowledge engenders both commercial and non-profit forms of tourism with varying discourses of perceived authenticity. Chapter four contended with the populist critique of authoritative productions of the past. It showed how mediums and ghost tourists who seek encounters with ghosts offer new ways of knowing and understanding the past. In chapter five, I showed how the touristic pursuit of haunted sites reveals a rich dialogue of English authenticity and belonging. Taken together, these practices of identifying and seeking out haunted sites and encountering and learning about ghosts produce haunted heritage. In this conclusion, I consider the populism of this haunted heritage and its implications for the growing field of ghost tourism throughout the world.

Haunted Heritage and Populism

Ultimately, the practices of ghost tourism produce a haunted heritage that is grounded in a populist critique. That such a critique should emerge in a European context in the early twenty-first century is not surprising. Anthropologists (Kalb 2009, 2011) and social theorists (Laclau 2005; Žižek 2006) have mapped the re-emergence of populism throughout much of Europe. While

Haunted Heritage: The Cultural Politics of Ghost Tourism, Populism, and the Past by Michele Hanks, 169–178. © 2015 Left Coast Press, Inc. All rights reserved.

many assume that populism entails a discreet set of political ideologies and practices, others have made clear that it can take less explicitly politicized, cultural forms. For example, regarding English populism during the Industrial Revolution, Craig Calhoun observed that "populism was not so much a distinct set of political opinions as a mobilization of people who shared a common understanding of how life ought to be. Not that all people were mobilized at any one time, but the mode of understanding was widespread" (1982, 98). Writing about the emergence of populist ideologies in contemporary Europe, Don Kalb observed that emergent forms of populism are "the somewhat traumatic expression of material and cultural experiences of dispossession and disenfranchisement in the neoliberal epoch" (2011, 1). This was the case for many of the ghost tourists I met. While few of the ghost tourists I met were active in explicitly political circles or vocalized more than passing critiques of Britain or the EU, their engagement with the ghostly emerged from a feeling of discontent and displacement in contemporary England. They felt undervalued and invisible and remained uncertain of why this was the case. The parallels between their turn to the ghostly and the practices of occult economies (Comaroff and Comaroff 1999) generally are strong. Ghost tourists' engagements with the occult mediated and engendered an implicit form of populist critique. As both Calhoun and Kalb emphasize, populism can take the form of expressive longing and subtle critique. This is the case for ghost tourists and haunted heritage.

Ghost tourism's populism manifests in two interrelated forms: a critique of the organization of public history and a destabilization of the expert authority of historians and other heritage officials. While heritage sites often present the past as a known, established story, ghost tourism contests this. Ghost tourism insists on multiple versions of an unknown past. From the presence of the Bubonic plague in the twentieth century to the proliferation of murderous torturers in the fifteenth century, ghost tourists present the past as more ambiguous and less certain than known histories. Such a range of claims provides an ideological alternative to the coherent histories more commonly found in the public sphere.

This destabilization of the past seems to be a generalizable trait of haunted heritage. It can be found in ghost tourism in the US as well. For instance, an art historian friend who researches the public presentation of the past in Gettysburg, Pennsylvania, shared a germane example of historical destabilization on a ghost walk with me. A ghost story about the Battle of Gettysburg begins with the claim that "no one knows who fired the first shot of the battle," and goes on to explore this historical uncertainty. My friend laughingly pointed to the fact that it is widely known and established who fired the first shot. The same destabilizing effect is evident in the story of

Harry Martindale and the Romans in the Basement of the Treasurer's House, with which I began this book. This destabilization is profoundly populist. Because the past is unknown, it creates the rhetorical space to include a different canon of historical figures.

This destabilization of the past leads to an expanding canon of historical figures throughout England. Individuals like John Sage, whom I discussed in chapter four, have a tenuous association with known, established history; however, a portion of the public embraced them as an accepted part of the past. While John Sage was widely known among ghost tourists, individual ghost hunting teams developed even more individualized canons of English history through their encounters with ghosts. There are many valid critiques of such history-making. Critics of pseudohistory worry about how such practices denigrate "the integrity of history" (Allchin 2004, 191), breed distrust of evidence (Shermer and Grobman 2009), and spread irrationality. When one considers the ghost tourism community's widespread acceptance of John Sage, a figure with little historical substantiation, the potential dangers of pseudohistory are clear.

These populist forms of history-making grounded in the ghostly may reveal something even more significant. Such forms of historical imagining reflect and seek to remedy ghost tourists' feelings of exclusion and isolation in the contemporary nation. Ghost tourists feel unrepresented in the forms of public heritage that they see as celebrating the elites of history. They respond by crafting a history that remedies these acts of historical exclusion. In recent years there has been a marked effort on the part of academic historians, as well as museum curators, to emphasize and explore the lives of the non-elite, but some ghost tourists expand the historical canon even further through encounters with ghosts. All forms of ghost tourism that I encountered foregrounded the ghosts of obscure or forgotten members of the working classes or the poor in their stories. On a ghost walk, tourists invariably hear stories about the lives of non-elites who lived, suffered, and died in the past, such as the little girl who fell to her death at a party (chapter two). While the historical reality of these stories remains at best unknown, they do highlight the real or imagined lives of workers and everyday citizens who are unlikely to factor into the grand, Monarchist histories that are such a mainstream tourist attraction in England. Ghost tourists who seek the opportunity to encounter ghosts themselves push this logic even further. As I showed in chapter four, mediums and experientially oriented tourists are especially vocal about their desire to encounter "ghosts like them."

While there are very real dangers associated with pseudohistory (Shermer and Grobman 2009), these historical claims can also be understood as a form of populist myth-making and commemorating. As scholars have long noted, the past, when presented as heritage, plays a powerful role in defining national identity through stereotyped images of peoples, sites, and mythology (Ashworth 1994; Palmer 1999). The historical figures that emerge through encounters with ghosts or in ghost stories reflect a desire for greater inclusion and focus on lives of the working class. This also reflects an implicit desire for greater emphasis on social history in the public sphere. It does more than simply reflect such a desire; it enacts it as well. Ghost tourists in York, for example, are likely to hear mythologized tales of suffering children and workers alongside mythologized stories of Roman and Viking invasions and Royal history.

Re-imagining and repopulating the past is only part of ghost tourism's populist project. Ghost tourism entails a populist critique of knowledge-producing practices. The producers of ghost tourism and ghost hunts, who eschew established histories and rely on either folklore or their own ghostly encounters to understand the past, offer new and sometimes contradictory visions of the past. In doing so, they explicitly challenge the expert authority of historians, archaeologists, and heritage officials. The tourists themselves extend this logic even further. The past, tourists argue, is something that can be experientially known through experiences with ghosts. While they embrace mediums as especially skilled at managing and understanding these encounters, they understand occult encounters as their own evidence of the past. Pointing to such events, they question assumptions about historians' expertise. Both by virtue of staging tours grounded in this expertise and the content of the tours, tourists and tour producers publicly and persuasively demonstrate their emergent expertise.

Ghost tourists critique the elitism of historians and heritage officials and point out their own ways of knowing the past that are grounded in mediumistic experiences. These ways of knowing and believing conform to many dominant cultural logics, particularly those of scientism and heritagization. Some might interpret the widespread emergence of ghost tourism, with its insistence on blind belief, as an indication of a widespread return to irrationality. This, however, is not the case. Much of ghost tourism, as I discussed in chapters two and three, depends on careful articulations of evidence and belief. The understanding that belief cannot be based on something that lacks evidence unites many of these practices while constituting a core component of modern scientism. As Charles Taylor (1989) argued, scientism, which he defines as the "sharp boundary between what one has good reason to give credence to and what goes beyond this limit" (1989, 405), remains a powerful form of cultural logic and ethics. In the contemporary North Atlantic world, scientism reveals itself in many forms; however, ghost tourism is a particularly compelling example. Ghost tourists engage in a quest (of varying degrees of seriousness) to amass the evidence necessary to substantiate the existence (or non-existence) of the ghostly. Ghost walks render belief as an interior state while commercial ghost hunts aim to provide the evidence or experience necessary to support transformations in states of belief. Non-profit ghost hunts are even more explicit in their attempts to define and produce evidence. This rhetorical and practical emphasis on the relationship between belief and evidence demonstrates the persistent role of scientism in shaping these practices. By explicitly seeking to conform to the values of scientism, ghost tourism avoids the public disregard that much of New Age tourism or pilgrimage attracts while maintaining a degree of legitimacy.

The Material Consequences of Spectral Heritagization

Ultimately, the populism of ghost tourism and its logic of scientism are more than simply ineffectual ideas. They enact and mobilize a logic of heritagization. While critics (Walsh 1992) of heritagization maintain that it is a destructive process that renders the real or authentic into the superficial or staged, anthropologists and religious studies scholars have usefully pointed to the way in which occult or spiritual encounters can reconfigure understandings of the past (Byrne 2009; Karlström 2013). In England, ghosts figure prominently in the process of heritagization. They provide a means of critiquing epistemic heritage authority and reconstituting the content of the past. Their impact is not merely discursive though. Perhaps surprisingly, these immaterial presences can have real material consequences.

Pubs that attract the attention of ghost tourists can translate this attention into new marketing schemes. Consider, for example, the Royal Oak in York. As I described in chapter five, the pub intrigued some of my friends in the paranormal investigating community. At the time, it had no reputation for hauntedness. While many York pubs, such as the Golden Fleece, capitalized on their haunted reputations with signs or their own ghost walks, the Royal Oak did not. Although the paranormal investigators knew of no ghosts associated with the pub, they hypothesized that the rich atmosphere of the pub—its physical, historical, and cultural merits—might translate into ghostly presences to investigate. At the time, the pub's landlord was unaware of any ghostly presences and allowed the paranormal investigators to spend the night at his pub for free. By 2014, this had changed. The pub's website advertised its (newfound) haunted reputation. The website reads:

> The Royal Oak offers locally sourced, home cooked food. We also offer a fine selection of real ales and a welcoming atmosphere, with real fires burning in the cold months. The building is reputedly haunted

by several mysterious ghosts that come as they please. There is an old prostitute in the front bar; ghosts of children playing by the fire; a tall, gaunt man in the back room and two female ghosts, one on the first floor called Alice and one in the flat called Mary. Staff have repeatedly heard someone walk up stairs but on investigation have found no one there, and staff have felt hands holding theirs as they pull pints. The tour bus stops close by Monk bar if you wish to get off and come for lunch or evening meal. (Royal Oak 2014)

The pub advertises its ghosts alongside all of the other markers of a "good" English pub, such as real ales and a welcoming atmosphere. While the pub does not (yet) offer explicitly paranormal experiences, it mentions its ghosts in much the same way it highlights its other positive attributes that are likely to attract patrons and tourists. The inclusion of its ghosts alongside its ales, food, and atmosphere points to the commercial significance of a haunted reputation. While my focus throughout this book has not been on the financial impact of ghost tourism, such a study would be fascinating.

Even more, paranormal investigators' access to the site became more limited. One group of local ghost hunters, after learning that a team of paranormal investigators spent the night in the Royal Oak, contacted the pub in 2011 about spending a night researching ghosts. According to Katie, a member of the ghost hunting club, spending the night ghost hunting at the pub would require "a steep fee," which her group could not afford. As I showed in chapter three, this is not an uncommon development. Sites leverage ghost tourists' interests into financial gain and a particular type of cultural capital.

In some cases, the material consequences of ghostly presences were even more pronounced. In 2009, a group of ghost hunters had plans to spend the night in a small pub, the Red Lion, in a village outside Whitby. As was the case with the Royal Oak in York, all of the members of the ghost hunting group expressed great enthusiasm about the atmosphere of the pub. One ghost hunter called the Red Lion a "canny old pub," and she praised its architecture and atmosphere. It had a roomy bar area with a large fireplace at the center and a beautiful wooden ceiling. There were lots of private nooks and crannies throughout the place. While there was no existing reputation for hauntedness, the ghost hunters anticipated that its atmosphere might signal the presence of ghosts. The pub itself was a family-run pub that had fallen into disrepair in recent years. The Red Lion attracted a lively local crowd, but the landlord worried about the pub's future. He cited competition from area chain pubs, changing patterns of nightlife, and changes to ales as causes of concern. He complained that he was already unable to keep up with the necessary renovations at the pub, and he worried about what the future would hold. He explicitly saw this ghost hunt as a potentially promising sign of his pub's future. At his urging, the team had brought along a local newspaper reporter whom the landlord knew. As the team set up their equipment for the night, the landlord remarked to me that he "hoped this would stir up some attention."

While at first glance this might seem like an instance of an opportunistic landlord capitalizing on the popularity of the paranormal, more is at work here. Other factors undeniably contribute to the renewed success of the pub; however, its emerging reputation for hauntedness played a role as well. In instances such as this, it is clear that ghost hunters and ghost tourists' pursuit of the occult at sites they find authentic enables a type of conservation and preservation. While their claims that a building is haunted do not land the site on the Register of Historic Parks and Gardens of Special Historic Interest in England, they do have some material consequences. Many pubs and sites capitalize on their haunted heritage simply through advertising, as was the case in the Royal Oak. Others, such as the Red Lion, go even further. By 2010, the pub's landlord not only advertised his pub's haunted reputation, but he also collaborated with commercial ghost hunting companies. Regular commercial ghost hunts, at which tourists pay £35 to spend the night with the building's ghosts, now occur at the pub. This collaboration brings direct revenue to the pub, as well as greater public attention; both factors contribute to its ongoing commercial viability and survival. Being successfully recognized as haunted by at least a small group of ghost hunters has the capacity to establish a site as haunted, which in turn signifies the site as worthy of attention, tourists, and revenue. As the market for commercial ghost hunting continues to expand, these companies will require access to an even greater number of properties. These expanding markets engender a type of haunted preservation, albeit a highly commercialized one.

This commercialization of haunted heritage responds to the conservational current of ghost tourism. As became clear throughout chapter five, ghost tourists fear that the public spaces they occupy are disappearing. By designating spaces such as the Red Lion as haunted, ghost tourists contribute to a logic of heritagization by rendering them into commodifiable heritage. As we arrived at the Red Lion in 2009 to investigate it, one ghost hunter remarked that "this is what a proper pub should be. It's a shame that places like this don't do a better business." By being there and by identifying it as haunted, she and her ghost hunting friends enabled it to do a better business. Paradoxically, this interplay of heritagization and ghost hunting replicates the neoliberal logic that contributes to the closure of public spaces that ghost hunters lament. By virtue of transforming such sites into commercially viable, publicly recognized haunted sites, ghost hunters' access to them becomes subject to their ability and willingness to pay to access them. As part of their populist imaginings, many ghost tourists, particularly ghost hunters, believe that their research interest in the paranormal should enable them free and unfettered access to sites that they imagine scientists enjoy. In some cases, the very success of their ability to establish a site's haunted heritage thwarts their ability to enjoy such access.

Ultimately, sites that have the most to gain from embracing ghost tourists' visions of the past are the ones most likely to do so, like the Red Lion. Of course, not all of ghost tourists' efforts result in such neat instances of preservation and heritagization. To return to the instances of trespassing that I mentioned in chapter five, there are many significant parallels between the acts of trespassing and the revitalization of pubs. Both acts are grounded in the populist democratization of space and history found throughout ghost tourism. When my friends in the ghost hunting community trespassed onto abandoned castles or closed heritage sites, they did so out of appreciation for the site. Such acts were an embodied enactment of their belief that the past belongs to everyone, and as such, they should have access to that past through their encounters with ghosts. That these visits were met with criminal inquires rather than appreciative landlords speaks to the limits of their critique and its efficacy.

The Recursivity of Ghosts and the Limitlessness of Haunted Heritage

The populist engagement with the past and its contribution to the commercialization of ghosts found in English ghost tourism provides a vital, if impartial, lesson on the nature of haunted heritage. As I showed in chapter one, museums and heritage sites are often eager to capitalize on haunted heritage by incorporating it into their sites, offering ghost walks, and publishing books about their ghosts. These interpretations tend to present the ghosts and hauntings as a complement to the known past rather than a contestation of it. While such deployments of ghosts are engaging and certainly appeal to a public that is eager to learn about ghosts, the populist critiques embedded in popular touristic engagement with haunted heritage must not be overlooked.

Ghosts' ability to change, disappear, and multiply must be reckoned with. Unlike forms of history-making grounded in the material past, ghosts are immaterial. Despite dogged interest and persistent research on the part of parapsychologists and psychical researchers—to say nothing of the efforts of amateur researchers I described here and elsewhere (Hanks 2011b)—little evidence has emerged that supports the existence of ghosts. Their existence remains a matter of belief or scientifically grounded theory. I mention this lack of evidence not to critique ghost tourists or paranormal investigators, but to point to the uncertain, ambiguous nature of ghosts. One can never say with any certainty that a certain ghost haunts a particular site. It is always a matter of belief, speculation, or legend. This indeterminacy lends itself to a recursive spiraling out of ghosts. When a site presents itself as haunted, perhaps by a known historical figure, this opens the door to other, lesser-known figures. Ghost tourists who visit the site seeking to encounter the known ghost may report any number of presences. In a sense, the presence of one ghost allows for the possibility of an endless stream of ghosts. Once the door is open, historians, museum curators, and others cannot in all fairness close it. In this book, I have argued that this recursive production of ghosts contributes to a populist critique and a destabilization of epistemic authority in the case of English ghost tourism. While ghost tourism in other cultural contexts may not be entrenched in the same populist politics, I suspect the recursivity of ghosts lends itself to various forms of culturally specific critiques. It certainly demands a rethinking of what constitutes historical knowledge.

This does not necessarily mean that heritage sites or museums should distance themselves from ghost stories, haunted heritage, or ghost tourists. Ghost tourists represent a segment of the public with a very real interest in the past, and museums, heritage sites, and historians should aim to engage this interest. But they should carefully consider and evaluate how they do so. Peterborough Museum's ghost walk and collaboration with commercial ghost hunting companies seem to be an especially successful way of managing the competing claims raised by ghosts. The Peterborough Ghost Walk, which is run by the Peterborough Museum, takes seriously the claims of more recent ghost stories; however, it tends to fit these new, emergent ghosts within a known historical context. In this way, it balances the demands of ghost tourists and a desire to maintain a degree of historical accuracy. It maintains a similar balance when hosting commercial ghost hunts. In my observations, commercial ghost hunts often fostered the most ahistorical claims about the past, and the emergent narratives that appeared on such events ran almost explicitly counter to the museums where they were held. (Consider my example of the discord between museum narratives and ghostly narratives on a commercial ghost hunt at the National Railway Museum that I described in chapter four.) The Peterborough Museum managed such tensions with great skill. A representative of the museum was present on the night of the commercial ghost hunt, and he participated enthusiastically in the ghostly experiences. He accepted tourists' experiences with ghosts without question or comment; however, when they made claims about the history of the museum or area that were ungrounded in the known past, he offered them full, rich explanations of the past. While such forms of collaboration are likely to anger skeptics and worry some about the spread of pseudoscience, they engendered positive and historically accurate dialogue about the nature of the past. An apt example about management of another set of conflicting interpretations of the past is Barbara Bender's (1999) now classic study of Stonehenge in which she demonstrated the viability of creating discursive and material space for multiple stakeholders. Given the abundance and accessibility of an array of vehicles of communication beyond authorized channels, Peterborough is exemplary in its balance of competing forces. Peterborough's approach is, in fact, the favored one in contemporary critical heritage studies, which argue strenuously for inclusivity.

While I did not encounter other museums or heritage sites mirroring Peterborough's thoughtful engagement with its commercial ghost tourists, perhaps their model of engagement is a crucial lesson for heritage officials who seek to capitalize on the haunted past. The success of the Peterborough model depends on accepting the demands of ghost tourists, complete with the ambiguous status of ghosts, and translating this into grounded historical knowledge. This inverts the ordering of experience found in many official heritage engagements with ghosts.

In England and the rest of the world, there is little evidence that popular interest in the paranormal is subsiding. Networks produce paranormal reality television shows at a steady rate. Films focus on paranormal events. New ghost hunting clubs form regularly. Tourist markets increasingly work to address this growing interest. Ghost walks appear in new cities each year. In the US and the UK, companies are working to address the desire for experiential encounters with ghosts. As the tourist and heritage industries increasingly work to include ghost tourists, scholars and heritage officials alike must contend with the nature of populist critique embedded in ghost tourism and its significance for these tours. While such critiques may seem to dangerously destabilize knowledge of the past and the expertise of historians, heritage producers can and should find productive ways to collaborate with ghost tourists.

NOTES

Chapter One

1 Guidebooks do not even agree on a spelling for Gaveston's last name. Some guides (e.g., Brooks 1994) include an "e" at the end of his last name, while others conform to the more orthodox spelling of Gaveston (Wray 2002).

2 This situation is not unique to England. It is not difficult to find similar books at tourist sites or bookstores in the United States.

3 This is not to say that these are the only genres of ghost books published in England. In recent years, guidebooks dedicated to explaining how to research ghosts have become a popular component of the market. However, such books have less of a direct connection to ghost tourism, and as such, I will not explore them here.

4 Acorah appeared on several series of *Most Haunted* as the resident medium. He has attracted significant public attention because of his role in the show, as well as persistent rumors of fraud.

5 While I focus here exclusively on guidebooks that address British ghosts, this trend is in no way limited to Britain. There is a parallel and thriving field in the US Titles, such as *The Minnesota Road Guide to Haunted Locations* (Lewis and Fisk 2005) and *The Wisconsin Road Guide to Haunted Locations* (Lewis and Fisk 2004), as well as the long-standing *Weird* travel guides to particular state's legends, hauntings, and oddities (e.g., *Weird N.J.: Your Travel Guide to New Jersey's Local Legends and Best Kept Secrets* [Moran and Sceurman 2009]) are just a few examples. I am aware of similar guides in Canada, Ireland, and Australia.

6 There is also a thriving field of guides to paranormal investigating. I do not consider those here because they rarely address specific haunted locations or ghosts or direct readers to them. They do, however, instruct readers on research techniques that some ghost tourists use.

7 Living has undergone several changes in its name. When the channel was first launched in 1993, it was called UK Living. It changed its name to Living in 1997, and then in 2001, it changed its name to Living TV. Its name reverted to Living in 2007. It was owned and launched by Virgin Media. The producers of the channel originally geared the programming toward women, although in the late 2010s, programming was increasingly geared toward expanding male viewership (especially with the introduction of several US serial crime shows, such as *CSI: Miami.*).

8 Some of the most famous participants include Yvette Fielding, Karl Beattie, Ciarán O'Keeffe, Derek Acorah, Phil Wyman, and Richard Felix.

9 The show featured several "parapsychologists." Sometimes the individual in question was, in fact, a parapsychologist that other parapsychologists would

have recognized as such, meaning an individual who received graduate training in parapsychology. In other cases, the parapsychologist seemed to be simply an individual who espoused slightly more skeptical interpretations of the phenomena in question.

10 As I noted earlier, the National Trust has even published a book of its ghosts, *Ghosts: Mysterious Tales from the National Trust* (Evans 2004). It can be purchased in some of National Trust gift shops. Interestingly, the ghost stories presented in the book, much like the textual references to ghosts found at National Trust sites such as the Treasurer's House in York, offer what I would call "sanitized" versions of ghost stories.

11 Interestingly, he does not offer any tips on how to investigate ghosts or negotiate a touristic visit at Heathrow Airport.

12 There are limits to this though. In any of the guides that I have reviewed, no chain stores or pubs are included. This is a fascinating omission.

Chapter Three

1 Some sociologists of science, most notably Harry Collins, have examined the practices of parapsychology in greater depth (Collins and Pinch 1979; Pinch 1979).

2 Of course, this critique was not entirely fair to or representative of the people who purchased commercial ghost hunts. As I showed in chapter two, the people who purchased commercial ghost hunts often did so as a means of addressing long-standing questions of faith and belief.

3 Venues imposed the only limits placed on the investigative activities, and they did this quite infrequently. A few sites requested that groups avoid using Ouija boards out of popular concerns about the association between Ouija boards and demonic possession.

4 Such debates and concerns were always hypothetical. During the course of my fieldwork, the coins never moved.

5 Possible environmental factors typically engendered a qualitative description of the location of the site and its proximity to sources of outside sound or light, such as a nearby road.

6 Since then, Facebook has become an increasingly important online site for networking and socializing. During the course of my research, however, teams were only beginning to create Facebook pages.

7 The reason for their lack of membership in formal research groups or teams is multiple and complex. In some cases, they simply did not want to invest the amount of time that membership often entailed. In other cases, they simply lacked the connections to join such a group.

Chapter Four

1 While I use the terms medium and mediumship throughout this text, it is imaginable that others might label such practices as forms of possession. The practices I chart in this chapter could easily fit within Janice Boddy's excellent definition of spirit possession as the "hold exerted over a human being by external forces

or entities more powerful than she. These forces may be ancestors or divinities, ghosts of foreign origin, or entities both ontologically and ethnically alien" (1994, 47). I use the terms for several reasons. First, the individuals in question label themselves mediums. They use the language of possession in far more limited contexts. I ultimately agree with Michael Brown who, in considering the relationship between channeling practices in the US and cross-cultural phenomena, such as shamanism and possession, noted that the "feel" of these practices is different (1997, 79).

2 Spiritualism is a contemporary religion founded on the belief that the personality or soul survives death and is able to communicate with living humans. The history of Spiritualism emerged as a new religious movement in the US in the 1840s and quickly spread to Britain and Europe. Spiritualist churches exist across the UK, and in the 2001 Census of Religious Affiliations in England and Wales, 32,404 people identified themselves as Spiritualists. Historians, anthropologists, and sociologists have provided excellent accounts and analyses of the religion (Braude 1989; Meintel 2007; Owen 1989; Porter 1995).

3 Many scholars, scientists, and popular skeptics have deconstructed the practices of mediumship or psychics and attempted to demonstrate that there is no empirical grounding for such endeavors (e.g., Hines 2003; Hyman 1977). Many of these critiques raise somewhat useful points about some of the ways mediums may engage in intentional fraud, although a significant number of them problematically conflate the practices of Spiritualists, a contemporary religious community, and for-profit psychics (see Hines 2003 as an example of this). Such analyses, which often veer toward the ethnocentric and tend to assume fraud on the part of the medium, are beyond the scope of this project. More recently, psychological anthropologists have fruitfully begun to examine the cognitive practice that may enable the emergence of cultural practices such as spirit possession or mediumship (Luhrmann 2011). While such work is productive and fascinating, my focus remains on analyzing the cultural politics of such acts of mediumship rather than mapping the underlying cognitive processes or detecting fraudulent practices.

4 Such engagements may increase the mediums' prestige though, and mediums can leverage this into financial compensation in commercial contexts.

5 Groups like CPI often revisited the sites, such as the Golden Fleece in York. In part, this was because some sites were especially welcoming to paranormal investigation groups. They charged reasonable fees, and groups found them easy to collaborate with. Additionally, groups simply *liked* particular sites better than others—a point I will return to later in this text.

6 The ghost section of the website details the ghost tours the Castle offers and briefly mentions some of its ghosts.

7 The 2013 anthropological controversy over *Dig Wars,* a television show featuring amateur archaeologists looting historical sites, demonstrates the continued tension in this field.

8 Orme eventually authored *Haunted Peterborough* in 2012. He drew on his own collection of local ghost stories and his knowledge of the regional past.

Chapter Five

1 Interestingly, they did not consider themselves tourists. While they identified others who visited York for a day outing as tourists, they excluded themselves from this group.

2 On open days, access to National Trust properties is free to the public.

3 This is not to say that they were the only favorites; rather, they are sites regularly visited and praised by investigators I knew. I also had the chance to observe multiple ghost hunts and investigations at each site, which recommends them as examples here.

4 Some of the management at Castle Keep are genuinely interested and periodically sit in on elements of the ghost hunt. Ghost hunters and investigators enthusiastically welcome this level of interest.

5 I am obscuring the name of the English Heritage Property here for a variety of reasons.

6 Of course, not all coverage adopted quite such a mournful tone. Some commentators suggested that pub closures were causes to celebrate. For example, Christine Bohan, writing in *The Guardian* in 2011, suggests that not all pubs are good pubs. She also adopts rhetoric of longing when noting that increasingly good pubs have "been usurped by formulaic and money-grabbing temples of blandness." She complains that "extortionate prices, crap music and early closing times, all provided in dull Ikea interiors with no atmosphere, are now the mainstays of the average pub experience" (2011). So, even some critics who resist the urge to mourn all pub closings maintain a degree of nostalgia for local, individuated pubs.

7 Pubs are so important to international imaginings of Englishness that a pub, The Rose and Crown, constitutes part of the England Pavilion at Disney World's Epcot.

8 Pubs are not unaware that these traits are much desired. In fact, they comprise key components of their marketing. For example, The Golden Slipper's website advertises that "The Golden Slipper Pub . . . is really quite special by the standards of most pubs. It is all too easy to claim that a pub offers a friendly and welcoming environment but we know that the Golden Slipper does . . . It really is the Slipper's unique ambiance and welcoming atmosphere that draws people to the pub" (2012). Such marketing strategies are fascinating and deserve further examination.

9 Both the BNP and UKIP made significant political inroads during the 2009 European Parliament elections in the UK. The UKIP won 6.5 % of the vote, or 2.49 million votes, which brought the party's total number of seats to thirteen. (Notably, they then had the same number of seats as the Labour Party). For the first time, the BNP won two seats in the European Parliament and several county council seats.

10 While this often takes exclusionary forms, this is not always the case, as Robin Mann (2011) has shown.

REFERENCES

Acorah, Derek. 2006. *Haunted Britain and Ireland*. London: Harper Element.

Ahmad, Aijaz. 1999. "Reconciling Derrida: 'Specters of Marx' and Deconstruction." In *Ghostly Demarcations: A Symposium on Jacques Derrida's Specters of Marx*, edited by Michael Sprinkler, 88–110. New York: Verso.

Aldermann, D. 2002. "Writing on the Graceland Wall: On the Importance of Authorship in Pilgrimage Landscapes." *Tourism Recreation Research* 27(2): 27–33.

Allchin, Douglas. 2004. "Pseudohistory and Pseudoscience." *Science and Education* 13:179–95.

Anderson, Benedict. 1983. *Imagined Communities: Reflections on the Origin and Spread of Nationalism*. London: Verso.

Ashworth, G. J. 1994. "From History to Heritage: From Heritage to Identity: In Search of Concepts and Models." In *Building a New Heritage: Tourism, Culture, and Identity in the New Europe*, edited by G. J. Ashworth and P. J. Larkham, 13–30. London: Routledge.

Bader, Christopher, F. Carson Mencken, and Joseph Baker. 2010. *Paranormal America: Ghost Encounters, UFO Sightings, Bigfoot Hunts, and Other Curiosities in Religion and Culture*. New York: New York University Press.

Badone, Ellen and Sharon Roseman, eds. 2004. *Intersecting Journeys: The Anthropology of Pilgrimage and Tourism*. Urbana and Chicago: University of Illinois Press.

Bailkin, Jordanna. 2002. "Radical Conservations: The Problem with the London Museum." *Radical History Review* 84:43–76.

BBC. 2004. "York: Most Haunted City in the World!" Last modified April 2004. http://www.bbc.co.uk/northyorkshire/uncovered/ghost/most_haunted.shtml

Beeton, Sue. 2005. *Film-Induced Tourism*. Clevedon, UK and Buffalo, NY: Channel View Publications.

Bender, Barbara. 1999. *Stonehenge: Making Space*. Oxford, UK: Berg.

Bennett, Gillian. 1999. *Alas, Poor Ghost: Traditions of Belief in Story and Discourse*. Logan: Utah State University Press.

Bergland, Renee L. 2000. *The National Uncanny: Indian Ghosts and American Subjects*. Hanover, NH: University Press of New England.

Bhattacharyya, D. 1997. "Mediating India: An Analysis of a Guidebook." *Annals of Tourism Research* 24:371–89.

Bird, S. Elizabeth. 2002. "It Makes Sense to Us: Cultural Identity in Local Legends of Place." *Journal of Contemporary Ethnography* 31:59–547.

Blanco, Maria del Pilar and Esther Peeren. 2013. "Introduction: Conceptualizing Spectralities." In *The Spectralities Reader*, edited by Maria del Pilar Blanco and Esther Peeren, 1–28. New York: Bloomsbury Publishing.

———, eds. 2013. *The Spectralities Reader*. New York: Bloomsbury Publishing.

Boddy, Janice. 1994. "Spirit Possession Revisited: Beyond Instrumentality." *Annual Review of Anthropology* 23:407–34.

Bohan, Christine. 2011. "There's No Need for Nostalgia over Closing Pubs." The *Guardian*, September 17. Accessed July 8, 2013. http://www.theguardian.com/commentisfree/2011/sep/17/pubs-closing-nostalgia

Bowman, Michael and Phaedra Pezzullo. 2010. "What's so 'Dark' about 'Dark Tourism?'" *Tourist Studies* 9(3):187–202.

Brandon, Ruth. 1984. *The Spiritualists: The Passion for the Occult in the Nineteenth and Twentieth Centuries*. Buffalo, NY: Prometheus Books.

Braude, Ann. 1989. *Radical Spirits: Spiritualism and Women's Rights in Nineteenth Century America*. Bloomington: Indiana University Press.

Bremer, Thomas S. 2003. *Blessed with Tourists: The Borderlands of Religion and Tourism in San Antonio*. Chapel Hill: University of North Carolina Press.

Brogan, Kathleen. 1998. *Cultural Haunting: Ghosts and Ethnicity in Recent American Literature*. Charlottesville: University of Virginia Press.

Brooks, John. 1994. *The Good Ghost Guide: A Gazetteer of Over a Thousand British Hauntings*. Norwich, UK: Jarrold Press.

Brooks, Cameron. 1999. "Glamis Castle Haunted? Not a Ghost of a Chance." *Daily Mail*, October 14.

Brown, Michael F. 1999. *The Channeling Zone: American Spirituality in an Anxious Age*. Cambridge, MA: Harvard University Press.

Bruce, Steve. 1995. "The Truth about Religion in Britain." *Journal for the Scientific Study of Religion* 34(4):417–30.

Bruner, Edward. 2005. *Culture on Tour: Ethnographies of Travel*. Chicago: University of Chicago Press.

Byrne, Bridget. 2007. "England – Whose England? Narratives of Nostalgia, Emptiness, and Evasion in Imaginations of National Identity." *The Sociological Review* 55(3):509–30.

Byrne, Dennis. 2009. "Archaeology and the Fortress of Rationality." In *Cosmopolitan Archaeologies*, edited by Lynn Meskell, 68–88. Durham, NC: Duke University Press.

Calhoun, Craig. 1982. *The Question of Class Struggle: Social Foundations of Popular Radicalism during the Industrial Revolution*. Chicago: University of Chicago Press.

Campbell, Vincent. 2000. "'You Either Believe it or You Don't...': Television Documentary and Pseudo Science." In *From Grierson to the Docu-Soap: Breaking the Boundaries*, edited by John Izod, Richard Kilborn, and Matthew Hibberd, 145–58. Luton, UK: University of Luton Press.

Cannell, Fenella. 2013. "Ghosts and Ancestors in the Modern West." In *A Companion to the Anthropology of Religion*, edited by Janice Boddy and Michael Lambek, 202–22. Malden, MA: Wiley Blackwell.

Carr, E. Summerson. 2010. "Enactments of Expertise." *Annual Review of Anthropology* 39:17–32.

Castricano, Jodey. 2003. *Cryptomimesis: The Gothic and Jacques Derrida's Ghost Writing.* Montreal: McGill Queens University Press.

Chatterton, Paul and Robert Hollands. 2003. *Urban Nightscapes: Youth Culture, Pleasure Spaces, and Corporate Power.* Florence, KY: Psychology Press.

Chillingham Castle. "Ghosts." http://www.chillinghamcastle.com/GhostsPg.asp?S =3&V=1&P=3 Accessed June 24, 2013

Clifford, James. 1986. "Introduction: Partial Truths." In *Writing Culture: The Poetics and Politics of Ethnography*, edited by James Clifford and George Marcus, 1–26. Chicago: University of Chicago Press.

———. 1992. "Traveling Cultures." In *Cultural Studies*, edited by Lawrence Grossberg, Cary Nelson, and Paula Treichler, 96-116. New York: Routledge.

Cohen, Robin. 1994. *Frontiers of Identity. The British and the Others*, London: Longman.

Collins, Harry. 2004. "Interactional Expertise as a Third Kind of Knowledge." *Phenomenology and the Cognitive Sciences* 3:125–43.

Collins, Harry and Robert Evans. 2002. "The Third Wave of Science Studies Studies of Expertise and Experience." *Social Studies of Science* 32(2):235–96.

Collins, Harry and Trevor Pinch. 1979. "The Construction of the Paranormal: Nothing Unscientific is Happening." In *On the Margins of Science*, edited by Roy Wallis, 237–70. Keele, UK: University of Keele Press.

Collins-Kreiner, Noga. 2010. "The Geography of Pilgrimage and Tourism: Transformations and Implications for Applied Geography." *Applied Geography* 30 (1):153–64

Comaroff, Jean and John Comaroff. 1999. "Occult Economies and the Violence of Abstraction: Notes from the South African Postcolony." *American Ethnologist* 26(2):279–303.

Crick, Bernard. 1991. "The English and the British." In *National Identities: The Constitution of the United Kingdom*, edited by Colin Crouch, David Marquand, and Bernard Crick, 90–105. Oxford, UK: Blackwell Publishers.

Culler, Jonathan. 1990. *Framing the Sign: Criticism and its Institutions.* Norman, OK: University of Oklahoma Press.

Davie, Grace. 1994. *Religion in Britain Since 1995: Believing without Belonging.* Oxford, UK: Blackwell Publishers.

Davies, Owen. 2007. *The Haunted: A Social History of Ghosts.* New York: Palgrave.

Davis, Colin. 2005. "État Présent: Hauntology, Spectres, and Phantoms." *French Studies* 59(3):373–79.

Dawkins, Richard. 2000. *Unweaving the Rainbow: Science, Delusion and the Appetite for Wonder.* New York: Mariner Books.

Deery, June. 2004. "Reality TV as Advertisment." *Popular Communication* 2(1): 1–20.

Dégh, Linda. 2001. *Legend and Belief: Dialectics of a Folklore Genre.* Bloomington: Indiana University Press.

Derrida, Jacques. 1994. *Specters of Marx: The State of the Debt, the Work of Mourning & the New International.* New York: Routledge.

Dickinson, Janis L., Benjamin Zuckerberg, and David N. Bonter. 2010. "Citizen Science as an Ecological Research Tool: Challenges and Benefits." *Annual Review of Ecology, Evolution, and Systematics* 41:149–72.

Dominguez, Virginia R. 2007. "When the Enemy is Unclear: US Censuses and Photographs of Cuba, Puerto Rico, and the Philippines from the Beginning of the 20th Century." *Comparative American Studies* 5(2):173–203.

Dunkley, Ria, Nigel Morgan, and Sheena Westwood. 2011. "Visiting the Trenches: Exploring Meanings and Motivations in Battlefield Tourism." *Tourism Management* 32(4):860–68.

Eagleton, Terry. 1999. "Marxism without Marxism." In *Ghostly Demarcations: A Symposium on Jacques Derrida's Specters of Marx*, edited by Michael Sprinkler, 83–88., New York: Verso.

Eade, John and Michael Sallnow. 1991. *Contesting the Sacred: The Anthropology of Christian Pilgrimage.* London: Routledge.

Edwards, Jeanette. 1998. "The Need for a 'Bit of History': Place and Past in English Identity." In *Locality and Belonging*, edited by Nadia Lovell, 147–67. London: Routledge.

———. 2000. *Born and Bred: Idioms of Kinship and New Reproductive Technologies in England.* Cambridge: Cambridge University Press.

———. 2012. "Ancestors, Class, and Contingency." *Focaal* 62:70-80.

Eliade, Mircea. 1987. *The Sacred and The Profane: The Nature of Religion.* Orlando, FL: Harcourt Inc.

Ellis, Bill. 1989. "Death by Folklore:Ostension, Contemporary Legend, and Murder." *Western Folklore* 48(3):201–220.

Else, David and Oliver Berry. 2005. *Lonely Planet England.* Oakland, CA: Lonely Planet.

Engelke, Matthew. 2002. "The Problem of Belief: Evans-Pritchard and Victor Turner on 'the Inner Life.'" *Anthropology Today* 18(6):3–8.

———. 2012. "Angels in Swindon: Public Religion and Ambient Faith in England." *American Ethnologist* 39(1):155–70.

English Heritage. 2011. "Ghostly Goings on After Dark." Last modified November 11. http://www.english-heritage.org.uk/about/news/a-ghost-is-for-life/

Evans, Gillian. 2012. "'The Aboriginal People of England': The Culture of Class Politics in Contemporary Britain." *Focaal* 62: 17–29.

Evans, Siân. 2006. *Ghosts: Mysterious Tales from the National Trust.* National Trust. London: Anova Books.

Finucane, R. C. 1996. *Ghosts: Appearances of the Dead and Cultural Transformations.* Amherst, NY: Prometheus Books.

Foley, Malcolm and Lennon J. John. 1996. "JFK and Dark Tourism: Heart of Darkness." *Journal of International Heritage Studies* 2(2):198–211.

Gable, Eric and Richard Handler. 1996. "After Authenticity at an American Heritage Site." *American Anthropologist* 98(3):568–78.

Garrett, Bradley L. 2013. "Undertaking recreational trespass: urban exploration and infiltration." *Transactions of the Institute of British Geographers* 39(1):1–13.

Gatewood, John and Catherine Cameron. 2004. "Battlefield Pilgrims at Gettysburg National Military Park." *Ethnology* 43(3):193–216.

Gentry, Glenn. 2007. "Walking with the Dead: The Place of Ghost Walk Tourism in Savannah, Georgia." *Southeastern Geographer* 47(2):222–38.

Ghost Story. "Chillingham Castle, Northumberland, England." http://www.ghost-story.co.uk/index.php/haunted-castles/200-chillingham-castle-northumberland-england Accessed June 24, 2013.

Ghost Northeast. "Chillingham Castle, Northumberland." http://www.ghostnortheast.co.uk/chilly.html Accessed June 24, 2013.

Gilroy, Paul. 1991. *There Ain't No Black in the Union Jack: The Cultural Politics of Race and Nation.* Chicago: University of Chicago Press.

———. (1982) 2013. *The Empire Strikes Back: Race and Racism in 1970s Britain.* London: Routledge.

Goffman, Erving. 1981. *Forms of Talk.* Philadelphia: University of Pennsylvania Press.

Goldstein, Diane E., Sylvia Ann Grider, and Jeannie Banks Thomas. 2007. *Haunting Experiences: Ghosts in Contemporary Folklore.* Logan: Utah State University Press.

Gordon, Avery. 1997. *Ghostly Matters: Haunting and the Sociological Imagination.* Minneapolis: University of Minnesota Press.

Gorer, Geoffrey. (1923) 2011. *Exploring English Character.* Charleston, SC: Nabu Press.

Gray, Jonathan. 2005. "Antifandom and the Moral Text: Television Without Pity and Textual Dislike." *American Behavioral Scientist* 48(7):840–58.

Grek, Sotiria. 2009. "'In and Against the Museum': The Contested Spaces of Museum Education for Adults." *Discourse: Studies in the Cultural Politics of Education* 30(2):195–211.

Gustafsson, Mai Lan. 2009. *War and Shadows: The Haunting of Vietnam.* Ithaca, NY: Cornell University Press.

Gutzke, David. 2005. *Pubs and Progressive: Reinventing the Public House in England, 1896-1960.* DeKalb, Illinois: Northern Illinois University Press.

Hall, Stuart. 1997. "The Local and the Global: Globalization and Ethnicity." In *Dangerous Liaisons: Gender, Nation, and Postcolonial Perspectives*, edited by Anne McClintock, Aamir Mufti, and Ella Shohat, 173–88. Minneapolis: University of Minnesota Press.

Hanks, Michele. 2011a. "Re-imagining the National Past: Negotiating the Roles of Science, Religion, and History in Contemporary British Ghost Tourism." In *Contested Cultural Heritage: Religion, Nationalism, Erasure, and Exclusion in a Global World*, edited by Helaine Silverman, 125–39. New York: Springer.

———. 2011b. "Between Belief and Science: The Production of Ghostly Knowledge in England." PhD Dissertation, University of Illinois.

Haraway, Donna. 1988. "Situated Knowledges: The Science Question in Feminism and the Privilege of Partial Perspective." *Feminist Studies* 14(3):575–99.

Harley, J. Brian. 2009. "Maps, knowledge, and power." In *Geographic Thought: A Praxis Perspective*, edited by George Henderson and Marvin Waterstone, 129–49. New York: Routledge.

Hawes, Jason, Grant Wilson, and Michael Jan Friedman. 2007. *Ghost Hunting: True Stories of Unexplained Phenomena from The Atlantic Paranormal Society*. New York: Gallery Books.

Hazelgrove, Jenny. 2000. *Spiritualism and British Society between the Wars*. Manchester, UK: University of Manchester Press.

Henley, John. 2010. "How the National Trust is Finding its Mojo." *The Guardian*, February 9. Accessed July 15, 2014. http://www.theguardian.com/culture/2010/feb/10/national-trust-opens-its-doors

Hewison, Robert. 1987. *The Heritage Industry: Britain in a Climate of Decline*. London: Methuen Publishing.

Higson, Andrew. 2001. "Heritage Cinema and Television." In *British Cultural Studies: Geography, Nationality, and Identity*, edited by David Morley and Kevin Robins, 249–60. Oxford, UK: Oxford University Press.

———. 2003. *English Heritage, English Cinema*. Oxford, UK: Oxford University Press.

Hines, Terrence. 2003. *Pseudoscience and the Paranormal*. Amherst, NY: Prometheus Books.

Hoskins, William G. 1959. *Local History in England*. Harlow, UK: Longman.

Hudson, Simon and J. R. Brent Ritchie. 2006. "Promoting Destinations via Film Tourism: An Empirical Identification of Supporting Marketing Initiatives." *Journal of Travel Research* 44:387–96.

Hunt, Geoffrey and Saundra Satterlee. 1986. "Cohesion and Division: Drinking in an English Village." *Man* 21(3):521–37.

Hyde, Kenneth and Serhat Harman. 2011. "Motives for a Secular Pilgrimage." *Tourism Management* 3(6):1243–351.

Hyman, Ray. 1977. "Cold Reading: How to Convince Strangers that You Know All about Them." *Skeptical Inquirer* 2(1):18-37.

Inglis, David and Mary Holmes. 2003. "Highland and Other Haunts: Ghosts in Scottish Tourism." *Annals of Tourism Research* 30(1):50–63.

Jameson, Fredric. 1999. "Marx's Purloined Letter." In *Ghostly Demarcations: A Symposium on Jacques Derrida's Specters of Marx*, edited by Michael Sprinkler, 26–68, New York: Verso.

Jay, Martin. 1998. *Cultural Semantics: Key Words for Our Time*. London: Atholone Press.

Jenkins, Henry. 2006. *Fans, Bloggers, and Gamers: Exploring Participatory Culture*. New York: New York University Press.

———. 2012. *Textual Poachers: Television Fans and Participatory Culture*. New York: Routledge.

Johnson, Andrew Alan. 2013. "Progress and its Ruins: Ghosts, Migrants, and the Uncanny in Thailand." *Cultural Anthropology* 28(2):299–319.

Jones, Graham. 2010. "Modern Magic and the War on Miracles in French Colonial Culture." *Comparative Studies in Society and History* 52(1):66–99.

Jones, Ian and Graham Symon. 2001. "Lifelong Learning as Serious Leisure: Policy, Practice, and Potential." *Leisure Studies* 20(4):269–83.

Jones, Richard. 2003. *Haunted Castles of Britain and Ireland*. London: New Holland Publishers Ltd.

Kalb, Don. 2009. "Conversations with a Polish Populist: Tracing Hidden Histories of Globalization, Class, and Dispossession in Postsocialism and Beyond." *American Ethnologist* 36(2):207–23.

———. 2011. "Headlines of Nation, Subtexts of Class: Working-Class Populism and the Return of the Repressed in Neoliberal Europe." In *Headlines of the Nation, Subtexts of Class*, edited by Don Kalb and Gabor Halmai, 1–36. London: Berghan Books.

Kapferer, Bruce. 2001. "Anthropology: The Paradox of the Secular." *Social Anthropology* 9(3):341–44.

Kaplan, Louis. 2003. "Where the Paranoid Meets the Paranormal: Speculations on Spirit Photography." *Art Journal* 62(3):18–29.

Karlstöm, Anna. 2013. "Spirits and the Ever Changing Heritage." *Material Religion* 9(3):395–99.

Keane, Webb. 2008a. "The Evidence of the Senses and the Materiality of Religion." *Journal of the Royal Anthropological Institute* 14(1):110 – 127.

———. 2008b. "Others, Other Minds, and Others' Theories of Other Minds: An Afterword on the Psychology and Politics of Opacity Claims." *Anthropological Quarterly* 81(2):473–82.

Kelley, Jane Holden. 1963. "Some Thoughts on Amateur Archaeology." *American Antiquity* 28(3): 394–96.

Kingsnorth, Paul. 2008. *Real England: The Battle Against the Bland*. London: Portobello Books.

Kirkup, Rob. 2008. *Ghostly Northumberland*. Gloucestershire: The History Press Ltd.

Koven, Mikel J. 1999. "Candyman Can: Film and Ostension." *Contemporary Legend New Series* 2:155–73.

———. 2002. "Filming Legends: A Revised Typology." *Contemporary Legend New Series* 5:114–35.

———. 2007. "*Most Haunted* and the Convergence of Traditional Belief and Popular Television." *Folklore* 118:183–202.

Krause, Stefan. 2012. "Pilgrimage to the Playas: Surf Tourism in Costa Rica." *Anthropology in Action* 19(3):37–48.

Kruse, Robert. 2003. "Imagining Strawberry Fields as a Place of Pilgrimage." *Area* 35(2):154–62.

Kumar, Krishan. 2003. *The Making of English Identity*, Cambridge, UK: Cambridge University Press.

Laclau, Ernesto. 1995. "The time is out of joint." *Diacritics* 25:85–96.

———. 2005. *On Populist Reason*. London: Verso.

Latour, Bruno. 1999. *Pandora's Hope: Essays on the Reality of Science Studies*. Cambridge, MA: Harvard University Press.

———. 2004. "Why has Critique Run out of Steam?" *Critical Inquiry* 30:225–48.

———. 2010. *On the Modern Cult of the Factish Gods*. Durham, NC: Duke University Press.

Lambek, Michael. 1998. "The Sakalava Poiesis of History: Realizing the Past Through Spirit Possession in Madagascar." *American Ethnologist* 25(2): 106–27.

Laycock, Mike. "Vandals Breach Security at Former Terry's Chocolate Factory." *The Press* February 13, 2013. Accessed March 20, 2013. http://www.yorkpress.co.uk/news/10227164.print/

Lennon, John J. and Foley Malcolm. 2000. *Dark Tourism: The Attraction of Death and Disaster*. London: Cassell. Routledge.

Lewis, Chad and Terry Fisk. 2004. *The Wisconsin Road Guide to Haunted Locations*. Eau Claire, WI: Unexplained Research Publishing Company.

———. 2005. *The Minnesota Road Guide to Haunted Locations*. Eau Claire, WI: Unexplained Research Publishing Company.

Liddell, Tony. 2004. *Otherworld North East: Ghosts and Hauntings Explored*. Newcastle, UK: Tyne Bridge Publishing.

Lippard, Lucy. 2000. *On the Beaten Track: Tourism, Art, and Place*. New York: New Press.

Lindahl, Carl. 2005. "Ostensive Healing: Pilgrimage to the San Antonio Ghost Tracks." *The Journal of American Folklore* 118:164–85.

Lough, Valerie. 2009. "Ghost-hunting teens charged with trespassing." *Springfield Sun-News*. Accessed online http://www.springfieldnewssun.com/news/news/crime-law/ghost-hunting-teens-charged-with-trespassing/nNsFr/.

Lowenthal, David. 1985. *The Past is a Foreign Country*. Cambridge, UK: Cambridge University Press.

Luckhurst, Roger. 2002. "The Contemporary London Gothic and the Limits of the 'Spectral Turn.'" *Textual Practice* 16(3):526–45.

Luhrmann, Tanya. 1989. *Persuasions of the Witch's Craft: Ritual Magic in Contemporary England*. Cambridge, MA: Harvard University Press.

Lyons, Linda. 2005. "Paranormal Beliefs Come (Super) Naturally to Some." *Gallup* Last modified November 1. http://www.gallup.com/poll/19558/Paranormal-Beliefs-Come-SuperNaturally-Some.aspx

MacCannell, Dean. 1973. "Staged Authenticity: On Arrangements of Social Space in Tourist Settings." *The American Journal of Sociology* 79(3):589–603.

———. 1999. *The Tourist: A New Theory of the Leisure Class*. Berkeley: University of California Press.

———. 2008. "Why it was Never Really about *Authenticity*." *Soc* 45:334–37.

Mageo, Jeanette. 1996. "Spirit Girls and Marines: Possession and Ethnopsychiatry as Historical Discourse in Samoa." *American Ethnologist* 23(1):61–82.

Maller, J. B. and G. E. Lundeen. 1933. "Sources of Superstitious Beliefs." *Journal of Educational Research* 26:321–43.

Mandler, Peter. 1997. *The Fall and Rise of the Stately Home*. New Haven: Yale University Press.

Mann, Robin. 2011. "'It just feels English rather than multicultural': Local interpretations of Englishness and non-Englishness." *Sociological Review* 59 (1): 128–147.

Mantz, Jeffery. 2007. "Enchanting Panics and Obeah Anxieties: Concealing and Disclosing Eastern Caribbean Witchcraft." *Anthropology and Humanism* 31(2):18–29.

Marsching, Jane D. 2003. "Orbs, Blobs, and Glows: Astronauts, UFOs, and Photography." *Art Journal* 62(3):57–65.

Martineau, Harriet. 1855. *A Complete Guide to the English Lakes*. London: Whittaker and Company.

Matoesian, Gregory. 1999. "The Grammaticalization of Participant Roles in the Constitution of Expert Identity." *Language in Society* 28:491–521.

Marx, Karl and Friedrich Engels. (1888) 2012. *The Communist Manifesto: A Modern Edition*. London: Verso.

McClenon, James. 1985. *Deviant Science: The Case of Parapsychology*. Philadelphia: University of Pennsylvania Press.

McGinty, Laura. 2010. "The National Trust is Not Just for the Middle Aged and Middle Class." *The Guardian*, February 22. Accessed July 15, 2014. http://www.theguardian.com/com/commentisfree/2010/feb/23/national-trust-middle-class-culture

Meintel, Deirdre. 2007. "When the Extraordinary Hits Home: Experiencing Spiritualism." In *Extraordinary Anthropology: Transformations in the Field*, edited by Jean-Guy Goulet and Bruce Granville Miller, 124–57. Lincoln: University of Nebraska Press.

Melleuish, Greg, Konstantin Sheiko, and Stephen Brown. 2009. "Pseudo History /Weird History: Nationalism and the Internet." *History Compass* 7(6):1484 –495.

Mitchell, David. 2010. "Why are the English Obsessed with Ghosts?" *The Guardian* October 16. Available online: http://www.theguardian.com/commentisfree/2010/oct/17/david-mitchell-english-ghost-obsession

Modood, Tariq. 2005. *Multicultural Politics: Racism, Ethnicity and Muslims in Britain*. Minneapolis: University Of Minnesota Press.

Moran, Michael. 2013 "Let's Hope it's Not Closing Time for the Traditional Pub." *The Guardian* August 29. Accessed September 1. http://www.theguardian.com/commentisfree/2013/aug/29/pub-traditional-boozer-community-life

Moran, Mark and Mark Sceurman. 2009. *Weird N.J.: Your Travel Guide to New Jersey's Local Legends and Best Kept Secrets*. Sterling.

"More Pubs 'in Danger of Closing.'" *The York Press* September 11, 2008. Accessed November 9. http://www.york press.co.uk/news/3665641. More_pubs_in_danger_of_closing_/

Mordue, T. 2009. "Television, Tourism, and Rural Life." *Journal of Travel Research* 47(3):332–345.

Morinis, Alan. 1992. "Introduction: The Territory of the Anthropology of Pilgrimage." In *Sacred Journeys: The Anthropology of Pilgrimage*, edited by Alan Morinis, 1–30. Westport, CT: Greenwood Press.

"Most Haunted Castle Turns its Back on Paranormal." *STV News*, September 28, 2009. Accessed August 11, 2011. http://news.stv.tv/scotland/126125-most-haunted-castle-turns-back-on-paranormal/

Needham, Rodney. 1973. *Belief, Language and Experience*. Chicago: University of Chicago Press.

Olsen, Kjell. 2002. "Authenticity as a Concept in Tourism Research: The Social Organization of the Experience of Authenticity." *Tourist Studies* 2(2):159–82.

Oppenheim, Janet. 1985. *The Other World: Spiritualism and Psychical Research in England, 1850–1914*. Cambridge, UK: Cambridge University Press.

Orme, Stuart. 2012. *Haunted Peterborough*. Gloucestershire, UK: The History Press.

Orwell, George. 1946. "The Moon under Water." *The Evening Standard*, February 9.

Osbaldiston, Nick and Theresa Petray. 2011. "The Role of Horror and Dread in the Sacred Experience." *Tourist Studies* 11(2):175–190.

Owen, Alex. 1989. *The Darkened Room: Women, Power, and Spiritualism in Late Victorian England*. Chicago: University of Chicago Press.

Owen, Alex. 2004. *The Place of Enchantment: British Occultism and the Culture of the Modern*. Chicago: University of Chicago Press.

Palmer, Catherine. 1999. "Tourism and the Symbols of Identity." *Tourism Management* 20:313–21.

Pinch, Trevor. 1979. "Normal Explanations of the Paranormal: The Demarcation Problem and Fraud in Parapsychology." *Social Studies of Science* 9:329–48.

Porter, Jennifer E. 1995. "Science" and Spiritual Vibrations." PhD dissertation, Department of Anthropology, McMaster University.

———. 2004. "Pilgrimage and the IDIC Ethic: Exploring Star Trek Convention Attendance as Pilgrimage." In *Intersecting Journeys: The Anthropology of Pilgrimage and Tourism*, edited by Ellen Badone and Sharon Roseman, 160–79. Urbana: University of Illinois Press.

Randi, James.1992. "Help Stamp Out Absurd Beliefs." *Time* 80 (April 13).

Readicker-Henderson, Edward. 2008. "The Most Haunted City in the World?" *National Geographic* (October):92–101.

Real British Ghosts. "Real Ghosts and Haunted Places in Britain." http://www.real-british-ghosts.com/ Accessed January 12, 2013.

Rice, Tom. 2003. "Believe it or Not: Religious and Other Paranormal Beliefs in the United States." *Journal for the Scientific Study of Religion* 42(1):95–106.

Richardson, Judith. 2003. *Possessions: The History and Uses of Hauntings in the Hudson Valley*. Cambridge: Harvard University Press.

Rittichainuwat, Bongkosh. 2011. "Ghosts: A Travel Barrier to Tourism Recovery." *Annals of Tourism Research* 38(2):437–59.

Roig, Miguel, K. Robert Bridges, Catherine Renner, and Cheryl Jackson. 1998. "Belief in the Paranormal and its Association with Irrational Thinking Controlled for Context Effects." *Personality and Individual Differences* 24(2):229–36.

Sanders, Todd. 2003. "Reconsidering Witchcraft: Postcolonial Africa and Analytic (Un)Certanties." *American Anthropologist* 105(2):338–52.

Sargent, Amy. 1998. "The Darcy effect: Regional Tourism and Costume Drama." *International Journal of Heritage Studies* 4(3–4):177–86.

Sather-Wagstaff, Joy. 2011. *Heritage that Hurts: Tourists in the Memoryscapes of September 11*. Walnut Creek, CA: Left Coast Press.

Seaton, A. V. 1996. "Guided by the Dark: From Thanatopsis to Thanatourism." *Journal of Heritage Studies* 2(4): 234–44.

Schoonover, Karl. 2003. "Ectoplasms, Evanescence, and Photography." *Art Journal* 62(3):31–43.

Scott, Joan. (1987) 1999. *Gender and the Politics of History*. New York: Columbia University Press.

Shaw, Rosalind. 1997. "The Production of Witchcraft/Witchcraft as Production: Memory, Modernity, and the Slave Trade in Sierra Leone." *American Ethnologist* 24(4):856–76.

Shermer, Michael. 2001. *The Borderlands of Science: Where Sense Meets Nonsense*. Oxford, UK: Oxford University Press.

Shermer, Michael and Alex Grobman. 2009. *Denying History: Who Says the Holocaust Never Happened and Why Do they Say It?* Berkeley: University of California Press.

Silverman, Helaine. 2011. "Contested Cultural Heritage: A Selective Historiography." In *Contested Cultural Heritage: Religion, Nationalism, Erasure, and Exclusion in a Global World*, edited by Helaine Silverman, 1–50. New York: Springer.

Smith, Daniel Jordan. 2001. "Ritual Killing, 419, and Fast Wealth: Inequality and the Popular Imagination in Southeastern Nigeria." *American Ethnologist* 28(4):803–26.

Smith, Jonathan Z. 1987. *To Take Place: Toward Theory in Ritual*. Chicago: University of Chicago Press.

Sontag, Susan. 1977. *On Photography*. New York: Picador.

Sparks, Glenn, Marianne Pellechia, and Chris Irvine. 1998. "Does Television News about UFOs Affect Viewers' UFO beliefs? An Experimental Investigation." *Communication Quarterly* 46(3):284–94.

Sparks, Glenn and Will Miller. 2001. "Investigating the Relationship Between Exposure to Television Programs that Depict Paranormal Phenomena and Beliefs in the Paranormal." *Communication Monographs* 68(1):98–113.

Stebbins, Robert. 1982. "Serious Leisure: A Conceptual Statement. "*Pacific Sociological Review* 25:251–72.

———. 2001. "Serious Leisure." *Society* 38(4):53–57.

Stevens, Hayley. 2013. "The Day that Ghost Hunting Died." *Hayley is a Ghost*. Updated December 6. http://hayleyisaghost.co.uk/the-day-that-ghost-hunting -died/

Stoler, Ann, ed. 2006. *Haunted by Empire: Geographies of Intimacy in North American History*. Durham, NC: Duke University Press.

Stoller, Paul. 1995. *Embodying Colonial Memories: Spirit Possession, Power, and the Hauka in West Africa*. New York: Routledge.

Stone, Philip. 2006. "A Dark Tourism Spectrum: Towards a Typology of Death and Macabre Related Tourist Sites, Attractions and Exhibitions." *Tourism* 54(2): 145–60.

———. 2009. "'It's Bloody Guide': Fun, Fear and a Lighter Side of Dark Tourism at the Dungeon Visitor Attractions, UK." In *The Darker Side of Travel: The Theory and Practice of Dark Tourism*, edited by Richard Sharpley and Philip Stone, 167–85. Bristol, UK: Channel View Publications.

Stone, Philip and Richard Sharpley. 2008. "Consuming Dark Tourism: A Thanatological Perspective." *Annals of Tourism Research* 35(2):574–95.

Sturken, Marita. 2007. *Tourists of History: Memory, Kitsch, and Consumerism from Oklahoma City to Ground Zero*. Durham, NC: Duke University Press.

Styers, Randall. 2004. *Making Magic: Religion, Magic, and Science in the Modern World*. Oxford: Oxford University Press.

Tankerville, Leonora. (1925) 2001. *The Ghosts of Chillingham Castle*. Northumberland Self Published.

Tarlow P. E. 2005. "Dark Tourism: The Appealing 'Dark Side' of Tourism and More." In *Niche Tourism – Contemporary Issues, Trends, and Cases*, edited by Marina Novelli, 47–58. Oxford, UK: Butterworth-Heinemann.

Taylor, Charles. 1989. *Sources of the Self: The Making of Modern Identity*. Cambridge, MA: Harvard University Press.

———. 2007. *A Secular Age*. Cambridge, MA: Harvard University Press.

Thompson, E. P. 1966. *The Making of the English Working Class*. New York: Vintage Books.

Thomspon, Robert. 2010. "'Am I Going to See a Ghost Tonight?' Gettysburg Ghost Tours and the Performance of Belief." *The Journal of American Culture* 33(2): 79–91.

Timms, Joanna. 2012. "Ghost-hunters and Psychical Research in Interwar England." *History Workshop Journal* 74(1):88–104.

Tinniswood, Adrian. 1989. *A History of Country House Visiting: Five Centuries of Tourism and Taste*. Oxford, UK: Basil Blackwell and the National Trust.

Tooke, Nichola and Michael Baker. 1996. "Seeing is Believing: The Effect of Film on Visitor Numbers to Screened Locations." *Tourism Management* 17(2):87–94.

Traweek, Sharon. 1988. *Beamtimes and Lifetimes: The World of High Energy Physics*. Cambridge, MA: Harvard University Press.

Trnka, Susanna. 2011. "Specters of Uncertainty: Violence, Humor, and the Uncanny in Indo-Fijian Communities Following the May 2000 Fiji Coup." *Ethos* 39(3): 331–48.

Turner, Edith. 1995. "Preface." *Image and Pilgrimage in Christian Culture*. xxiii–xxi. New York: Columbia University Press.

Turner, Victor. 1979. *Process, Performance, and Pilgrimage: A Study in Comparative Symbology*. New Delphi: Concept.

Turner, Victor and Edith Turner. (1978) 1995. *Image and Pilgrimage in Chiristian Culture*. New York: Columbia University Press.

Urry, John. 1990. *The Tourist Gaze: Leisure and Travel in Contemporary Societies*. London: Sage Publication.

Venbrux, Eric. 2010. "Cemetery Tourism: Coming to Terms with Death?" *La Ricerca Folklorica* 61:41–49.

Wales, Katie. 2009. "Unnatural Conversations in Unnatural Conversations: Speech Reporting in the Discourse of Spiritual Mediumship." *Language and Literature* 18(4):347–56.

Walker, Emily. 2007. "Uncovering Things that Go Bump in the Night." *Swindon Advertiser*, March 7. Accessed August 11, 2013. http://www.swindonadverti ser.co.uk/news/1242785.uncovering_things_that_go_bump_in_the_night/

Walsh, Kevin. 1992. *The Representation of the Past: Museums and Heritage in a Postmodern World*. New York: Routledge.

Wardlow, Holly. 2002. "Headless Ghosts and Roving Women: Specters of Modernity in Papua New Guinea." *American Ethnologist* 29(1):5–32.

Watson, Sheila. 2011. "'Why Can't We Dig Like They Do on Time Team?' The Meaning of the Past Within Working-Class Communities." *International Journal of Heritage Studies* 17(4):364–79.

Weiss, Margo. 2011. *Techniques of Pleasure: BDSM and the Circuits of Sexuality*. Durham, NC: Duke University Press.

White, Paul. 1996. *Classic Devon Ghost Stories*. Redruth, Cornwall, UK: Tor Mark Press.

Wilder, Kelley. 2009. "Photography and the Art of Science." *Visual Studies* 24(2): 163–68.

Winsper, Ann, Steven Parsons, and Ciaran J. O'Keeffe. 2008. "Have the Lunatics Taken Over the (Haunted) Asylum?" Paper presented at the meeting of the Society for Psychical Research and the Parapsychological Association, University of Winchester, Winchester, August 13–17.

Wiseman, Richard, Caroline Watt, Paul Stevens, Emma Greening, and Ciaran O'Keeffe. 2003. "An Investigation into Alleged 'Hauntings.'" *British Journal of Psychology* 94:195–211.

Wooffitt, Robin. 2006. *The Language of Mediums and Psychics: The Social Organization of Everyday Miracles*. Hampshire, UK: Ashgate Publishing.

———. 2007. "Communication and Laboratory Experience in Parapsychology Experiments: Demand Characteristics and the Social Organization of Interaction." *British Journal of Social Psychology*. 46(3):477–98.

Wray, Michael. 2002. *The Haunted Coast*. Wells, ME: East Coast Books.

———. 2004. *Ghosts and Ghouls of the East Riding*. Whitby, UK: The Caedmon Storytellers and East Coast Books.

Wright, Patrick. (1985) 2009. *On Living in an Old Country*. Oxford, UK: Oxford University Press.

Young, R. J. C.1995. *Colonial Desire. Hybridity in Theory, Culture and Race*. London: Routledge.

Žižek, Slavoj. 2006. "Against the Populist Temptation." *Critical Inquiry* 32(3): 551–74.

INDEX

Page numbers in *italics* refer to illustrations.
Italicized *n* refers to note number.

E

Eagleton, Terry, 19
Eastern Ghost Researchers (EGR), 28, 104, 112, 131
Edinburgh Vaults, 56–57
Edwards, Jeanette, 117–118
electromagnetic energy, 98–99, 111
embodiment, 34, 60, 93–94, 119
emotion, 129–130
encyclopedias, 37–39
English Heritage, 34, 50–53, 149–150
Englishness, 167
    nostalgia and, 151–152
    place and, 163–166
    pubs and, 152–153, 154–155
ethnicity, 29
    See also Englishness
Evans, Siân, 46, 47
experience, 14–15, 120–121
    embodied of investigators, 93–94
    embodied of tourists, 34, 60
    of ghost hunts, 74–77
    as nonscientific, 105–106
expertise, 88, 105–106
    in public investigations, 110–111, 115–116
extrasensory perception, 119
    See also mediums

F

Facebook, 180n6
fear, 96–97
Felix, Richard, 55, 56
Fielding, Yvette, 42
fieldwork, 27–28

G

Gaveston, Piers (ghost), 33, 34, 179n1
geography, 44–45, 82
    urban exploration and, 164–165

geography, con't.
    See also place and space; sites (haunted)
Gettysburg, Pennsylvania, 16, 17, 170
Ghost Doctors, 28, 148
Ghost Hunters (reality TV show), 39
ghosts, 12–13, 79, 92
    academic study of, 15–16, 18, 19–22
    ambiguity of, 176–177
    belief in, 17–19, 59–60, 83–84
    defined, 14, 70
    in English culture, 17
    as fractured, 79–80, 82
    identity of, 100, 127–128, 130, 172
    as liminal, 82
    as metaphor, 21
    Roman, 11–12
Ghosts (Evans), 46, 47
Ghosts and Ghouls of the East Riding (Wray), 37
ghost hunts and hunting, 13, 28–29, 62–63, 81
    advertising and, 63–64
    belief and, 59–60, 83–84
    cost of, 69, 107–110, 111
    as experiential, 74–77
    hosts of, 75–76
    as pilgrimage, 59, 64, 70
    at railway museum, 124–126
    as transformative, 70, 84–85
    See also paranormal investigations
Ghost Research Foundation International, 11
Ghost Seekers, 111–112, 113
ghost stories, 12, 17, 36–37, 74
    ghost walks and, 70–71
ghost tourism. *See* tourism
ghost walks, 22, 29, 61–62
    advertising and, 65, 66, 66–67, 68
    belief and, 59–60, 70, 83
    cost of, 68–69

S

Sage, John (ghost), 133–136, 171
Savannah, Georgia, 16, 17
Scarborough Castle, 33, 34
scientism, 172–173
Seaton Delaval Hall, 145
secularization, 18, 26
self, 94. *See also* embodiment
senses, 94–95, 119
sightseeing (negative), 26
　See also tourism
sites (haunted)
　access to, 148–151, 160, 161–163, 166
　authenticity of, 143, 145–146, 168
　commercialized, 108–110, 173–176
　contested, 123–126, 125, 137–138
　heritage, 50–53, 122–123
　inclusive history of, 177–178
　reputation of, 142, 145–146
　selection of, 142–143
　See also place and space; *and specific sites*
Smith, Jonathan Z., 61
South Bridge Vaults (Edinburgh Vaults), 56–57
space and place. *See* place and space; pubs; sites (haunted)
Specters of Marx (Derrida), 15, 19
spectral turn, 19–21
Spiritualism, 18, 48, 118, 119, 181n2
spirituality, 119
　See also Spiritualism
Spooks, 149, 160, 161
Stebbins, Robert, 89–90
Stevens, Hailey, 108
Swindon, 139

T

Tankerville, Leonora, 135
Taylor, Charles, 19, 94, 172

technology, 77–78, 111
television, 39–43, 63–64
　See also Most Haunted (TV reality show)
temperature, 98–99, 105
terrorism, 27
testing, 98, 99
thanatourism, 26
Tinniswood, Adrian, 122–123
tourism, 12, 16–17, 26
　as critique, 170–172
　dark, 26–27
　heritage sites and, 50–51, 137–138, 139–140
　media and, 35
　photography and, 78
　travel and, 43–45
　types of, 13, 16–17
　See also ghost hunts and hunting; ghost walks
tragedy, 26, 27
transformation, 61, 70, 84–85
　See also liminality; pilgrimage
travel, 43–45
Treasurer's House (York), 80–81, 150
　haunting of, 11, 51, 52, 53
trespassing, 160–163, 166, 176
Turner, Edith, 60–61, 84–85
Turner, Victor, 60
Tutbury Castle, 41–42
TV, 39–43, 63–64
　See also Most Haunted (TV reality show)

U, V, W

Urry, John, 35, 78

walks (as paranormal training), 95–97
　See also ghost walks
websites, 38–39, 63–64, 136

C urrently a SAGES Fellow in the Department of Anthropology at Case Western Reserve University, **Michele Hanks** received her PhD in sociocultural anthropology in 2011 from the University of Illinois at Urbana-Champaign. Her research interests and experiences have centered on tourism, knowledge production, and cultural politics. She has been fascinated by how forms of knowledge or interpretations of the past become authoritative in the past and present. Her dissertation research centered on the production and circulation of paranormal knowledge in England. From 2006 to 2009, she conducted ethnographic research with ghost hunters, ghost tour guides, and other paranormal researchers in England to learn about the processes of producing and sharing new knowledge of the ghostly.

 green
press
I N I T I A T I V E

Left Coast Press, Inc. is committed to preserving ancient forests and natural resources. We elected to print this title on 30% post consumer recycled paper, processed chlorine free. As a result, for this printing, we have saved:

2 Trees (40' tall and 6-8" diameter)
1 Million BTUs of Total Energy
146 Pounds of Greenhouse Gases
788 Gallons of Wastewater
53 Pounds of Solid Waste

Left Coast Press, Inc. made this paper choice because our printer, Thomson-Shore, Inc., is a member of Green Press Initiative, a nonprofit program dedicated to supporting authors, publishers, and suppliers in their efforts to reduce their use of fiber obtained from endangered forests.

For more information, visit www.greenpressinitiative.org

Environmental impact estimates were made using the Environmental Defense Paper Calculator. For more information visit: www.papercalculator.org.